RAILWAY LAWS OF INDIA

Shubham Sinha

The Railway Laws of India

Contains

- THE RAILWAYS ACT, 1989
- THE RAILWAY CLAIMS TRIBUNAL ACT, 1987
- THE RAILWAY COMPANIES (EMERGENCY PROVISIONS) ACT, 1951
- THE RAILWAY PROPERTY (UNLAWFUL POSSESSION) ACT, 1966
- THE RAILWAY PROTECTION FORCE ACT, 1957
- THE RAILWAYS (EMPLOYMENT OF MEMBERS OF ARMED FORCES) ACT, 1965
- THE TERMINAL TAX ON RAILWAY PASSENGERS ACT, 1956
- THE CALCUTTA METRO RAILWAY (OPERATION AND MAINTENANCE) TEMPORARY PROVISIONS ACT, 1985
- THE CHAPARUMUKH-SILGHAT RAILWAY LINE AND THE KATAKHAL LALA BAZAR RAILWAY LINE (NATIONALISATION) ACT, 1982
- THE METRO RAILWAYS (CONSTRUCTION OF WORKS) ACT, 1978
- THE INDIAN RAILWAY COMPANIES ACT, 1895
- THE INDIAN TRAMWAYS ACT, 1902
- THE INDIAN RAILWAY BOARD ACT, 1905
- THE RAILWAYS (LOCAL AUTHORITIES' TAXATION) ACT, 1941
- THE RAILWAY COMPANIES (SUBSTITUTION OF PARTIES IN CIVIL PROCEEDINGS)ACT, 1946
- THE COTTON TRANSPORT ACT, 1923

By : Shubham Sinha

Published by:
Shubham Sinha

©Shubham Sinha

The Publication is sold with the understanding that author and publishers are not responsible for the result of any action taken on the basis of this work nor for any error or omission to any person whether a purchaser of this publication or not. No part of this book may be reproduced or copied in any form or by any means without he written permission of the publishers.

Marketing by:
Amazon, Google, Apple and other online advertisers.

The Railways Act, 1989

CHAPTER I
PRELIMINARY

	Sections	*page*
1.	Sort title and commencement	1
2.	Definitions	1

CHAPTER II
RAILWAY ADMINISTRATION

3.	Zonal Railways	3
4.	Appointment of General Manager	4

CHAPTER III
COMMISSIONERS OF RAILWAY SAFETY

5.	Appointment of Chief Commissioner of Railway Safety and Commissioners of Railway Safety.	5
6.	Duties of Commissioner	5
7.	Powers of Commissioner	5
8.	Commissioner to be public servant	5
9.	facilities to be afforded to Commissioners	5
10.	Annual report of Commissioners	5

CHAPTER IV
CONSTRUCTION AND MAINTENANCE OF WORKS

11.	Power of railway administrations to execute all necessary woks	5
12.	Power to alter the position of pipe, electric supply line, drain or sewer, etc	7
13.	Protection for Government property	7
14.	Temporary entry upon)and to remove obstruction, to repair or to prevent accident	7
15.	Payment of amount for damage or loss	8
16.	Accommodation works	9
17.	Power of owner, occupier, State Government or local authority to cause additional accommodation works to be made	9
18.	Fences, gates and bars	10
19.	Over bridges and under-bridges	10
20.	Fewer of Central Government to give directions for safety	10

Sections *page*

CHAPTER V
OPENING OF RAILWAYS

21.	Sanction of the Central Government to the opening of railway	10
22.	Formalities to be complied with before giving sanction to the opening of a railway	10
23.	Sections 21 and 22 to apply to the opening of certain works	11
24.	Temporary suspension of traffic	11
25.	Power to close railway opened for the public carriage of passengers	11
26.	Re-opening of closed railway	12
27.	Use of rolling stock	12
28.	Delegation of powers	12
29.	Power to make rules in respect of matters in this Chapter	12

CHAPTER VI
FIXATION OF RATES

30.	Power to fix rates	13
31.	Power to classify commodities or alter rates	13
32.	Power of railway administration to charge certain rates	13

CHAPTER VII
RAILWAY RATES TRIBUNAL

33.	Constitution of the Railway Rates Tribunal	13
34.	Staff of the Tribunal	14
35.	Sittings of the tribunal	14
36.	Complaints against a railway administration	14
37.	Matters not within the jurisdiction of the Tribunal	15
38.	Powers of the Tribunal	15
39.	Reference to the Tribunal	15
40.	Assistance by the Central Government	15
41.	Burden of proof, etc.	15
42.	Decision, etc., of the Tribunal	16
43.	Bar of jurisdiction of courts	16
44.	Reliefs which the Tribunal may grant	16
45.	Revision of decisions given by the Tribunal	16
46.	Execution of decisions or orders of the Tribunal	16
47.	Report of the Central Government	16
48.	power of the Tribunal to make regulations	16

CHAPTER VIII
CARRIAGE OF PASSENGERS

49.	Exhibition of certain timings and Tables of fares at stations	17
50.	Supply of tickets on payment of fare	17
51.	Provision for case in which ticket is issued for class or train not having accommodation for additional passengers	18
52.	Cancellation of ticker and refund	18
53.	Prohibition against transfer of certain tickets	18
54.	Exhibition and surrender of passes and tickets	18
55.	Prohibition against travelling without pass or ticker	18
56.	Power to refuse to carry persons suffering from infectious or contagious diseases	18
57.	Maximum number of passengers for each compartment	19
58.	Earmarking of compartment, etc., for ladies	19
59.	Communications between passengers and railway servant in charge. of train	19
60.	Power to make rules in respect of matters in this Chapter	19

CHAPTER IX
CARRIAGE OF GOODS

61.	Maintenance of rate-books, etc., for carriage of goods	20
62.	Conditions for receiving, etc., of goods	20
63.	Provision of risk rates	20
64.	Forwarding note	20
65.	Railway receipt	21
66.	Power to require statement relating to the description of goods	21
67.	Carriage of dangerous or offensive goods	22
68.	Carriage of animals suffering from infectious or contagious diseases	22
69.	Deviation of route	22
70.	Prohibition of undue preference	22
71.	Power to give direction in regard to carriage of certain goods	22
72.	Maximum carrying capacity for wagons and trucks	23
73.	Punitive charge for over-loading a wagon	23
74.	Passing of property in the goods covered by railway receipt	23
75.	Section 74 not to affect right of stoppage in transit or claims for freight	24
76.	Surrender of a railway receipt	24
77.	Power of railway administration to deliver goods or sale proceeds thereof in certain cases	24
78.	Power to measure, weigh, etc.	24
79.	Weighment of consignment on request of the consignee or endorsee	24
80.	Liability of railway administration for wrong delivery	24
81.	Open delivery of consignments	25

82.	Partial delivery of consignments	25
83.	Lien for freight or any other sum due	25
84.	Unclaimed consignment	25
85.	Disposal of Perishable consignments in certain circumstances.	26
86.	Sales under sections 63 to 85 not to affect the right to Suit	26
87.	Power to make rules in respect of matters in this Chapter	26

CHAPTER X
SPECIAL PROVISIONS AS TO GOODS BOOKED TO NOTIFIED STATIONS

88.	Definitions	27
89.	Power to declare notified stations	27
90.	Disposal of unremoved goods at notified stations	28
91.	Price to be paid to person entitled after deducting dues	29
92.	Power to make rules in respect of matter in this Chapter	30

CHAPTER XI
RESPONSIBILITIES OF RAILWAY ADMINISTRATION AS CARRIERS

93.	General responsibility of a railway administration as carrier of goods	30
94.	Goods to be loaded or delivered at a siding not belonging to a railway administration	31
95.	Delay or retention in transit	31
96.	Traffic passing over railways in India and railways in foreign countries	32
97.	Goods carried at owner's risk rate	32
98.	Goods in defective condition or defectively packed	32
99.	Responsibility of a railway administration after termination of transit	33
100.	Responsibility as carrier of luggage	34
101.	Responsibility as a carrier of animals	34
102	Exoneration from liability in certain cases	34
103.	Extent of monetary liability in respect of any consignment	34
104.	Extent of liability in respect of goods carried in open wagon	35
105.	Right of railway administration-to check contents of certain consignment or luggage	35
106.	Notice of claim for compensation and refund of overcharge	35
107.	Applications for compensation for loss, etc., of goods	35
108.	Person entitled to claim compensation	36
109.	Railway administration against which application for compensation for personal injury is to be filed	36
110.	Burden of proof	36
111.	Extent of liability of railway administration in respect of accidents at sea	36

| 112 | Power to make rules in respect of matters in this Chapter | 37 |

CHAPTER XII
ACCIDENTS

113.	Notice of railway accident	37
114.	Inquiry by Commissioner	37
115.	Inquiry by railway administration	38
116.	Powers of Commissioner in relation to inquiries	38
117.	Statement made before Commissioner	38
118.	Procedure, etc	38
119.	No inquiry, investigation, etc. to be made if the Commission of Inquiry is appointed	38
120.	Inquiry into accident not covered by section	39
121.	Returns	39
122	Power to make rules in respect of matters in this Chapter	39

CHAPTER XIII
LIABILITY OF RAILWAY ADMINISTRATION FOR DEATH AND INJURY TO PASSENGERS DUE TO ACCIDENTS

123	Definitions	39
124	Extent of liability	40
124 A.	Compensation on account of untoward incident	40
125.	Application for compensation	41
126.	Interim relief by railway administration	41
127.	Determination of compensation in respect of any injury or loss of goods	42
128.	Saving as to certain rights	42
129.	Power to make rules in respect of matters in this Chapter	42

CHAPTER XIV
REGULATION OF HOURS OF WORK AND PERIOD OF REST

130.	Definitions	42
131.	Chapter not to apply to certain railway servants	43
132.	Limitation of hours of work	43
133.	Grant of periodical rest	43
134.	Railway servant to remain on duty	44
135.	Supervision of railway labour	44
136.	Power to make rules in respect of matter in this Chapter	44

CHAPTER XV
PENALTIES AND OFFENCES

137.	Fraudulently traveling or attempting to travel without proper pass or ticket	45
138	Levy of excess charge and fare far travelling without proper pass or ticket or beyond authorised distance	45
139.	Power to remove persons	46
140.	Security for good behaviour in certain cases	46
141.	Needlessly interfering with means of communication in a train	46
142	Penalty for transfer of tickets	47
143.	Penalty for unauthorised carrying on of business of procuring and supplying of railway tickets	47
144.	Prohibition on hawking, etc., and begging	48
148.	Drunkenness or nuisance	48
146.	Obstructing railway servant in his duties	48
147.	Trespass and refusal to desist from trespass	48
148.	Penalty for mating a false statement in an application for compensation	49
149.	Making a false claim for compensation	49
150.	Maliciously wrecking or attempting to wreck a train	49
151.	Damage to or destruction of certain railway properties	50
152	Maliciously hurting or attempting to hurt persons travelling by railway	50
153.	Endangering safety of persons travelling by railway by wilful act or omission	50
154.	Endangering safety of persons travelling by railway by rash or negligent act or omission	50
155.	Entering into a compartment reserved or resisting entry into a compartment not reserved	50
156	Traveling on roof, step or engine of strain	51
157.	Altering or defacing pass or ticket	51
158.	Penalty for contravention of any of the provision of Chapter XIV	51
159.	Disobedience of driven or conductor of vehicles to directions of railway servant etc.	51
160.	Opening or breaking a level crossing gate	51
161.	Negligently crossing unmanned level crossing	51
162.	Entering carriage or other place reserved for females	51
163.	Giving false account of goods	52
164.	Unlawfully bringing dangerous goods on a railway	52
165.	Unlawfully bringing offensive goods on a railway	52
166.	Defacing public notices	52
167.	Smoking	52
168.	Provision with respect to commission of offence by the children of acts endangering safety of person travelling on railway	52
169.	Levy of penalty on non Government railway	53

170.	Recovery of penalty	53
171.	Section 169 or 170 not to preclude Central Government from taking any other action	53
172	Penalty for intoxication	53
173.	Abandoning train etc. without authority	53
174.	Obstructing naming of train, etc.	53
175.	Endangering the safety of persons	53
176.	Obstructing level crossing	54
177.	False returns	54
178.	Making a false report by a railway servant	54
179.	Arrest for offences under certain sections	54
180.	Arrest of persons likely to abscond etc.	54
181	Magistrate having jurisdiction under the Act.	55
182.	Place of trial.	55

CHAPTER XVI
MISCELLANEOUS

183.	Power to provide other transport services.	55
184.	Taxation on railways by local authorities.	55
185.	Taxation on railways for advertisement.	55
186.	Protection of action taken in good faith.	56
187.	Restriction on execution against railway property	56
188.	Railway servants to Se public servants for the proposes of Chapter 1X and section 409 of the Indian Penal Code	56
189.	Railway servants not to engage in trade	56
190.	Procedure for delivery to railway administration of property detained by a railway servant.	56
191.	Proof of entries in records and documents	56
192.	Service of notice, etc., on railway administration	57
193.	Service of notice, etc., by railway administration	57
194.	Presumption where notice is served by post	57
195.	Representation of railway administration	57
196.	Power to exempt railway from Act	57
197.	Matters supplemental to the definitions of "railways" and "railway servant"	57
198.	General power to make rules	58
199.	Rules to be laid before Parliament	58
200.	Repeal and saving	58

CHAPTER XVII
AMENDMENTS TO THE RAILWAYS ACT'

31.	Amendment of section 3	69

32.	Amendment of section 78A.	69
33.	Substitution (if new section for section 80	69
34.	Omission of section 82B, 82D and 82F.	69
35.	Amendment of section 82C	69
36.	Amendment of sections 82.E, 82G and 82HH	69
37.	Amendment of section 82I	69
38.	Amendment of section 82I	69

APPENDIX

THE RAILWAYS ACT, 1989
(24 OF 1989)

[3rd June, 1989.]

An Act to consolidate and amend the law relating to Railways.
Be it enacted by Parliament in the Fortieth Year of the Republic of India as follows:-

CHAPTER I
PRELIMINARY

1. Short title and commencement. -- (i) This Act may be called the Railways Act,
(2) It shall come into force on such date[1] as the Central Government may, by notification in the Official Gazette, appoint :

Provided that different dates may be appointed for different provisions of this Act, and any reference in any such provision to the commencement of this Act shall be construed as a reference to the coming into force of that provision.

2. Definitions. -- In this Act, unless the context otherwise requires,-
(1) "authorised" means authorised by a railway administration;
(2) "carriage" means the carriage of passengers or goods by a railway administration;
(3) "Claims Tribunal" means the Railway Claims Tribunal established under section 3 of the Railway Claims Tribunal Act, (54 of 1987);
(4) "classification" means the classification of commodities made under section 31 for the purpose of determining the rates to be charged for carriage of such commodities;
(5) "class rates" means the rate fixed for a class of commodity in the classification;
(6) "Commissioner" means the Chief Commissioner of Railway Safety or the Commissioner of Railway Safety appointed under Section 5;
(7) "commodity" means a specific item of goods;
(8) "consignee" means the person named as consignee in a railway receipt;
(9) "consignment" means goods entrusted to a railway administration for carriage;
(10) "consignor" means the person, named in a railway receipt as consignor, by whom or on whose behalf goods covered by a railway receipt are entrusted to a railway administration for carriage;
(11) "demurrage" means the charge levied for the detention of any rolling stock 'after the expiry of free time, if any, allowed for such detention;
12) "endorsee" means the person in whose favour an endorsement is made, and in .the case of successive endorsements, the person in whose favour the last endorsement is made;

---

1. July t, 1990 [vide S.O. 475(E) dated 12.6.1990.]

(13) "endorsement" means the signing by the consignee or the endorsee after adding a direction on a railway receipt to pass the property in the goods mentioned in such receipt to specified person;

(14) "Tare" means the charge levied for the carriage of passengers;

(15) "ferry" includes a bridge of boats, pontoons or rafts, a swing bridge, a fly bridge and a temporary bridge and the approaches to, and landing places of a Ferry;

(16) "forwarding note" means the document executed under section 64;

(17) "freight" means the charge levied for the carriage of goods including transshipment charges, if any;

(18) "General Manager" means the General Manager of a Zonal Railway appointed under section 4;

(19) "goods" includes-;
- (i) containers, pallets or similar articles of transport used to consolidate ; goods; and
- (ii) animals;

(20) "Government railway" means a railway owned by the Central Government;

(21) "in transit", in relation to the carriage of goods by railway, means the period between the commencement and the termination of transit of such goods, and unless otherwise previously determined -
- (a) transit commences as soon as the railway receipt is issued or the consignment is loaded, whichever is earlier;
- (b) transit terminates on the expiry of the free time allowed for unloading of consignment from any rolling stock and where such unloading has been completed within such free time, transit terminates on the expiry of the free time allowed, for the removal of the goods from the railway premises;

(22) "level crossing" means an inter-section of a road with lines of rails at the same level;

(23) "luggage" means the goods of a passenger either carried by him in his charge or entrusted to a railway administration for carriage;

(24) "lump sum rate" means the rate mutually agreed upto between a railway administration and a consignor for the carriage of goods and for any service in relation to such carriage;

(25) "non-Government railway" means a railway other than a Government railway;

(26) "notification" means a notification published in the Official Gazette; (27) "parcel" means goods entrusted to a railway administration for carriage by a passenger or a parcel train;

(28) "pass" means an authority given by the Central Government or a railway administration to a person allowing him to travel as a passenger but does not include a ticket;

(29) "passenger" means a person travelling with a valid pass or ticket; (30) "prescribed" means prescribed by rules made under this Act; (31) "railway" means a railway, or any portion of a railway, for the public carriage of passengers or goods, and includes--

(a) all lands within the fences or other boundary marks indicating the limits of the land appurtenant to a railway;

b) all lines of rails, sidings or yards or branches used for the purposes of, or in connection with, a railway;

(c) all electric traction equipments, power supply and distribution installations used for the purposes of, or in connection with, a railway;

(d) all rolling stock, stations, offices, warehouses, wharves, workshops, manufactories, fixed plant and machinery, roads and streets, running rooms, rest houses, institutes, hospitals, water works and water supply installations, staff dwellings and any other works constructed for the purpose of, of in connection with, a railway;

(e) all vehicles which are used on any road for the purposes of traffic of a railway and owned, hired or worked by a railway; and

(f) all ferries, ships, boats and rafts, which are used on any canal, river, lake or other navigable inland waters for the purposes of the traffic of railway and owned, hired or worked by a railway administration,

but does not include -
  (i) a tramway wholly within a municipal area; and
  (ii) lines of rails built in any exhibition ground, fair, park, or any other place solely for the purpose of recreation;

(32) "railway administration", in relation to -
  (a) - a Government railway, means the General Manager of a Zonal Railway; and
  (b) a non-Government railway; means the person who is die owner or lessee of the railway or the person working the railway under an agreement;

(33) "railway receipt" means the receipt issued under section 65;

(34) "railway servant" means any person employed by the Central Government or by a railway administration in connection with the service of a railway;

(35) "rate" includes any fare, freight or any other charge for the carriage of any passenger or goods;

(36) "regulations" means the regulations made by the Railway Rates Tribunal under this Act;

(37) "rolling stock" includes locomotives, lenders, carriages, wagons, rail-cars, containers, trucks, trolleys and vehicles or all kinds moving on rails;

(38) "station to station rate" means a special reduced rate applicable to a specific commodity booked between specified stations;
(39) "traffic" includes rolling stock of every description, as well as passengers and goods;
(40) "Tribunal" means the Railway Rates Tribunal constituted under section 33;
(41) "wharfage" means the charge levied on goods for not removing them from the railway after the expiry of the free time for such removal;
(42) "Zonal Railway" means a Zonal Railway constituted under section 3.

COMMENTS

Cabinman is a railway servant. A.I.R. 1941 Sindh 117.

One who is paid partly by railway and partly by contractor is a railway servant. A.I.R. 1924 Rangoon 373.

Stations and railway carriage are public place but not public properly. A.I.R. 1972 S.C. P792.

"Railway administration" is neither a legal entity nor a juristic person. A.I.R. 1976 S.C. 2538.

The term "railway" is of a wide amplitude . A.I.R. 1963 Orissa 20. A suit lies against the Union of India'. A.I.R. 1965 Kerala 277.

Station Master or General Manager is not competent railway administration. A.I.R. 1975 Gauhati 74.

Duty pass is issued for a special purpose. A.I.R. 1971 Madras 488.

CHAPTER II
RAILWAY ADMINISTRATION

3. Zonal Railways. -- (1) The Central Government may, for the purpose of the efficient administration of the Government railways, by notification, constitute such railways into as many Zonal Railways as it may deem fit and specify in such notification the names and headquarters of such Zonal Railways and the areas in respect of which they shall exercise jurisdiction.

(2) The Zonal Railway existing immediately before the commencement of this Act shall be deemed to be Zonal Railways constituted under sub-section (1).

(3) The Central Government may, by notification, declare any unit of the railways engaged in research, development, designing, construction or production of rolling stock, its parts or other equipment used on a railway, to be a Zonal Railway.

(4) The Central Government may, by notification, abolish any Zonal Railway or constitute any new Zonal Railway out of any existing Zonal Railway or Zonal Railways, Change the name or headquarters if any Zonal Railway or determine the areas in respect of which a Zonal Railway shall exercise jurisdiction.

4.. Appointment of General Manager. -- (1) The Central Government shall, by notification, appoint a person to be the General Manager of a Zonal Railway.

(2) The general superintendence and control of Zonal Railway shall vest in the General Manager.

CHAPTER III
COMMISSIONERS OF RAILWAY SAFETY

5. Appointment of Chief Commissioner of Railway Safety and Commissioners of Railway Safety. -- The Central Government may appoint a person to be the Chief Commissioner of Railway Safety and such other persons as it may consider necessary to be the Commissioners of Railway Safety.

6. Duties of Commissioner. -- The Commissioner shall--
(a) inspect any railway with a view to determine whether it is fit to be opened for the public carriage of passengers and report thereon to the Central Government as required by or under this Act;
(b) make such periodical or other inspections of any railway or of any rolling stock used thereon as the Central Government may direct;
(c) make an inquiry under this Act into the cause of any accident on a railway; and
(d) discharge such other duties as are conferred on him by or under this Act.

7.. Powers of Commissioner. -- Subject to the control of the Central Government, the Commissioner, whenever it is necessary so to do for any of the purpose of this Act, may:
(a) enter upon and inspect any railway or any rolling stock used thereon;
(b) by order in writing addressed to a railway administration, require the attendance before him or any railway servant and to require answers or returns to such inquiries as he-links fit to make from such railway servant or from the railway administration; and
(c) require the production of any book, document or material object belonging to or in the possession control of any railway administration which appears to him to be necessary to inspect.

8. Commissioner to be public servant. -- The Commissioner shall be deemed to be a public servant within the meaning of section 21 of the Indian Penal Code, [45 of 1860].

9. Facilities to be afforded to Commissioners. -- A railway administration shall afford to the Commissioner all reasonable facilities for the discharge of the duties or for the exercise of the powers imposed or conferred on him by or under this Act.

10. Annual report of Commissioners. --The Chief Commissioner of Railway Safety shall prepare in each financial year an annual report giving a full account of the activities of the Commissioners during the financial year immediately preceding the financial year in which such that report is prepared and forward, before such date as may be specified by the Central Government, copies thereof to the Central Government, and that Government shall cause that report to be laid, as soon as may be, alter its receipt before each House of Parliament.

CHAPTER IV
CONSTRUCTION AND MAINTENANCE OF WORKS

11. Power of railway administrations to execute all necessary works. - Notwithstanding anything contained in any other law for the time being in force, but subject to the provisions of this Act and the provisions of any law for the acquisition of land for a public purpose or for companies, and subject also, in the case of a non Government railway, to the provisions of any contract between the non-Government railway and the Central Government, a railway administration may, for the purposes of constructing or maintaining a railway

(a) make or construct in or upon, across under or over any lands, or any streets, hills, valleys, roads, railway, tramways, or any rivers, canals, brooks, streams or other waters, or any drains, water pipes, gas-pipes, oil-pipes, sewers, electric supply lines, or telegraph lines, such temporary or permanent inclined-planes, bridges, tunnels, culverts, embankments, acquaducts, roads, lines of railways, passages, conduits, drains, piers, cuttings and fences, in-take wells, tube wells, dams, river training and protection works as it thinks proper;

(b) alter the course of any rivers, brooks, streams or other water courses, for the purpose of constructing and maintaining tunnels, bridges, passages or other works over or under them and divert or alter either temporarily or permanently, the course of any rivers, brooks, streams or other water courses or any roads, streets or ways, or raise or sink the level thereof, in order to carry them more conveniently over or under or by the side of the railway;

(c) make drains or conduits into, through or under any lands adjoining the railway for the purpose of conveying water from or to the railway;

(d) erect and construct such houses, warehouses, offices and other buildings, and such yards, stations, wharves, engines, machinery apparatus and other works and conveniences as the railway administration thinks proper;

(e) alter, repair or discontinue such buildings, works and conveniences as aforesaid or any of them and substitute others in their stead;

(f) erect, operate, maintain or repair any telegraph and telephone lines in connection with the working of the railway;

(g) erect, operate, maintain or repair any electric traction equipment, power supply and distribution installation in connection with the working of the railway; and

(h) do all other acts necessary for making, maintaining, altering or repairing and using the railway.

COMMENTS

Instances of negligence on the part of the railway administration and its liability there for. A.I.R. 1963 Patna 167; A.I.R. 1983 Rajasthan 17; A.I.R. 1992 Bombay 471.

12. Power to alter the position of pipe, electric supply line, drain or sewer, etc.-- (1) A railway administration may, for the purpose of exercising the powers conferred on it by this Act, alter the position of any pipe for the supply of gas, water, oil or compressed air, or the position of any electric supply line, drain on sewer :

Provided that before altering the position of any such pipe, electric supply line, drain or sewer, the railway administration shall give a notice indicating the time at which the work of such alteration shall commence, to the local authority or other person having control over the pipe, electric supply line, drain or sewer.

(2) The railway administration shall execute the work referred to in sub-section (1) to the reasonable satisfaction of the local authority or the person receiving the notice under the proviso to sub-section (1).

13. Protection for Government property. -- Nothing in sections 11 and 12 shall authorise

(a) a railway administration of the Government railway to do anything on or to any works, lands or buildings vested in, or in the possession of, a State Government without the consent of that Government; and

(b) a railway administration of a non-Government railway to do anything on or to any works, lands or buildings vested in, or in the possession of, the Central Government or a Stale Government without the consent of the Government concerned.

14. Temporary entry upon land to remove obstruction, to repair or to prevent accident. -- (1) Where in the opinion of a railway administration -

(a) there is imminent danger that any tree, post or structure may fall on the railway so as to obstruct the movement of rolling stock; or
(b) any tree, post, structure or light obstructs the view of any signal provided for movement of rolling stock; or
(c) any tree, post or structure obstructs any telephone or telegraph line maintained by it,

it may take such steps as may be necessary to avert such danger or remove such obstruction and submit a report thereof to the Central Government in such manner and within such time as may be prescribed.

(2) Where in the opinion of a railway administration-
(a) a slip or accident has occurred; or
(b) there is apprehension of any slip or accident to any cutting embankment or other work on a railway.

it may enter upon any lands adjoining the railway and do all such works as may be necessary for the purpose of repairing or preventing such slip or accident and submit a report thereof to the Central Government in such manner and within such time as may be prescribed.

(3) The Central Government may, after considering the report under sub-section (1) or sub-section (2), in the interest of public safety, by order, direct the railway administration that further action under sub-section (1) or sub-section (2) shall be stopped or the same shall be subject to such conditions as may be specified in that order.

15. Payment of amount for damage or loss. -- (1) No suit shall lie against a railway administration to recover any amount for any damage or loss caused in the exercise of the powers conferred by any of the foregoing provisions of this Chapter.

(2) A railway administration shall pay or tender payment for any damage or loss caused in the exercise of the powers conferred by any of the foregoing provisions of this

Chapter, and in case of a dispute as to the sufficiency of any amount so paid or tendered or as to the persons entitled to receive the amount, it shall immediately refer the dispute for the decision of the District Judge of the district and his decision thereon shall be final:

Provided that where the railway administration fails to make a reference within sixty days from the date of commencement of the dispute, the District Judge may, on an application made to him by the person concerned. direct the railway administration to refer the dispute for his decision.

(3) The reference under sub-section (2) shall be treated as an appeal under section 96 of the Code of Civil Procedure, [5 of 1908] and shall be disposed of accordingly.

(4) Where any amount has been paid as required by sub-section (2), the railway administration shall, notwithstanding anything in any other law for the time being in force, be discharged from all liabilities to any person whatsoever in respect of any amount so paid.

COMMENTS

A suit is barred against the railway administration for recovery of compensation from it in certain circumstances. I.L.R. 27 Bombay 344; (1874) 14 B.LR.

16. Accommodation works. -- (1) A railway administration shall make and maintain the following works for the accommodation of the owners and occupiers of lands adjoining the railway, namely:-

(a) such crossings, bridges, culverts and passages over, under or by the sides of, or leading- to or from, the railway as may, in the opinion of the State Government, be necessary for the purpose of making good any interruptions caused by the railway to the use of the lands through which the railway is made; and

(b) all necessary bridges, tunnels, culverts, drains, water sources or other passages, over, under or by the sides of the railway, or such dimensions as will, in the opinion of the State Government, be sufficient at all times to convey water as freely from or to the lands lying near or affected by the railway as it was before the making of the railway or as nearly as possible.

(2) Subject to the other provisions of this Act, the works specified in sub-section (1) shall be made at the cost of the railway administration during or immediately after the laying out or formation of the railway over the lands traversed and in such a manner as to cause, as little damage or inconvenience as possible to persons interested in the lands or affected .by the works:

Provided that -

(a) a railway administration shall not be required to make any accommodation works in such a manner as would prevent or obstruct the working or using of the railway, or to make any accommodation works with respect to which the owners or occupiers of the lands have been paid compensation in consideration of their not requiring the said works to be made;

(b) save as hereinafter, in this Chapter: provided, no railway administration shall be liable to execute any further or additional accommodation works for the use of the owners or occupiers of the lands after the expiration of ten years from the date on which the railway passing through the lands was first opened for public traffic;

(c) where a railway administration has provided suitable accommodation work for the crossing of a road or stream and the road or stream is afterwards diverted by the act Or neglect of the person having the control thereof, the railway administration shall not be compelled to provide any other accommodation work for the crossing of such road or stream.

(3) The State Government may specify a dale for the commencement of any work to be executed under sub-section (i) and, if within three months next after that date, the railway administration fails to commence the work or having commenced it, fails to proceed diligently to execute it, the Central Government shall, on such failure being brought to its notice by the State Government, issue such directions to the railway administration as it thinks fit.

Explanations--For the purposes of this section, the expression "lands" shall include public roads.

17. Power of owner, occupier, State Government or local authority to cause additional accommodation works to be made. -- (1) If an owner or occupier of any land affected by a railway considers the works made under section 16 to be insufficient for the use of the land, or if the State Government or a local authority desires to construct a public road or other work across, under or over a railway, such owner or occupier, or, as the case may be, the State Government or the local authority may, at any time, require the railway administration to make at the expense of the owner or occupier or of the State Government or the local authority, as the case may be, such further accommodation works as are considered necessary and are agreed to by the railway administration.

(2) The accommodation works made under sub-section (1) shall be maintained at the cost of the owner or occupier of the land, the State Government or the local authority, at whose request the works were made.

(3) In the case of any difference of opinion between the railway administration and the owner or occupier, the State Government or the local authority, as the case may be, in relation to -

(i) the necessity of such further accommodation works; or
(ii) the expenses to be incurred on the construction of such further accommodation works; or
(iii) the quantum of expenses on the maintenance of such further accommodation works,

it shall be referred to the Central Government whose decision thereon shall be final.

COMMENTS

This section applies only where accommodation works have already been made. I.L.R. 23 Bombay 358.

18. Fences, gates and bars. -- The' Central Government may, within such time as may be specified by it or within such further time, as it may grant, require that -

(a) boundary marks or fences be provided or renewed by a railway administration for a railway or any part thereof and for roads constructed in connection therewith;

(b) suitable gates, chains, bars, stiles or hand-rails be erected or renewed by a railway administration at level crossings;

(c) persons be employed by a railway administration to open and shut gates, chains or bars.

COMMENTS

The statutory duty of the Railway administration is not automatic but arises as and when the Central Government requires it to do so. A.I.R. 1959 Madhya Pradesh 125.

19. Over bridges and under-bridges. -- (1) Where a railway administration has constructed lines of rails across a public road at the same level, the State Government or the local authority maintaining the road, may, at any time, in the interest of public safety, require the railway administration to take the road either under or over the railway by means of a: bridge or arch with Convenient ascents and descents and other convenient approaches, instead of crossing the road on the level, or to execute such other works as may, in, the circumstances of the case, appear to the State Government or the local authority maintaining the road to be best adapted for removing or diminishing the danger arising from the level crossing.

(2) Tile railway administration may require the Stale Government or the local authority, as the case may be, as a condition of executing any work under sub-section (1), to under take to pay the whole of the cost of the work and the expense of maintaining the work, to the railway administration or such proportion of the cost and expenses as the Central Government considers just and reasonable.

(3) In the case of any difference of opinion between the railway administration and the State Government or the local authority, as the case may be, over any of the matters mentioned in sub-section (1), it shall be referred to the Central Government, whose decision thereon shall be Final.

COMMENTS

Any interference with the railway employees' duty is impermissible. A.I.R. 1994 Allahabad 83.

20. Power of Central Government to give directions for safety. -- Notwithstanding anything contained in any other law, the Central Government may, if it is of the opinion that any work undertaken or may be undertaken, is likely to alter or impede the natural course of water flow or cause an increase in the volume of such now endangering any cutting, embankment or other work on a railway, issue directions in writing to any person, officer or authority responsible for such work to close, regulate or prohibit that work.

CHAPTER V
OPENING OF RAILWAYS

21. Sanction of the Central Government to the opening of railway. -- No railway shall be opened for the public carriage of passengers until the Central Government has, by order, sanctioned the opening thereof for that purpose.

22. Formalities to be complied with before giving sanction to the opening of a railway. - (1) The Central Government shall, before giving its sanction to the opening of a railway under section 21, obtain a report from the Commissioner that -

(a) he has made a careful inspection of the railway and the rolling stock that may be used thereon;
(b) the moving and fixed dimensions as laid down by the Central Government have not been infringed;
(c) the structure of lines of rails, strength of bridges, general structural character of the works and the size of, and maximum gross load upon, the axles of any rolling stock, comply with the requirements laid down by the Central Government; and
(d) in his opinion, the railway can be opened for the public carriage of passengers without any danger to the public using it.

(2) If the Commissioner is of the opinion that the railway cannot be opened without any danger to the public using it, he shall in his report, state the grounds therefor, as also the requirements which, in his opinion, are to be complied with before sanction is given by the Central Government.

(3) The Central Government, after considering the report of the Commissioner, may sanction the opening of a railway under section 21 as such or subject to such conditions as may be considered necessary by it for the safety of the public.

23. Sections 21 and 22 to apply to the opening of certain works. -- The provisions of sections 21 and 22 shall apply to the opening of the following works if they form part of, or rue directly connected with a railway used for the public carriage of passengers and have been constructed subsequent to the giving of a report by the Commissioner under section 22, namely:
(a) opening of additional lines of railway and deviation lines;
(b) opening of stations, junctions and level crossings:
(c) re-molding of yards and re-building of bridges;
(d) introduction of electric traction; and
(c) any alteration or reconstruction materially affecting the structural character of any work to which the provisions of sections 21 and 22 apply or are extended by this section.

24. Temporary suspension of traffic. -- When an accident has occurred on a railway resulting in a temporary suspension of traffic, and either the original lines of rails and works have been restored to their original standard or a temporary diversion has been laid, for the purpose of restoring communication, the original lines of rails and works so restored, or the temporary diversion, as the case may be, may, without prior inspection by the Commissioner, be opened for the public carriage of passengers, subject to the following conditions, namely :-

(a) the railway servant incharge of the works undertaken by reason of the accident has certified in writing that the opening of the restored lines of rails and works, or of the temporary diversion will not in his opinion be attended with danger to the public; and
(b) a notice of the opening of the lines of rails and works or the diversion shall be sent immediately to the Commissioner.

25. Power to close railway opened for the public carriage of passengers.-Where, after the inspection of any railway opened and used for the public carriage of passengers or any rolling stock used thereon, the Commissioner is of the opinion that the use of the railway or of any rolling stock will be attended with danger to the public using it, the Commissioner shall send a report to the Central Government who may thereupon direct that -

(i) the railway be closed for the public carriage of passengers: or
(ii) the use of the rolling stock be discontinued; or
(iii) the railway or the rolling stock may be used for the public carriage of passengers subject to such conditions as it may consider necessary for the safety of the public.

26. Re-opening of closed railway. -- When the Central Government has, under section 25, directed the closure of a railway or the discontinuance of the use of any rolling stock -

(a) the railway shall not be re-opened for the public carriage of passengers until it has been inspected by the Commissioner and its re-opening is sanctioned in accordance with the provisions of this Chapter; and
(b) the rolling stock shall not be used until it has been inspected by the Commissioner and its re-use is sanctioned in accordance with the provisions of this Chapter.

27. Use of rolling stock. -- A railway administration may use such rolling stock as it may consider necessary for the construction, operation and working of a railway:
Provided that before using any rolling stock of a design or type different from that already running on any section of the railway, the previous sanction of the Central Government shall not be obtained for such use:

Provided further that before giving any such sanction, the Central Government shall obtain a report from the Commissioner that he has made a careful inspection of the rolling stack and, in his opinion, such rolling stock can be used.

28. Delegation of powers. -- The Central Government may, by notification, direct that any of its powers or functions under this chapter, except section 29, or the rules made thereunder shall, in relation to such matters and subject to such conditions, if any, as may be specified in the notification, be exercised or discharged also by a Commissioner.

29. Power to make rules in respect of matters in this Chapter. -- (1) The Central Government may, by notification, make rules to carry out the purposes of this Chapter.
(2) In particular, and without prejudice to the generality of the foregoing power, such rules may provide for all or any of the following matters, namely :-

(a) the duties of a railway administration and the Commissioner in regard to the opening of a railway for the public carriage of passengers;
(b) the arrangements to be made for and the formalities to be complied with before opening a railway for the public carriage of passengers;
(c) for regulating the mode in which, and the speed at which rolling stock used on railways is to be moved or propelled; and
(d) the cases in which and the extent to which the procedure provided in this Chapter may be dispensed with.

CHAPTER VI
FIXATION OF RATES

30. Power to fix rates. --(1) The Central Government may, from time to time, by general or special order fix, for the carriage of passengers and goods, rates for the whole or any part of the railway and different rates may be fixed for different classes of goods and specify in such order the conditions subject to which such rates shall apply.

(2) The Central Government may, by a like order, fix the rates of any other charges incidental to or connected with such carriage including demurrage and wharfage for the whole or any part of the railway and specify in the order the conditions subject to which such rates shall apply.

31. Power to classify commodities or alter rates. -- The Central Government shall I have power to -

(a) classify or reclassify any commodity for the purpose of determining the rates to be charged for the carriage of such commodities; and
(b) increase or reduce the class rates and other charges.

COMMENTS

Powers of the Central Government are quasi-judicial in nature. A.I.R. 1970 Patna 109.

Rates, even if fixed by agreement, may be altered on such grounds as escalation of costs. A.I.R. 19(38 S.C. 1832.

32. Power of railway administration to change certain rates. -- Notwithstanding anything contained in this Chapter, a railway administration may, in respect of the carriage of any commodity and subject to such conditions as may be specified.--

(a) quote a station to station rate;
(b) increase or reduce or cancel, after due notice in the manner determined by the Central Government, a station to station rate, not being a station to station rate introduced in compliance with an order made by the Tribunal;
(c) withdraw, alter or amend the conditions attached to a station to station rate other than conditions introduced in compliance with an order made by the Tribunal; and
(d) charge any lump sum rate.

CHAPTER VII
RAILWAY RATES TRIBUNAL

33. Constitution of the Railway Rates Tribunal. -- (1) There shall he a Tribunal to be called the Railway Rules Tribunal, for the purpose or: discharging the functions specified in this Chapter.

(2) The Tribunal shall consist of a Chairman and two other members to be appointed by the Central Government.

(3) A person shall not be qualified for appointment as the Chairman of the Tribunal unless he is, or has been, a Judge of the Supreme Court or of a High Court and of the other two members, one shall be a person, who, in the opinion of the Central Government, has special knowledge of the commercial, industrial or economic conditions of the country, and the other shall be a person, who in the opinion of the Central Government, has special, knowledge and experience of the commercial-working of the railways.

(4) The Chairman and the ether members of the Tribunal shall hold office for such period, not exceeding five years, as may be prescribed.

(5) in-case the Chairman or any other member is, by infirmity or otherwise, rendered incapable of carrying out his duties or is absent on leave or otherwise in circumstances not involving the vacation of his office, the Central Government may appoint another person to act in his place during his absence,

(6) A person who holds office as the Chairman or other member of the Tribunal shall, on the expiration of the term of his office (not being an office to fill a casual vacancy), be ineligible for re-appointment to that office.

(7) Subject to the provisions of sub-sections (5) and (6), the Chairman and other members of the Tribunal shall hold office on such terms and conditions as may be prescribed.

(8) No act or proceeding of the Tribunal shall be invalidated merely by reason of-

(a) any vacancy in, or any defect in the constitution of, the Tribunal; or

(b) any defect in the appointment of a person acting as a Chairman or other member of the Tribunal.

COMMENTS

The levy of any charges is not liable to be assailed in a writ petition. A.I.R. 1992 Orissa

34. Staff of the Tribunal. -- (1) The Tribunal may, with the previous approval of the Central Government, appoint such officers and employees as it considers necessary for the efficient discharge of its functions under this Chapter.

(2) The terms and conditions of service of the officers and employees of the Tribunal shall be such as may be determined by regulations.

35. Sittings of the Tribunal. -- The Tribunal may sit at such place or places as it may find convenient for the transaction of its business.

36. Complaints against a railway administration. -- Any complaint that a railway administration -

(a) is contravening the provisions of section 70; or

(b) is charging for the carriage of any commodity between two stations a rate which is unreasonable; or

(c) is levying any other charge which is unreasonable, may be made to the Tribunal, and the Tribunal shall hear and decide any such complaint in accordance with the provisions of this Chapter.

COMMENT'S

Railways are commercial undertakings intending to earn profits. A.I.R. 1969 S.C. 630.

Rates charged should always be reasonable. A.I.R. 1971 S.C. 349; A.I.R. 1987 S.C. 2·114.

37. Matters not within the jurisdiction of the Tribunal. -- Nothing in this Chapter shall confer jurisdiction on the Tribunal in respect of -

(a) classification or re-classification of any commodity;

(b) fixation of wharfage and demurrage charges (including conditions attached to such charges);

(c) fixation of fares levied for the carriage of passengers and freight levied for the carriage of luggage, parcels, railway material and military traffic; and

(d) fixation of lump sum rates.

COMMENTS

Jurisdiction of Civil Courts is ousted. A.I.R. 1939 Nagpur 141.

Supreme Court cannot go into the question of fact A.I.R. 1968 S.C. 22.

Tribunal's order may take effect from the date of complaint. A.I.R. 1979 Madras 28.

38. Powers of the Tribunal. - (1) The Tribunal shall have the powers of a Civil Court under the Code of Civil Procedure, 1908 [5 or 1908] for the purposes of taking evidence on oath, enforcing the attendance on witnesses, compelling the discovery and protection of documents, issuing commissions for the examination of witnesses and of view and shall be deemed to be a civil court for all the purposes of section 195 and chapter XXXV of the Code of Criminal Procedure, 1973 [2 of 1974] and any reference i In such section or Chapter to the presiding officer of a court shall be deemed to include a reference to the Chairman for the Tribunal.

(2) The Tribunal shall also have power to pass such interim and final orders as the circumstances may require, including orders for the payment of costs.

39. Reference to the Tribunal. -- Notwithstanding anything contained in section 37, the Central Government may make a reference to the Tribunal in respect of any of the matter specified in that section and where any such reference is made in respect of any such matter, the Tribunal shall made an inquiry into that matter and submit its report thereon to the Central Government.

40.. Assistance by the Central Government.-- (1) The Central Government shall give to the Tribunal such assistance as it may require and shall also place at its disposal any information in the possession of the Central Government which that Government may think relevant to any matter before the Tribunal.

(2) Any person duly authorised in this behalf by the Central Government shall be entitled to appear and be heard in any proceedings before the Tribunal.

41. Burden of proof, etc. -- In the case of any complaint under clause (a) of section 36,-

(a) Whenever it is shown that a railway administration charges one trader or class of traders or the traders in any local area, lower rates for the same or similar goods or lower charges for the same or similar services than it charges to other traders in any other local area, the burden of providing that such lower rate or charge does not amount to an undue preference, shall lie on the railway administration;

(b) in deciding whether a lower rate or charge does not amount to an undue preference, the Tribunal may, in addition to any other considerations affecting the case, take into consideration whether such lower rate or charge is necessary in the interests of the public.

COMMENTS

Reasonability of rates depends on various factors such as working costs and principle of profit-making. A.I.R. 1968 S.C. 22.

42. Decision, etc., of the Tribunal .- The decisions or orders of the Tribunal shall be by a majority of the members sitting and shall be final.

43. Bar of jurisdiction of courts. -- No suit shall be instituted or proceeding taken in respect of any matter which the Tribunal is empowered to deal with, or decide, under this Chapter.

COMMENTS

Civil Court is competent to interpret an agreement and decide validity thereof. A.I.R. 1973 S.C 1281.

44. Relief which the Tribunal may grant. -- In the case of any complaint made under clause (b) or clause (c) of section 36, the Tribunal may -

(i) fix such rate or charge as it considers reasonable from any date as it may deem proper, not being a date earlier to the date of the filing of the complaint;
(ii) direct a refund of amount, if any, as being the excess of the rate or charge fixed by the Tribunal under clause (i).

45. Revision of decisions given by the Tribunal. -- Where a railway administration considers that since the date of decision by the Tribunal, there has been a material change in the circumstances on which it was based, it may, after the expiry of one year from such date, make an application to the Tribunal and the Tribunal may, alter making such inquiry as it considers necessary, vary or revoke the decision.

46. Execution of decisions or orders of the Tribunal. -- The Tribunal may transmit any decision or order made by it to a civil court having local jurisdiction and such civil court shall execute the decision or order as if it were a decree made by that court.

COMMENTS

Civil Court has jurisdiction to execute the Tribunal's order which is transmitted to it. A.I.R. 1963 S.C. 217.

47. Report of the Central Government. -- The Tribunal shall present annually a report to the Central Government of all its proceedings under this Chapter.

48. Power of the Tribunal to make regulations. -- (1) The Tribunal may, with the previous approval of the Central Government, make regulations consistent with this Act and rules generally to regulate its procedure for the effective discharge of its functions under this Chapter.

(2) In particular, and without prejudice to the generality of the foregoing power, such regulations may provide for all or any of the following matters, namely:-

(a)   the terms and conditions of service of the officers and employees of the Tribunal;

(b)   the award of costs by the Tribunal in any proceedings before it;

(c) the reference of any question to a member or to an officer of the Tribunal or any other person appointed by the Tribunal, for report after holding a local inquiry;

(d) the right of audience before the Tribunal, provided that any party shall be entitled to be heard in person, or by a representative duly authorised in writing, or by a legal practitioner;

(e) the disposal by the Tribunal of any proceedings before it, notwithstanding that in the course thereof there has been a change in the persons sitting as members of the Tribunal;

(f) a scale of fees for and in connection with the proceedings before the Tribunal.

CHAPTER VIII
CARRIAGE OF PASSENGERS

49. Exhibition of certain timings and Tables of fares at stations. --

(1) Every railway administration shall cause to be pasted in a conspicuous and accessible place at every station in Hindi and English and also in the regional language commonly in use in the area where the station is situated.-

(i) a table of times of arrival and departure of trains which carry passengers and stop at that station, and

(ii) list of fares from such station to such other stations as it may consider necessary.

(2) At every station where tickets are issued to passengers, a copy of the timetable in force shall be kept in the office of the station master.

50. Supply of tickets on payment of fare. -- (1) Any person desirous of travelling on a railway shall, upon payment of the fare, be supplied with a ticket by a railway servant or an agent authorised in this behalf and such ticket shall contain the following particulars, namely :

(i) the date of issue;
(ii) the class of carriage;
(iii) the place from and the place to which it is issued; and
(iv) the amount of the fare.

(2) Every railway administration shall display the hours during which booking windows at a station shall be kept open for the issue of tickets to passengers.

(3) The particulars required to be specified on a ticket under clauses (ii) and (iii) of sub-section (1) shall-

(a) if it is for the lowest class of carriage, be set forth in Hindi, English and the regional language commonly in use at the place of issue of the ticket; and

(b) if it is for any other class of carriage, be set forth in Hindi and English :

Provided that where it is not feasible to specify such particulars in any such language due to mechanisation or any other reason, the Central Government may exempt such particulars being specified in that language.

COMMENTS

The charges paid for excess luggage are not a "fare". 128 Punjab Law Reporter 1903.

A person who travels without a ticket, can be removed from the train as a trespasser. I.LR. I Bombay 52.

51. Provision for case in which ticket is issued for class or train not having accommodation for additional passengers. -- (1) A ticket shall be deemed to have been issued subject to the condition of availability of accommodation in the class of carriage and the train for which the ticket is issued.

(2) If no accommodation is available in the class of carriage for which a ticket is issued, and the holder thereof travels in a carriage of a lower class, he shall, no returning such ticket, be entitled to a refund of the difference between the fare paid by him and the fare payable for the class of carriage in which he travels.

52. Cancellation of ticket and refund. -- If a ticket is returned for cancellation, the railway administration shall cancel the same and refund such amount as may be prescribed.

53. Prohibition against transfer of certain tickets. -- A ticket issued in the name of a person shall be used only by that person :

Provided that nothing contained in this section shall prevent mutual transfer of a seat or berth by passengers travelling by the same train :

Provided further that a railway servant authorised in this behalf may permit change of name of a passenger having reserved a seat or berth subject to such circumstances as may be prescribed.

54. Exhibition and surrender of passes and tickets. -- Every passenger shall, on demand by any railway servant authorised in this behalf, present his pass or ticket to such railway servant for examination during the journey or at the end of the journey and surrender such ticket -

(a) at the end of the journey, or

(b) if such ticket is issued for a specified period, on the expiration of such period.

55. Prohibition against travelling without pass or ticket. -- (1) No person shall enter or remain in any carriage on a railway for the purpose of travelling therein as a passenger unless he has with him a proper pass or ticket or obtained permission of a railway servant authorised in this behalf for such travel.

(2) A person obtaining permission under sub-section (!) shall ordinarily get a certificate from the railway servant referred to in that sub-section that he has been permitted to travel in such carriage on condition that he subsequently pays the fare payable for the distance to be travelled.

56. Power to refuse to carry persons suffering from infectious or contagious diseases. -- (1) A person suffering from such infectious or contagious diseases, as may be prescribed, shall not enter or remain in any carriage on a railway or travel in train without the permission of a railway servant authorised in this behalf.

(2) The railway servant giving permission under sub-section (1), shall arrange for the separation of the person suffering from such disease from other persons in the train and such person shall be carried in the train subject to such other conditions as may be prescribed.

(3) Any person who enters or remains in any carriage or travels in a train without permission as required under sub-section (1) or in contravention of any condition prescribed under sub-section (2), such person and a person accompanying him shall be liable to the forfeiture of their passes or tickets and removal from railway by any railway servant.

57. Maximum number of passengers for each compartment. -- Subject to the approval of the Central Government, every railway administration shall fix the maximum number of passengers which may be carried in each compartment of every description of carriage, and shall exhibit the number so fixed in a conspicuous manner inside or outside each compartment in Hindi, English and also in one or more of the regional languages commonly in use in the areas served by the railway.

58. Earmarking of compartment, etc., for ladies -- Every railway administration shall, in every main carrying passengers, earmark for the exclusive use of females, one compartment or such number of berths or seats, as the railway administration may think fit.

59. Communications between passengers and railway servant in charge of train. -- A railway administration shall provide and maintain in every train carrying passengers, such efficient means of communication between the passengers and the railway servant in charge of the train as may be approved by the Central Government :

Provided that when: the railway administration is satisfied that the means of communication provided in a train are being misused, it may cause such means to be disconnected in that train for such period as it thinks fit :

Provided further that the Central Government may specify the circumstances under which a railway administration may be exempted from providing such means of communication in any train.

60. Power to make rules in respect of matters in this Chapter. -- (1) The Central Government may, by notification, make rules to carry out the purposes of this Chapter.

(2) In particular, and without prejudice to the generality of the foregoing power, such rules may provide for all or any of the following matters, namely :

(a) the convenience and accommodation (including the reservation of seats or berths in trains) to passengers :

(b) the amount of refund for the cancellation of a ticket;

(c) the circumstances under which change of names of passengers, having reserved seats or berths, may be permitted;

(d) the carriage of luggage and the conditions subject to which luggage may be kept in the cloak rooms at the stations;

(e) diseases which are infectious or contagious;

(f) the conditions subject to which a railway administration may carry passengers suffering from infectious or contagious diseases and the manner in which carriages used by such passengers may be disinfected;

(g) generally, for regulating the travelling upon, and the use, working and management of the railways.

(3) Any rule made under this section may provide that a contravention thereof shall be punishable with fine which shall not exceed five hundred rupees.

(4) Every railway administration shall keep at every station on its railway a copy of all the rules made under this section and shall also allow any person to inspect it free or' charge.

COMMENTS

The Appointment of Railway Tourist Agent Rules, 1980 are reasonable. A.I.R. 1984 S.C. 415.

CHAPTER IX
CARRIAGE OF GOODS

61. Maintenance of rate-books, etc., for carriage of goods. -- Every railway administration shall maintain. at each station and at such other places where goods are received for carriage, the rate-books or other documents which shall contain the rate authorised for the carriage: of goods from one station to another and make them available for the reference of any person during all reasonable hours without payment of any fee.

62. Conditions for receiving, etc., of goods. -- (1) A railway administration may impose, conditions, not inconsistent with this Act or any rules made thereunder, with respect to the receiving, forwarding, carrying or delivering of any goods.

(2) A railway administration shall maintain, at each station and at such other places where goods are received for carriage, a copy of the conditions for the time being in force under sub-section (1) and make them available for the reference of any person during all reasonable hours without payment of any fee.

COMMENTS
A copy of the "conditions" which are statutory in character, must be maintained at each station and other places. A.I.R. 1971 Delhi 79.

63. Provision of risk rates. -- (i) Where any goods are entrusted to a railway administration for carriage, such carriage shall, except where owner's risk rate is applicable in respect of such goods, be at railway risk rate.

(2) Any goods, for which owner's risk rate and railway risk rate are in force, may be entrusted for carriage at either for the rates and if no rate is opted, the goods shall be deemed to have been entrusted at owner's risk rate.

64. Forwarding note. -- (1) Every person entrusting any goods to a railway administration for carriage shall execute a forwarding note in such form as may be specified by the Central Government :

Provided that no forwarding note shall be executed in the case of such goods as may be prescribed.

(2) The consignor shall he responsible for the correctness of the particulars furnished by him in the forwarding note.

(3) The consignor shall indemnify the railway administration against any damage suffered by it by reason of the incompleteness or incompleteness of the particulars in the forwarding note.

65. Railway receipt. -- (1) A railway administration shall, -
  (a) in a case where the goods are to be loaded by a person entrusting such goods, on the completion of such loading; or
  (b) in any other case, on the acceptance of the goods by it, issue a railway receipt in such form as may be specified by the Central Government.

(2) A railway receipt shall be prima facie evidence of the weight and the number of packages staled therein:

Provided that in the case of a consignment in wagon-load or train load and the weight or the number of packages is not checked by a railway servant authorised in this behalf, and a statement to that effect is recorded in such railway receipt by him, the burden of proving the weight or, as the case may be, the number of packages scaled therein, shall lie on the consignor, the consignee or the endorsee.

COMMENTS

The factum of entrusting the goods to the railway for carriage must have to be established in certain circumstances. A.I.R. 1988 Orissa 261.

66. Power to require statement relating to the description of goods. -- (1) The owner or a person having charge of any goods which are brought upon a railway for the purposes of carriage by railway and the consignee or the endorsee of any consignment shall on the request of any railway servant authorised in this behalf, deliver to such railway servant a statement in writing signed by such owner or person or by such consignee or endorsee, as the case may be, containing such description of the goods as would enable the railway servant to determine the rate of such carriage.

(2) If such owner or person refuses or neglects to give the statement as required under sub-section (1) and refuses to open the package containing the goods, i f so required by the railway servant, if shall be open to the railway administration to refuse to accept such goods for carriage unless such owner or person pays for such carriage the highest rate for any class of goods;

(3) If the consignee or endorsee refuses or neglects to give the statement as required under sub-section (i) and rcfuscs to open the package containing the goods, if so required by the railway servant, it shall be open to the railway administration to charge in respect of the carriage of the goods the highest rate for any class of goods.

(4) If the statement delivered under sub-section (1) is materially false with respect to the description of any goods to which it purports to relate, the railway administration may charge in respect of the carriage of such Goods such rate, not exceeding double the highest rate for any class of goods as may be specified by the Central Government.

(5) If any difference arises between a railway servant and such owner or person, the consignee or tile endorsee, as the case may be, in respect of the description of the goods for which :I statement has been delivcrcd under sub-section (1), the railway servant may detain and examine, the goods.

(6) Where any goods have been detained under sub-section (5) for examination and upon such examination it is found that the description of the goods is different from that given in the statement delivered under sub-section (1): the cost of such detention and examination shall be done by such owner or person, the consignee or the endorsee, as the case may be, and the railway administration shall not be liable for any loss, damage or deterioration which may be caused by such detention or examination.

67. Carriage of dangerous or offensive goods. -- (1) No person shall take with him on a railway, or require a railway administration to carry such dangerous or offensive goods, as may be prescribed, except in accordance with the provisions of this section.

(2) No person shall Lake with him on a railway the goods referred to in sub-section (1) unless he gives a notice in writing of their dangerous or offensive nature to the railway servant authorised in this behalf.

(3) No person shall entrust the goods referred to in sub-section (1) to a railway servant authorised in this behalf for carriage unless he distinctly marks on the outside of the

package containing such goods their dangerous or offensive nature and gives a notice in writing of their dangerous or offensive nature to such railway servant.

(4) IF any railway servant has reason to believe that goods contained in a package are dangerous or offensive and notice as required under sub-section (2) or sub-section (3), as the case may be, in respect of such goods in not given, he may cause such package to be opened for the purpose of ascertaining its contents.

(5) Notwithstanding anything contained in this section, any railway servant may refuse to accept any dangerous or offensive goods for carriage or stop, in transit, such goods or cause the same to be removed, as the case may be, if he has reason to believe that the provisions of this section for such carriage are not complied with.

(6) Nothing in this section shall be construed to derogate from the provisions of the Indian Explosives Act, 1884 [4 of 1884]1 or any rule or order made under that Act, and nothing in sub-sections (4) and (5) shall be construed to apply to any goods entrusted for carriage by order or on behalf of the Government or to any goods which a soldier, sailor, airman or any other officer of the armed forces of the Union or a police officer or a member of the Territorial Army or of the National Cadet Corps may take with him on a railway in the course of his employment or duty as such.

68. Carriage of animals suffering from infectious or contagious diseases.- A railway administration shall not be bound to carry any animal suffering from such infectious or contagious disease as may be prescribed.

69. Deviation of route. -- Where due to any cause beyond the control of a railway administration or due to congestion in the yard or any other operational reasons, goods are carried over a route other than the route by which such goods are booked, the railway administration shall not be deemed to have committed a breach of the contract of carriage by reason only of the deviation of the route.

70. Prohibition of undue preference. -- A railway administration shall not make or give any undue or unreasonable preference or advantage to, or in favour of, any particular person or any particular description of traffic in the carriage of goods.

71. Power to give direction in regard to carriage of certain goods. -- (1) The Central Government may, if it is of the opinion that it is necessary in the public interest so to do, by general or special order, direct any railway administration-
  (a) to give special facilities for, or preference to, the carriage of such goods or class of goods consigned by or to the Central Government or the Government of any Stale or of such other goods or class of goods;
  (b) to carry any goods or class of goods by such route or routes and at such rates;
  (c) to restrict or refuse acceptance of such goods or class of goods at or to such station for carriage,

(2) Any order made under sub-section (1) shall cease to have effect after the expiration of a period of one year from the date of such order, but may by a like order, be renewed from time to time for such period not exceeding one year at a time as may be specified in the order.

(3) Not withstanding anything contained in this Act, every railway administration shall be bound to comply with any order given under sub-section (1) and any action taken by a railway administration in pursuance of any such order shall not be deemed to be 3 contravention of section 70.

72. Maximum carrying capacity for wagons and trucks. --(1) The gross weight of every wagon or truck bearing on the axles when the wagon or truck is loaded to its maximum carrying capacity shall not exceed such limit as may be Fixed by the Central Government for the class of axle under the wagon or truck.

(2) Subject to the limit fixed under sub-section (1), every railway administration shall determine the normal carrying capacity for every wagon or truck in its possession and shall exhibit in words and figures the normal carrying capacity so determined in a conspicuous manner on the outside of every such wagon or truck.

(3) Every person owning a wagon or truck which passes over a railway shall determine and exhibit the normal carrying capacity for the wagon or truck in the manner specified in sub-section (2).

(4) Notwithstanding anything contained in sub-section (2) or sub-section (3), where a railway administration considers it necessary or expedient so to do in respect of any wagon or truck carrying any specified class of goods or any class of wagons or trucks of any specified type, it may vary the normal carrying capacity for such wagon or truck or such class of wagons or trucks and subject to such conditions as it may think fit to impose, determine for the wagon or truck or class of wagons or trucks such carrying capacity as may be specified in the notification and it shall not he necessary to exhibit the words and figures representing the carrying capacity so determined on the outside of such wagon or truck or such class of wagons or trucks.

73. Punitive charge for over-loading a wagon. -- Where a person loads goods in a wagon beyond its permissible carrying capacity as exhibited under sub-section (2) or sub-section (3), or notified under sub-section (4), of section 72, a railway administration may, in addition to the freight and other charges, recover from the consignor, the consignee or the endorsee, as the case may be, charges by way of penalty at such rates, as may be prescribed, before the delivery of the goods:

Provided that it shall be lawful for the railway administration to unload the goods loaded beyond the capacity of the wagon, if detected at the forwarding station or at any place before the destination station and to recover the cost of such unloading and any charge for the detention of any wagon on this account.

74. Passing of property in the goods covered by railway receipt .- The properly in the consignment covered by a railway receipt shall pass to the consignee or the endorsee, as the case may be, on the delivery of such railway receipt to him and he shall have all the rights and liabilities of the consignor.

75. Section 74 not to affect right of stoppage in transit or claims for freight, - Nothing contained in section 74 shall prejudice or affect
  (a) any right of the consignor for stoppage of goods in transit as an unpaid vendor (as defined under the Sale of Goods Act, 3930) [3 of 19301 on his written request to the railway administration;
  (b) any right of the railway to claim freight from the consignor; or

(c) any liability of the consignee or the endorsee, referred to in that section by reason of his being such consignee or endorses.

76. Surrender of a railway receipt. -- The railway administration shall deliver the consignment under a railway receipt on the surrender of such railway receipt :

Provided that in case the railway receipt is not forthcoming, the consignment may be delivered to the person, entitled in the opinion of the railway administration to receive the goods, in such manner as may be prescribed.

77. Power of railway administration to deliver goods or sale proceeds thereof in certain cases. --Where no railway receipt is forthcoming and any consignment or the sale proceeds of any consignment are claimed by two or more persons the railway administration may withhold delivery of such consignment or sale proceeds, as the case may be, and shall deliver such consignment or sale proceeds in such manner as may be prescribed.

78. Power to measure, weigh, etc.- Notwithstanding anything contained in the railway receipt, the railway administration may, before the delivery of the consignment, have the right to
  (i) re-measure, re-weigh or re-classify any consignment;
  (ii) re-calculate the freight and other charges; and
  (iii) correct any other error or collect any amount that may have been omitted to be charged.

79. Weighment of consignment on request of the consignee or endorsee, -A railway administration may, on the request made by the consignee or endorsee, allow weighment of the consignment subject to such conditions and on payment of such charges as may be prescribed and the demurrage charges, if any :

Provided that except in cases where a railway servant authorised in this behalf considers it necessary so to do, no weighment shall be allowed of goods booked at owner's risk rate or goods which are perishable and are likely to lose weight in transit:

Provided further that no request for weighment of consignment in wagon-load or train-load shall be allowed if tile weighment is not feasible due to congestion in the yard or such other circumstances as may be prescribed.

80. Liability of railway administration for wrong delivery. -- Where a railway administration delivers the consignment to the person who produces the railway receipt, it shall not be responsible for any wrong delivery on the ground that such person is not entitled thereto or that the endorsement on the railway receipt is forged or otherwise defective.

81. Open delivery of consignments.--Where the consignment arrives in a damaged condition or shows signs of having been tampered with and the consignee or the endorsee demands open delivery, the railway administration shall give open delivery in such manner as may be prescribed.

82. Partial delivery of consignments. --(1) The consignee or endorsee shall, as soon as the consignment or part thereof is ready for delivery, take delivery of such consignment or part thereof notwithstanding that such consignment or part thereof is damaged .

(2) In the case of partial delivery under sub-section (I), the railway administration shall furnish a partial delivery certificate, in such form as may be prescribed.

(3) if the consignee or endorsee refuses to take delivery under sub-section (1), the consignment or part thereof shall be subject to wharfage charges beyond the time allowed for removal.

83. Lien for freight or any other sum due. -- (1) If the consignor, the consignee or the endorsee fails to pay on demand any freight or other charges due from him in respect of any consignment, the railway administration may detain such consignment or part thereof, or, if such consignment is delivered, it may detain any other consignment of such person which is in, or thereafter comes into, its possession.

(2) The railway administration may, if the consignment detained under sub-section (1) is-

(a) perishable in nature, sell at once; or

(b) not perishable in nature, sell by public auction,

such consignment or part thereof, as may be necessary to realise a sum equal to the freight or other charges:

Provided that where a railway administration for reasons to be recorded in writing is of the opinion that it is not expedient to hold the auction, such consignment or part thereof may be sold in such manner as may be prescribed.

(3) The railway administration shall give a notice of not less that seven days of the public auction under clause (b) of sub-section (2) in one or more local newspapers or where there are no such newspapers in such manner as may be prescribed.

(4) The railway administration may, out of the sale proceeds received under subsection (2), retain a sum equal to the freight and other charges including expenses for the sale due to it and the surplus of such proceeds and the part of the consignment, if any, shall be rendered to the person entitled thereto.

84. Unclaimed consignment. -- (1) If any person fails to take delivery of -

(a) any consignment; or

(b) the consignment released from detention made under sub-section (1) of section 83; or

(c) any remaining part of the consignment under sub-section (2) of section 83, such consignment shall be treated as unclaimed. (2) The railway administration may,-

(a) in the case of an unclaimed consignment which is perishable in nature, sell such consignment in the manner provided in clause (a) of sub-section (2) of section 83; or

(b) in the case of an unclaimed consignment which is not perishable in nature, cause a notice to be served upon the consignee if his name and address are known, and upon the consignor in thc name and address of the consignee are not known, requiring him to remove the goods within a period of seven days from the receipt thereof and if such notice cannot be served or there is a failure to comply with the requisition in the notice, sell such consignment in the manner provided in clause (b) of sub-section (2) of section 83.

(3) The railway administration shall, out of the sale proceeds received under subsection (2), retain a sum equal to the freight and other charges including expenses for the sale due to it and the surplus, if any, of such sale proceeds shall be rendered to the person entitled thereto.

85. Disposal of perishable consignments in certain circumstances. --(1) Where by reason of any flood, land-slip, breach of any lines of rails, collision between trains, derailment of, or other accident to a train or any other cause, traffic on any route is interrupted and there is no likelihood of early resumption of such traffic, nor is there any other reasonable route whereby traffic of perishable consignment may be diverted to prevent, loss or deterioration of, or damage to, such consignment, the railway administration may sell them in the manner provided in clause (a) of sub-section (2) of section 83.

(2) The railway administration shall, out of the sale proceeds received under subsection (1), retain a sum equal to the freight and other charges including expenses for the sale due to it and the surplus, if any, of such sale proceeds, shall be rendered to the person entitled thereto.

86. Sales under sections 83 to 85 not to affect tile right to suit. --Notwithstanding anything contained in this Chapter, the right of sale under sections 83 to 85 shall be without prejudice to tile right of the railway administration to recover by suit, any freight charge, amount or other expenses due to it.

87. Power to make rules in respect of matters in this Chapter. --(1) The Central Government may, be notification, make rules to carry out the purposes of this Chapter.

(2) In particular, and without prejudice to the generality of the foregoing power, such rules may provide for all or any of the following matters, namely :
(a) goods in respect of which no forwarding note shall be executed under proviso to sub-section (1) of section 64:
(b) dangerous and offensive goods for the purposes of sub-section (1) of section 67;
(c) infectious or contagious diseases for the purposes of section 68;
(d) rates of penalty charges under section 73;
(e) the manner in which the consignment may be delivered without a railway receipt under section 76;
(f) the manner of delivery of consignment or the sale proceeds to the person entitled thereto under section 77;
(g) the conditions subject to which and charges payable for allowing weighment and circumstances for not allowing wcighment of consignment in wagon-load or train-load under section 79;

(h) the manner of giving open delivery under sub-section 81;

(i) the form of partial delivery certificate under sub-section (2) of section 82;

(j) the manner of sale of consignment or part thereof under the proviso to sub-section (2) of section 83;

(k) the manner in which a notice under sub-section (3) of section 83 may be given;

(1) generally, for regulating-the carriage of goods by the railways.

(3) Any rule made under this section may provide that a contravention thereof shall be punishable with fine which may extend to one hundred and fifty rupees.

(4) Every railway administration shall keep at each station a copy of the rules for the time being in force under this section, and shall allow any person to refer to it free of charge.

CHAPTER X

SPECIAL PROVISIONS AS TO GOODS BOOKED TO NOTIFIED STATIONS

88. Definitions, --In this Chapter, unless the context otherwise requires,-

(a) "essential commodity" means an essential commodity as defined in clause (a) section 2 of the Essential Commodities Act, 1955; [10 of]955].
(b) "notified station" means a station declared to be a notified station under section 89;
(c) "State Government", in relation to a notified station, means the Government of the State in which such station is situated, or where such station is situated in a Union territory, the administrator of that Union territory appointed under article 239 of the Constitution.

89. Power to declare notified stations. -- (1) The Central Government may, if it is satisfied that it is necessary that goods entrusted for carriage by train intended solely for the carriage of goods to any railway station should he removed without delay from such railway station, declare, by notification, such railway station to be a notified station for such period as may be specified in the notification;

Provided that before declaring any railway station to be a notified station under this sub-section, the Central Government shall have regard to all or any of the following factors, namely :

(a) the volume of traffic and the storage space available at such railway station;
(b) the nature and quantities of goods generally booked to such railway station;
(c) the scope for causing scarcity of such goods by not removing them for long periods from such railway station and the hardship which such scarcity may cause to the community;
(d) the number of wagons likely to be held hp at such railway station if goods are not removed therefrom quickly and the need for quick movement and availability of such wagons;
(e) such other factors (being relevant from the point of view of the interest of the general public) as may be prescribed:

Provided further that the period specified in any notification issued under this subsection in respect of any railway station shall not exceed six months in the first instance, but such period may, be notification, be extended from time to time by a period not exceeding six months on each occasion.

(2) If any person entrusting any goods to a railway administration to be carried to a notified station makes an application in such form and manner as may be prescribed and specifics therein the address of the person to whom intimation by registered post of the arrival of the goods at the notified station shall be given and pays the postage charges required for giving such intimation, the railway administration shall, as soon as may be after the arrival of the goods at the notified station, send such intimation accordingly.

(3) There shall be exhibited at a conspicuous place at each notified station a statement in the prescribed form setting out the description of the goods which by reason of the fact that they have not been removed from the station within a period of seven days from the termination of transit thereof are liable to be sold. in accordance with the provision, of sub-section (1) of section 90 by public auction and the dates on which they would be sold:

Provided that different statements may be so exhibited in respect of goods proposed to be sold on different dates.

(4) If the goods specified in any statement to be exhibited under sub-section (3) include essential commodities, the railway servant preparing the statement shall, as soon as may be after the preparation of such statement, forward a copy thereof to-
- (a) the representative of the Central Government nominated by that Government in this behalf;
- (b) the representative of the State Government, nominated by that Government in this behalf; and
- (c) the District Magistrate within the local limits of whose jurisdiction the railway station is situated.

90. Disposal of unremoved goods at notified stations. --(1) If any goods entrusted for carriage to any notified station by a train intended solely for the carriage of goods are not, removed from such station by a person entitled to do so within a period of seven days after the termination of transit thereof at such station, the railway administration may, subject to the provisions of sub-section (2), sell such goods by public auction and apart from exhibiting, in accordance with the provisions of sub-section (3) of section 89, a statement containing a description of such goods, it shall not be necessary to give any notice of such public auction, but the date on which such auction may be held under this sub-section may be notified in one or more local newspapers. or where there are no such newspapers, in such manner as may be prescribed:

Provided that if at any time before the sale of such goods under this sub-section the person entitled thereto pays the freight and other charges and the expenses due in respect thereof to the railway administration, he shall be allowed to remove such goods.

(2) If any goods which may be sold by public auction under sub-section (1) at a notified station, being essential commodities. are required by the Central Government or the State Government for its own use or if the Central Government or such State Government considers that it is necessary for securing the availability of all or any such essential commodities at fair prices so to do, it may, by order in writing, direct the railway servant in-charge of such auction to transfer such goods to ii or to such agency, cooperative society or other person (being an agency, co-operative society or other person subject to the control of the: Government) engaged in the business of selling such essential commodities as may be specified in the direction.

(3) Every direction issued under sub-section (2) in respect of any essential commodity shall be binding on the railway servant to whom it is issued and the railway administration and it shall be a sufficient defence against any claim by the person entitled to

the goods that such essential commodities have been transferred in compliance with such direction:

Provided that--

(a) such direction shall not be binding on such railway servant or the railway administration--

(i) if it has not been received by the railway servant sufficiently in time to enable him to prevent the sale of the essential commodities to which it relates; or

(ii) if before the time appointed for such sale, the person entitled to such goods pays the freight and other charges and the expenses due in respect thereof and claims that he be allowed to remove the goods; or

(iii) if the price payable for such goods (as estimated by the Central Government or, as the case may be, the State Government) is not credited to the railway administration in the prescribed manner and the railway administration is not indemnified against any additional amount which it may become liable to pay towards the price by reason of the price not having been computed in accordance with the provisions of sub-section (4);

(b) where directions are issued in respect of the same goods both by the Central Government and the State Government, the directions received earlier shall prevail.

(4) The price payable for any essential commodity transferred in compliance with a direction issued under sub-section (2) shall be the price calculated in accordance with the provisions of sub-section (3) of section 3 of the Essential Commodities Act, 1955: [10 of 1955j:

Provided that -

(a) in the case of any essential commodity being a food-stuff in respect whereof a notification issued under sub-section (3A) of section 3 of the Essential Commodities Act, 1955, [10 of 2955], is in force in the locality in which the notified station is situated, the price payable shall be calculated in accordance with the provisions of clauses (iii) and (iv) of that sub-section;

(b) in the case of an essential commodity being any grade or variety of food grains, edible oil-seeds or edible oils in respect whereof no notification issued under subsection (3A) of section 3 of the Essential Commodities Act, 1955, [10 of 1955], is in force in the locality in which the notified station is situated, the price payable shall be calculated in accordance with the provisions of sub-section (3B) of that section;

(c) in the case of an essential commodity being any kind of sugar in respect whereof no notification issued under sub-section (3A) of section 3 of the Essential Commodities Act, 1955, [10 of 1955], is in force in the locality in which the notified station is situated, the price payable shall, if such sugar has been booked by the producer to himself, be calculated in accordance with the provisions of sub-section (3C) of that section.

Explanation.--For the purposes of this clause, the expressions "producer" and "sugar" shall have the meanings assigned to these expressions in the *Explanation* to subsection (3C) of section 3, and clause (e) of section 2 of the Essential Commodities Act, 1955, [10 of 1955], respectively.

91. Price to be paid to person entitled after deducting dues. -- (1) Out of the proceeds of any sale of goods under sub-section (1) of section 90 or the price payable therefor under sub-section (4) of that section, the railway administration may retain a sum equal to the freight and other charges due in respect of such goods and the expenses incurred in respect of the goods and the auction thereof and render the surplus, if any, to the person entitled thereto.

(2) Notwithstanding anything contained in sub-section (1), the railway administration may recover by suit any such freight or charge or expenses referred to therein or balance thereof.

(3) Any goods sold under sub-section (1) of section 90 or transferred in compliance with the directions issued under sub-section (2) of that section shall vest in the buyer or the transferee free from all encumbrances but subject to a priority being given for the sum which may be retained by a railway administration under sub-section (1), the person in whose favour such encumbrance subsists may have a claim in respect of such encumbrance against the surplus, if any, referred in that sub-section.

92. Power to make rules in respect of matter in this Chapter. -- (1) The Central Government may, be notification, make rules to carry out the purposes of this Chapter, (2) In particular, and without prejudice to the generality of the foregoing power, such rules may provide for all or any of the following matters, namely :-

- (a) the factors to which the Central Government shall have regard under clause (e) of the first proviso to sub-section (1) of section 89;
- (b) the form and manner in which an application may be made under sub-section (2) of section 89;
- (c) the form in which a statement is required to be exhibited under sub-section (3) of section 89;
- (d) the manner in which the dates of public auctions may be notified under subsection (1) of section 90;
- (e) the manner of crediting to the railway administration the price of goods referred to in sub-clause (iii) of clause (a) of the proviso to sub-section (3) of section 90.

CHAPTER XI
RESPONSIBILITIES OF RAILWAY ADMINISTRATION AS CARRIERS

93. General responsibility of a railway administration as carrier of goods. - Save as otherwise provided in this Act, a railway administration shall be responsible for the loss, destruction, damage or deterioration in transit, or non-delivery of any consignment, arising from any cause except the following, namely :-

(a) act of God;
(b) act of war;
(c) act of public enemies;
(d) arrest, restraint or seizure under legal process;
(e) orders or restrictions imposed by the Central Government or a Slate Government or by an officer or authority subordinate to the Central Government or a State Government authorised by it in this behalf;
(f) act or omission or negligence of the consignor or the consignee or the endorsee or the agent or servant of the consignor or the consignee or the endorsee;
(g) natural deterioration or wastage in bulk or weight due to inherent defect, quality or vice of the goods;
(h) latent defects;
(i) fire explosion or any unforeseen risk :

Provided that even where such loss, destruction, damage, deterioration or non-delivery is proved to have arisen from any one or more of the aforesaid causes, the railway administration shall not be relieved of its responsibility for the loss, destruction, damage, deterioration or non-delivery unless the railway administration further proves that it has used reasonable foresight and care in the carriage of the goods.

COMMENTS
Special provisions exclude the general provisions. A.I.R. 1967 Calcutta 133.

94. Goods to be loaded or delivered at a siding: not belonging to a railway administration. -- (1) Where goods rue required to be loaded at a siding not belonging to a railway administration for carriage by railway, the railway administration shall not be responsible for any loss, destruction, damage or deterioration of such goods from whatever cause arising, until the wagon confining the goods has been placed at the specified point of interchange or wagons between the siding and the railway administration and a railway servant authorised in this behalf has been informed in writing accordingly by the owner of the siding.

(2) Where any consignment is required to be delivered by a railway administration at a siding not belonging to a railway administration, the railway administration shall not be responsible for any loss, destruction, damage or deterioration or non-delivery of such consignment from whatever cause arising after the wagon containing the consignment has been placed at the specified point of interchange of wagons between the railway and the siding and the owner of the siding has been informed in writing accordingly by a railway servant authorised in this behalf.

95. Delay or retention in transit.--A railway administration shall not be responsible for the loss, destruction, damage or deterioration of any consignment proved by the owner to have been caused by the delay or detention in their carriage if the railway administration proves that the delay or detention arose for reasons beyond its control or without negligence or misconduct on its part or on the part of any of its servants,

COMMENTS

Railway administration is responsible for deterioration in quality of the goods. *A.I.R. 1981 Allahabad 268.*

96. Traffic passing over railways in India and railways in foreign countries.- Where in the course of carriage of any consignment from a place in India to a place, outside India or from a place outside India to a place in India or from one place outside India to another place outside India or from one place in India to another place in India over any territory outside India, it is carried over the railways of any railway administration in India, the railway administration shall not be responsible under any of the provisions of this Chapter for the loss, destruction, damage or deterioration of the goods, from whatever cause arising, unless it is proved by the owner of the goods that such loss, destruction, damage or deterioration arose over the railway of the railway administration.

97. Goods carried at owner's risk rate.- Notwithstanding anything contained in section 93, a railway administration shall not responsible for any loss, destruction, damage, deterioration or non-delivery in transit, of any consignment carried at owner's risk rate, from whatever cause arising except upon proof, that such loss, destruction, damage, deterioration or non-delivery was due to negligence or misconduct to its part or on the part of any of its servants :

Provided that--

(a) where the whole of such consignment or the whole of any package forming part of such consignment is not delivered to the consignee or the endorsee and such non-delivery is not proved by the railway administration to have been due to fire or to any accident to the train; or

(b) where in respect of any such consignment or of any package forming part of such consignment which had been so covered or protected that the covering or protection was not readily removable by hand, it is pointed out to the railway administration on or before delivery that any part of that consignment or package had been pilfered in transit,

the railway administration shall be bound to disclose to the consignor, the consignee of the endorsee how the consignment or the package was dealt with throughout the time it was in its possession or control, but if negligence or misconduct on the part of the railway administration or of any of its servants cannot be fairly inferred from such disclosure, the burden of proving such negligence or misconduct shall lie on the consignor, the consignee or the endorsee.

COMMENTS

The railway administration is bound to Lake as much care of the consignment as it would have taken of its own goods. A.I.R. 1965 S.C. 1666.

98. Goods in defective condition or defectively packed.-- (1) Notwithstanding anything contained in the foregoing provisions of this Chapter, when any goods entrusted to 3 railway administration for carriage -

(a) are in a defective condition as a consequence of which they are liable to damage, deterioration, leakage or wastage; or

(b) are either defectively packed or not packed in such manner as may be prescribed and as a result of such defective or improper packing are liable to damage, deterioration, leakage of wastage,

and the fact of such condition or defective or improper packing has been recorded by the consignor or his agent in the forwarding note, the railway administration shall not be responsible for an y damage, deterioration, leakage or wastage or for the condition in which such goods are available for delivery at destination :

Provided that the railway administration shall be responsible for any such damage, deterioration, leakage or wastage or for the condition in which such goods are available for delivery at destination if negligence or misconduct on the part of the railway administration or of any of its servants is proved.

(2) When any goods entrusted to a railway administration for carriage are found on arrival at the destination station to have been damaged or to have suffered deterioration, leakage or wastage, the railway administration shall not be responsible for the damage, deterioration, leakage or wastage of the goods on proof by railway administration,--

(a) that the goods were, at the time of entrustment to the railway administration, in a defective condition, or were at that time either defectively packed or not packed in such manner as may be prescribed and as a result of which were liable to damage, deterioration, leakage or wastage; and

(b) that such defective condition or defective or improper packing was not brought to the notice of railway administration or any of its servants at the time of entrustment of entrustment of the goods to the railway administration for carriage by railway:

Provided that the railway administration shall be responsible for any such damage, deterioration, leakage or wastage if negligence or misconduct on the part of the railway administration or of any its servants is proved.

COMMENTS

The Forwarding Note alone can show whether the packing was defective or not. A.I.R. 1978 Patna 213.

99. Responsibility of a railway administration after termination of transit.--(1) A railway administration shall be responsible as a bailee under sections 151, 152 and 161 of the Indian Contract Act, 1872 [9 of 1872], for the loss, destruction, damage, deterioration or non-delivery of any consignment up to a period of seven days after the termination of transit :

Provided that where the consignment is at owner's risk rate, the railway administration shall not be responsible as a bailee for such loss, destruction, damage, deterioration or non-delivery except on proof of negligence or misconduct on the part of the railway administration or of any of its servants.

(2) The railway administration shall not be responsible in any case for the loss, destruction, damage, deterioration or non-delivery of any consignment arising after the expiry of a period of seven days after the termination of transit.

(3) Notwithstanding anything contained in the foregoing provisions of this section, a railway administration shall not be responsible for the loss, destruction, damage,

deterioration or non-delivery of perishable goods, animals, explosives and such dangerous or other goods as may be prescribed, after the termination of transit.

(4) Nothing in the foregoing provisions of this section shall affect the liability of any person to pay any demurrage or wharfage, as the case may be, for so long as the consignment is not unloaded from the railway wagons or removed from the railway premises.

COMMENTS

The railway's liability under section 93 is subjected to alteration or variation. 1981 A.C.C. 431 (M.P.)].

100. Responsibility as carrier of luggage.--A railway administration shall not be responsible for the loss, destruction, damage, deterioration or non-delivery of any luggage unless a railway servant has booked the luggage and given a receipt therefor and in the case of luggage which is carried by the passenger in his charge, unless it is also proved that the loss, destruction, damage or deterioration was due to the negligence or misconduct on its Dart or on the part of any of its servants.

101. Responsibility as a carrier of animals.--A railway administration shall not be responsible for any loss or destruction of, or injuries to, any animal carried by railway arising from fright or restiveness of the animal or from overloading of wagons by the consignor.

102. Exoneration from liability in certain cases. Notwithstanding anything contained in the foregoing provisions of this Chapter, a railway administration shall not be responsible for the loss, destruction, damage deterioration or non-delivery of any consignment,
- (a) when such loss, destruction, damage, deterioration or non-delivery is due to the fact that a materially false description of the consignment is given in the statement delivered under sub-section (1) of section 66; or
- (b) where a fraud has been practiced by the consignor or the consignee or the endorsee or by an agent of the consignor, consignee or the endorsee; or
- (c) where it is proved by the railway administration to have been caused by, or to have arisen from -
    - (i) improper loading or unloading by the consignor or the consignee or the endorsee or by an agent of the consignor, consignee or the endorsee;
    - (ii) riot, civil commotion, strike, lock-out, stoppage or restraint of labour from whatever cause arising whether partial or general; or (d) for any indirect or consequential loss or damage or for loss of particular market.

COMMENTS

The liability of an ordinary carrier for damage is exonerable in certain circumstances. 1976 (3) S.C.C. 108.

103. Extent of monetary liability in respect of any consignment.--(1) Where any consignment is entrusted to a railway administration for carriage by railway and the value of such consignment has not been declared as required under sub-section (2) by the consignor, the amount of liability of the railway administration for the loss, destruction, damage, deterioration or non-delivery of the consignment shall in no case exceed such amount calculated with reference to the weight of the consignment as may be prescribed, and where such consignment consists of an animal, the liability shall not exceed such amount as may be prescribed.

(2) Notwithstanding anything contained in sub-section (1), where the consignor declares the value of any consignment at the time of its entrustment to a railway administration for carriage by railway, and pays such percentage charge as may be prescribed on so much of the value of such consignment as is in excess of the liability of the railway administration as calculated or specified, as the case may be, under subsection (1), the liability of the railway administration for the loss, destruction, damage, deterioration or non-delivery of such consignment shall not exceed the value so declared.

(3) The Central Government may, from time to time, by notification, direct that such goods as may be specified in the notification shall not be accepted for carriage by railway unless the value of such goods is declared and percentage charge is paid as required under sub-section (2).

104. Extent of liability in respect of goods carried in open wagon.- Where any goods, which, under ordinary circumstances, would be carried in covered wagon and would be liable to damage, if carried otherwise, are with the consent of the consignor, recorded in the forwarding note, carried in open wagon, the responsibility of railway administration for destruction, damage or deterioration which may arise only by reason of the goods being so carried, shall be one-half of the amount of liability for such destruction, damage of deterioration determined under this Chapter.

105. Right of railway administration to check contents of certain consignment or luggage.-- Where the value has been declared under section 103 in respect of any consignment a railway administration may make it a condition of carrying such consignment that a railway servant authorised by it in this behalf has been satisfied by examination or otherwise that the consignment tendered for carriage contain the articles declared.

106. Notice of claim for compensation and refund of overcharge.--(l) A person shall not be entitled to claim compensation against a railway administration for the loss, destruction, damage, deterioration or non-delivery of goods carried by railway, unless a notice thereof is served by him or on his behalf,-

(a) to the railway administration to which the goods are entrusted for carriage; or
(b) to the railway administration on whose railway the destination station lies, or the loss, destruction, damage or deterioration occurs, within a period of six months from the date of entrustment of the goods.

(2) Any information demanded or enquiry made in writing from, or any complaint made in writing to, any of the railway administrations mentioned in sub-section (1) by or on behalf of the person within the said period of six months regarding the non-delivery or delayed delivery of the goods with particulars sufficient to identify the goods shall, for the purpose of this section, be deemed to be a notice of claim for compensation.

(3) A person shall not be entitled to a refund of an overcharge in respect of goods carried by railway unless a notice therefor has been served by him or on his behalf to the railway administration to which the overcharge has been paid within six months from the date of such payment or the date of delivery of such goods at the destination station, whichever is later.

107. Applications for compensation for loss, etc., of goods.--An application for compensation for loss, destruction, damage, deterioration or non-delivery of goods shall be filed against the railway administration on whom a notice under section 106 has been served.

108. Person entitled to claim com pension. -- (i) If a railway administration pays compensation for the loss, destruction, damage, deterioration or non-delivery of goods entrusted to it for carriage, to the consignee or the endorsee producing the railway receipt, the railway administration shall be deemed to have discharged its liability and no application before the Claims Tribunal or any other legal proceeding shall lie against the railway administration on the ground that the consignee or the endorsee was not legally entitled to receive such compensation.

(2) Nothing in sub-section (i) shall affect the right of any person having any interest in the goods to enforce the same against the consignee or the endorsee receiving compensation under that sub-section.

109. Railway administration against which application for compensation for personal injury is to be filed.--An application before the Claims Tribunal for compensation for the loss of life or personal injury to a passenger, may be instituted against,

(a) the railway administration from which the passenger obtained his pass or purchased his ticket, or

(b) the railway administration on whose railway the destination station lies or the loss or personal injury occurred.

110. Burden of proof-- In an application before the Claims Tribunal for compensation for loss, destruction, damage, deterioration or non-delivery of any goods, the burden of proving--

(a) the monetary loss actually sustained; or (b) where the value has been declared under sub-section (2) of section 103 in respect of any consignment that the value so declared is its true value, shall lie on the person claiming compensation, but subject to the other provisions contained in this Act, it shall not be necessary for him to Drove how the loss, destruction, damage, deterioration or non-delivery was caused.

111. Extent of liability of railway administration in respect of accidents at sea.-(1) When a railway administration contracts to carry passengers or goods partly by railway and partly be sea, a condition exempting the railway administration from responsibility for any loss of life, personal injury or loss of or damage to goods which may happen during the carriage by sea from act of Cod, public, enemies, fire, accidents from machinery, boilers and steam and all and every other dangers and accidents of the seas, rivers and navigation of whatever nature and kind shall, without being expressed, be deemed to be part of the contract, and, subject to that condition, the railway administration shall, irrespective of the nationality or ownership of the ship used for the carriage by sea, be responsible for any loss of life, personal injury or loss of or damage to goods which may happen during the carriage by sea, to the extent to which it would be responsible under the Merchant Shipping Act,

1958, [43 of 1958] if the ships were registered under that Act and the railway administration were owner of the ship and not to any greater extent.

(2) The burden of proving that any such loss, injury or damage as is mentioned in sub-section (1) happened during the carriage by sea shall lie on the railway administration.

112. Power to make rules in respect of matters in this Chapter.-- (l) The Central Government may, be notification, make rules to carry out the purposes of this Chapter.

(2) In particular, and without prejudice to the generality of the foregoing power, such rules may provide for all or any of the following matters, namely:

- (a) the manner of packing of goods entrusted to a railway administration under clause (b) sub-section (1) of section 98;
- (b) the goods for the purposes of sub-section (3) of section 99; and
- (c) the maximum amount payable by the railway administration for the loss, destruction, damage, deterioration or non-delivery of any consignment under sub-section (1) of section 103.

CHAPTER XII

ACCIDENTS

113. Notice of railway accident.-- (1) Where, in the course of working a railway, -

(a) any accident attended with loss of any human life, or with grievous hurt, as defined in the Indian Penal Code, [45 of 1860] or with such serious injury to property as may be prescribed; or

(b) any collision between trains of which one is a train carrying passengers; or

(c) the derailment of any train carrying passengers, or of any part of such train; or

(d) any accident of a description usually attended with loss of human life or with such grievous hurt as aforesaid or with serious injury to property; or

(e) any accident of any other description which the Central Government may notify in this behalf in the Official Gazette,

occurs, the station master of the station nearest to the place at which the accident occurs or where there is no station master, the railway servant in charge of the section of the railway on which the accident occurs shall, without, delay, give notice of the accident to the District Magistrate and Superintendent of Police, within whose jurisdiction the accident occurs, the officer in charge of the police station within the local limits of which the accident occurs and to such other Magistrate or police officer as may be appointed in this behalf by the Central Government.

(2) The railway administration within whose jurisdiction the accident occurs, as also the railway administration to whom the train involved in the accident belongs, shall without delay, give notice of the accident to the State Government and the Commissioner having jurisdiction over the place of the accident.

114. Inquiry by Commissioner.--(1) On the receipt of a notice under section 113 of the occurrence of an accident to a train carrying passengers resulting in loss of human life or grievous hurt causing total or partial disablement of permanent nature to a passenger or serious damage to railway property, the Commissioner shall, as soon as may be, notify the railway administration in whose jurisdiction the accident occurred of his intention to hold an inquiry into the causes that led to the accident and shall at the same time fix and communicate the date, time and place of inquiry:

Provided that it shall be open to the Commissioner to hold an inquiry into any other accident which, in his opinion, requires the holding of such an inquiry.

(2) If for any reason, the Commissioner is not able to hold an inquiry as soon as may be after the occurrence of the accident, he shall notify the railway administration accordingly.

115. Inquiry by railway administration.-Where no inquiry is held by the Commissioner under sub-section (1) of section 114 or where the Commissioner has informed the railway administration under sub-section (2) of that section that he is not able to hold an inquiry, the railway administration within whose jurisdiction the accident occurs, shall cause an inquiry to be made in accordance with the prescribed procedure.

116. Powers of Commissioner in relation to inquiries.--(l) For the purpose of conducting an inquiry under this Chapter into the causes of any accident on a railway, the Commissioner shall, in addition to the powers specified in section 7, have the powers as are vested in a civil court while trying a suit under the Code of Civil Procedure, 1908, [5 of 1908] in respect of the following matters, namely :-

(a) summoning and enforcing the attendance of persons and examining them on oath;
(b) requiring the discovery and production of documents;
(c) receiving evidence on affidavits;
(d) requisitioning any public record or copies thereof from any court or office;
(e) any other matter which may be prescribed.

(2) The Commissioner while conducting an inquiry under this Chapter shall be deemed to be a Civil Court for the purposes of section 195 and Chapter XXVX of the Code of Criminal Procedure, 1973, [2 of 1974].

117. Statement made before Commissioner.--No statement made by a person in the course of giving evidence in an inquiry before the Commissioner shall subject him to, or be used against him in, any civil or criminal proceeding, except a prosecution for giving false evidence by such statement :

Provided that the statement is -

(a) made in reply to a question which is required by the Commissioner to answer;
(b) relevant to the subject-matter of the inquiry.

118. Procedure, etc--Any railway administration or the Commissioner conducting an inquiry under this Chapter may send notice of the inquiry to such persons, follow such procedure, and prepare the report in such manner as may be prescribed.

119. No inquiry, investigation, etc, to be made if the Commission of Inquiry is appointed.-Notwithstanding anything contained in the foregoing provisions of this Chapter, where a Commission of Inquiry is appointed under the Commissions of Inquiry Act, 1952, [3 of 1952] to inquire into an accident, any inquiry, investigation or other proceeding pending in relation to that accident shall not be proceeded with, and all records or other documents relating to such inquiry shall be forwarded to such authority as may be specified by the Central Government in this behalf.

120. Inquiry into accident not covered by section 113.--Where any accident of the nature not specified in section 113 occurs in the course of working a railway, the railway administration within whose jurisdiction the accident occurs, may cause such inquiry to be made into the causes of the accident, as may be prescribed.

121. Returns.--Every railway administration shall send to the Central Government, a return of accidents occurring on its railway, whether attended with injury to any person or not, in such form and manner and at such intervals as may be prescribed.

122. Power to make rules in respect of matters in this Chapter,--(l) The Central Government may, by notification, make rules to carry out the purposes of this Chapter.

(2) In particular, and without prejudice to the generality of the foregoing power, such rules may provide for all or any of the following matters, namely :-

- (a) the injury to property which shall be considered serious under clause (a) of subsection (1) of section 113;
- (b) the forms of notice of accidents to be given under section 1 13 and the particulars of the accident such notices shall contain;
- (c) the manner of sending the notices of accidents, including the class of accidents to be sent immediately after the accident;
- (d) the duties of the Commissioner, railway administration, railway servants, police officers and Magistrates on the occurrence of an accident;
- (c) the persons to whom notices in respect of any inquiry under this Chapter are to be sent, the procedure to be followed in such inquiry and the manner in which a report of such inquiry shall be prepared;
- (f) the nature of inquiry to be made by a railway administration into the causes of an accident under section 120;
- (g) the form and manner of sending a return of accidents by a railway administration under section]21.

CHAPTER XIII

LIABILITY OF RAILWAY ADMINISTRATION FOR DEATH AND INJURY TO PASSENGERS DUE TO ACCIDENTS

123. Definitions.--In this Chapter, unless the context otherwise requires, (a) "accident" means an accident of the nature described in section 124; (b) "dependant" means any of the following relatives of a deceased passenger, namely :-

(i) the wife, husband, son and daughter, and in case the deceased passenger is unmarried or is a minor, his parent,

(ii) the parent, minor brother or unmarried sister, widowed sister, widowed daughter-in-law and a minor child of a pre-deceased son, if dependant wholly or partly on the deceased passenger;

(iii) a minor child of a pre-deceased daughter, if wholly dependant on the deceased passenger;

---

1. 'Ins. by Act No. 28 of 1994. S. 2. (w.e.f.. 1.8.1994).

(iv) the paternal grand parent wholly dependant on the deceased passenger. 1[(c)"untoward incident" means-(1) (i) the commission of a terrorist act within the meaning of sub-section (1) of section 3 of the Terrorist and Disruptive Activities (Prevention) Act, 1987 (28 of 1987) ,or

(ii) the making of a violent attack or tile commission of robbery or dacoity; or

(iii) the indulging in rioting, shoot-out or arson,

by any person in or any train carrying passengers, or in a waiting hall, cloak room or reservation or booking office or on any platform or in any other place within the precincts of a railway station; or

(2) the accidental falling of any passenger from a train carrying passenger]

COMMENT

This section defines the words "accident " and "dependant" used in Chapter XIII.

124. Extent of liability.--When in the course of working a railway, an accident occurs, being either a collision between trains of which one is a train carrying passengers or the dcrailmcnt of or other accident to a train or any part of a train carrying passengers, then whether or not there has been any wrongful act, neglect or default on the part of the railway administration such as would entitle a passenger who has been injured or has suffered a loss to maintain an action and recover damages in respect thereof · the railway administration shall, not withstanding anything contained in any other law, be liable to pay compensation to such extent as may be prescribed and to that extent only for loss occasioned by the death of a passenger dying as a result of such accident, and for personal injury and loss, destruction, damage or deterioration of goods owned by the passenger and accompanying him in his compartment or on the train, sustained as a result of such accident.

Explanation.--For the purposes of this section "passenger" includes a railway servant on duty.

²[**124A. Compensation on account of untoward incidents.**--When in the course of working a railway untoward incident occurs, then whether or not there has been any wrongful act, neglect or default on the part of the railway administration such as would entitle a passenger who has been injured or the dependant of a passenger who has been killed to maintain an action and recover damages in respect thereof the railway administration shall, notwithstanding any thing contained in any other law, be liable to pay compensation to such extent as may be prescribed and to that extent only for loss occasioned by the death of, or injury to, a passenger as a result of such untoward incident:

Provided that no compensation shall be payable under this section by the railway administration if the passenger dies or suffers injury due to-

(a) suicide or attempted suicide by him;
(b) self-inflicted injury;

---

1. Ins. by Act No. 28 of 1994 s. 2. (w.e.f. 1.8.1994).
2. Ins. by Act No. 28 of 1994 s. 3 (w.c.f. 1.R.1994).

(c) his own criminal act;
(d) any act committed by him in a state of intoxication or insanity;
(e) any natural cause or disease or medical or surgical treatment unless such treatment becomes necessary due to injury caused by the said untoward incident.

Explanation.--For the purposes of this section "passenger" includes-
   (i) a railway servant on duty; and
   (ii) a person who has purchased a valid ticket for travelling, by a train carrying passengers, on any date or a valid platform ticket and becomes a victim of an untoward incident.]

COMMENTS

Guard is not entitled to compensation. *A.I.R. 1988 Patna 130.*

125. Application-for compensation (1) An application for compensation under section 124 [1][or section 124 A] may be made to the Claims Tribunal-

(a) by the person who has sustained the injury or suffered any loss, or
(b) by any agent duly authorised by such person in this behalf, or
(c) where such person is a minor, by his guardian, or
(d) where death has resulted from the accident [2][or the untoward incident], by any dependant of the deceased or where such a dependant is a minor, by his guardian.

(2) Every application by a dependant for compensation under this section shall be for the benefit of every other dependant.

126. Interim relief by railway administration.--(l) Where a person who has made an application for compensation under section 125 desires to be paid interim relief, he may apply to the railway administration for payment of interim relief alongwith a copy of the application made under that section.

(2) Where, on the receipt of an application made under sub-section (1) and after making such inquiry as it may deem fit, the railway administration is satisfied that circumstances exist which require relief to be afforded to the applicant immediately, it may, pending determination by the Claims Tribunal of the actual amount of compensation payable under section 124 [3][or section 124A] pay to any person who has sustained the injury or suffered any loss, or where death has resulted from the accident, to any dependant of the deceased, such sum as it considers reasonable for affording such relief, so however, that the sum paid shall not exceed the amount of compensation payable at such rates as may be prescribed.

(3) The railway administration shall, as soon as may be, after making an order regarding payment of interim relief under sub-section (2), send a copy thereof to the Claims Tribunal.

(4) Any sum paid by the railway administration under sub-section (2) shall be taken into

---
1. Ins. by Act No. 28 of 1994 s.4 (a), (w.c.f 1.8.1994).
2. Ins. by Act No. 28 of 1994 s.4 (b), (w.e.f 1.8.1994).
3. Ins. by Act No. 28 of 1994 s.5. (w.e.f 1.8.1994).

account by the Claims Tribunal while determining the amount of compensation payable.

127. Determination of compensation in respect of any injury or loss of goods.-(1) Subject to such rules as may be made, the rates of compensation payable in respect of any injury shall be determined by the Claims Tribunal.

(2) The compensation payable in respect of any loss of goods shall be such as the Claims Tribunal may, having regard to the circumstances of the case, determine to be reasonable.

COMMENTS

The Claims Commissioner is a Special Tribunal with limited powers. *AIR. 1973 Allahabad 342.*

128. Saving as to certain rights.--(l) The Fight of any person to claim compensation under section 124 ¹[or section 124A] shall not affect the right of any such person to recover compensation payable under the Workmen's Compensation Act, 1923, [8 of 1923] or any other law for the time being in force; but no person shall be entitled to claim compensation more than once in respect of the same accident.

(2) Nothing in sub-section (1) shall affect the right of any person to claim compensation payable under any contract or scheme providing for payment of compensation for death or personal injury or for damage to property or any sum payable under any policy of insurance.

129. Power to make rules in respect of matters in this Chapter.--(l) The Central Government may, by notification make rules to carry out the purposes of this Chapter.

(2) In particular, and without prejudice to the generality of the foregoing power, such rules may provide for all or any of the following matters, namely:

(a) the compensation payable for death ;

(b) the nature of the injuries for which compensation shall be paid and the amount of such compensation.

CHAPTER XIV
REGULATION OF HOURS OF WORK AND PERIOD OF REST

130. Definitions;-In this Chapter, unless the context otherwise requires, -

(a) the employment of a railway servant is said to be "continuous" except when it is excluded or has been declared to be essentially intermittent or intensive;

(b) the employment of a railway servant is said to be "essentially intermittent" when it has been declared to be so by the prescribed authority on the ground that the daily hours of duty of the railway servant normally include periods of inaction aggregating to fifty per cent or more (including at least one such period of not less than one hour or two such periods of not less than half an hour each) in a tour of twelve hours duty (on the average over seventy-two consecutive hours), during which the railway servant may be on duty, but is not called upon to display either physical activity or sustained attention;

---

1. Ins. by Act No. 28 of 1994 S.6. (w.e.f 1.8.1994).

(c) the employment of a railway servant is said to be "excluded" , if he belongs to any one of the following categories, namely :-

    (i) railway servants employed in a managerial or confidential capacity;
    (ii) armed guards or other personnel subject to discipline similar to that of any of the armed police forces;
    (iii) staff of the railway schools imparting technical training of academic education;
    (iv) such staff as may be specified as supervisory under the rules;
    (v) such other categories of staff as may be prescribed;

(d) the employment of a railway servant is said to be "intensive" when it has been declared to be so by the prescribed authority on the ground that it is of strenuous nature involving continued concentration or hard manual labour with little or no period of relaxation.

131, Chapter not to apply to certain railway servants--Nothing in this Chapter shall apply to any railway servant to whom the Factories Act, 1948[63 of 1948], or Mines Act, 1952 [35 of 1952] or the Railway Protection Force Act, 1957 [23 of 1957] or the Merchant Shipping: Act, 1958 [44 of 1958], applies.

132. Limitation or hours of work.--(l) A railway servant whose employment is essentially intermittent shall not be employed for more than seventy-five hours in any week.

(2) A railway servant whose employment is continuous shall not be employed for more than fifty-four hours a week on an average in a two-weekly period of fourteen days.

(3) A railway servant whose employment is intensive shall not be employed for more than forty-five hours a week on an average in a two-weekly period of fourteen days.

(4) Subject to such rules as may be prescribed, temporary exemptions of railway servants from the provisions of sub-section (1) or sub-section (2) or sub-section (3) may be made by the prescribed authority if it is of opinion that such temporary exemptions are necessary to avoid serious interference with the ordinary working of the railway or in cases

of accident, actual or threatened, or when urgent work is required to be done to the railway or to rolling stock or in any emergency which could not have been foreseen or prevented, or in other cases of exceptional pressure of work:

Provided that where such exemption results in the increase of hours of employment of a railway servant referred to in any of the sub-sections, he shall be paid overtime at not less than two times his ordinary rate of pay for the excess hours of work.

133. Grant of periodical rest.--(1) Subject to the provisions of this section, a railway servant -

(a) whose employment is intensive or continuous shall, for every week commencing on a Sunday, be granted a rest of not less than thirty consecutive hours;
(b) whose employment is essentially intermittent shall, for every week commencing on a Sunday, be granted a rest of not less than twenty-four consecutive hours including a full night.

(2) Notwithstanding anything contained in sub-section (1),

(i) any locomotive or traffic running staff shall be granted, each month, a rest of at least four periods of not less than thirty consecutive hours each or at least five periods of not less than twenty-two consecutive hours each, including a full night;
(ii) the Central Government may, be rules, specify the railway servants to whom periods of rest on scales less than those laid down under sub-section (1) may be granted and the periods thereof.

(3) Subject to such rules as may be made in this behalf, if the prescribed authority is of the opinion that such circumstances as are referred to in sub-section (4) of section 132 are present, it may exempt any railway servant from the provisions of sub-section (1) or clause (i) of sub-section (2):

Provided that a railway servant so exempted shall, in such circumstances as may be prescribed, be granted compensatory periods of rest for the periods he has forgone.

134. Railway servant to remain on duty.-Nothing in this Chapter or the rules made thereunder shall, where due provision has been made for the relief of a railway servant, authorise him to leave his duty until he has been relieved.

135. Supervisors of railway labour.--(1) Subject to such rules as may be made in this behalf, the Central Government may appoint supervisors of railway labour.

(2) The duties of supervisors of railway labour shall be -

(i) to inspect railways in order to determine whether the provisions of this Chapter or of the rules made thereunder are duly observed; and
(ii) to perform such other functions as may be prescribed.

(3) A supervisor of railway labour shall be deemed to be a Commissioner for the purposes of sections 7 and 9.

136. Power to make rules in respect of matters in this Chapter.--(1) The Central Government may, by notification, make rules to carry out the purposes of this Chapter.

(2) In particular, and without prejudice to the generality of the foregoing power, such rules may provide for all or any of the following matters, namely :--

- (a) the authorities who may declare the employment of any railway servant essentially intermittent or intensive;
- (b) the appeals against any such declaration and the manner in which, and the conditions subject to which any such appeal may be filed and heard;
- (c) the categories of staff that may be specified under sub-clauses (iv) and (v) of clause (c) of section 130;
- (d) the authorities by whom exemptions under sub-section (4) of section 132 or subsection (3) of section 133 may be made;
- (e) the delegation of power by the authorities referred to in clause (d);
- (f) the railway servants to whom clause (ii) of sub-section (2) of section 133 apply and the periods of rest to be granted to them;
- (g) the appointment of supervisors of railway labour and their functions.

CHAPTER XV
PENALTIES AND OFFENCES

137. **fraudulently travelling or attempting to travel without proper pass or ticket**--(i) If any person, with intent to defraud a railway administration,-(

a) enters or remains in any carriage on a railway or travels in a train in contravention of section 55, or

b) uses or attempts to use a single pass or a single ticket which has already been used on a previous journey, or in the case of a return ticket, a half thereof which has already been so used,

he shall be punishable with imprisonment for a term which may extend to six months, or with fine which may extend to one thousand rupees, or with both :

Provided that in the absence of special and adequate reasons to the contrary to be mentioned in the judgment of the court, such punishment shall not be less than a fine of five hundred rupees.

(2) The person referred to in sub-section (1) shall also be liable to pay the excess charge mentioned in sub-section (3) in addition to the ordinary single fare for the distance which he has travelled, or where there is any doubt as to the station from which he started, the ordinary single fare from the station from which the train originally started, or if the tickets of passengers travelling in the train have been examined since the original starting L of the train, the ordinary single fare from the place where the tickets were so examined or, in case of their having been examined more than once, were last examined.

(3) The excess charge referred to in sub-section (2) shall be a sum equal to the ordinary single fare referred to in that sub-section or fifty rupees, whichever is more.

(4) Notwithstanding anything contained in section 65 of the Indian Penal Code, [45 of 1860], the court convicting an offender may direct that the person in default of payment of any fine inflicted by the court shall suffer imprisonment for term which may extend to six months.

138. Levy of excess charge and fare for travelling without proper pass or ticket or beyond authorised distance. - (l) If any passenger,-

(a) being in or having alighted from a train, fails or refuses to present for examination or to deliver up his pass or ticket immediately on a demand being made therefor under section 54, or

(b) travels in a train in contravention of the provisions of section 55, he shall be liable to pay, on the demand of any railway servant authorised in this behalf, the excess charge mentioned in sub-section (3) in addition to the ordinary single fare for the distance which he has travelled or, where there is any doubt as to the station from which he started; the ordinary single fare from the station from which the train originally started, or, if the tickets of passengers travelling in the train have been examined since the original starting of the train, the ordinary single fare from the place where the tickets were so examined or in the case of their having been examined more than once, were last examined.

(2) If any passenger,--

(a) travels or attempts to travel in or on a carriage, or by a train, of a higher class than that for which he has obtained a pass or purchased a ticket; or

(b) travels in or on a carriage beyond the place authorised by his pass or ticket,

he shall be liable to pay, on the demand of any railway servant authorised in this behalf, any difference between the fare paid by him and the fare payable in respect of the journey he has made and the excess charge referred to in sub-section (3).

(3). The excess charge shall be a sum equal to the amount payable under sub-section (1) or sub-section (2), as the case may be, or fifty rupees, whichever is more :

Provided that if the passenger has with him a certificate granted under sub-section (2) of section 55, no excess charge shall be payable.

(4) If any passenger liable to pay the excess charge and the fare mentioned in subsection (1), or the excess charge and any difference of fare mentioned in sub-section (2), fails or refuses to pay the same on a demand being made therefor under one or other of these sub-sections, as the case may be, any railway servant authorised by the railway administration in this behalf may apply to any Metropolitan Magistrate or a Judicial Magistrate of the first or second class, as the case may be, for the recovery of the sum payable as if it were a fine, and the Magistrate if satisfied that the sum is payable shall order it to be so recovered, and may order that the person liable for the payment shall in default of payment suffer imprisonment of either description for a term which may extend to one month but not less than ten days.

(5) Any sum recovered under sub-section (4) shall, as and when it is recovered, be paid to the railway administration.

COMMENTS

Neither 'criminal intention' nor 'offence' is implied. *A.I.R. 1950 Allahabad 441.*

139. Power to remove persons--Any person failing or refusing to pay the fare and the excess charge referred to in section 138 may be removed by any railway servant authorised in this behalf who may call to his aid any other person to effect such removal:

Provided that nothing in this section shall be deemed to preclude a person removed from a carriage of a higher class from continuing his journey in a carriage of a class for which he holds a pass or ticket :

Provided further that a woman or a child if unaccompanied by a male passenger, shall not be so removed except either at the station from where she or he commences her or his journey or at a junction or terminal station or station at the headquarters of a civil district and such removal shall be made only during the day.

140. Security for good behaviour in certain cases.--(l) When a court convicting a person for an offence under section 137 or section i38 finds that he has been habitually committing or attempting to commit that offence and the court is of the opinion that it is necessary or desirable to require that person to execute a bond for good behaviour, such court may, at the time of passing the sentence on the person, order him to execute a bond with or without sureties, for such amount and for such period not exceeding three years as it deems fit.

(2) An order under sub-section (1) may also be made by an appellate court or by the High Court when exercising its powers of revision.

141. Needlessly interfering with means of communication in a train.--If any passenger or any other person, without reasonable and sufficient cause, makes use of, or interferes with. any means provided by a railway administration in a train for communication between passengers and the railway servant in charge of the train, he shall be punishable with imprisonment for a term which may extend to one year, or with fine which may extend to one thousand rupees, or with both:

Provided that, in the absence of special and adequate reasons to the contrary to be mentioned in a judgment of the court. where a passenger, without reasonable and sufficient cause, makes use of the alarm chain provided by a railway administration, such punishment shall not be less than-

(a) a fine of five hundred rupees, in the case of conviction for the first offence; and

(b) imprisonment for three months in case of conviction for the second or subsequent offence.

142. Penalty for transfer of tickets.--(l) If any person not being a railway servant or an agent authorised in this behalf--

(a) sells or attempts to sell any ticket or any half of a return ticket; or

(b) parts or attempts to part with the reservation of a seat or berth has been made or any half of a return ticket or a season ticket,

in order to enable any other person to travel therewith, he shall be punishable with imprisonment for a term which may extend to three months, or with fine which may extend to five hundred rupees, or with both, and shall also forfeit die ticket which he sells or attempts to sell or parts or attempts to part.

(2) If any person purchases any ticket referred to in clause (a) of sub-section (1) or obtains the possession of any ticket referred to in clause (b) of that sub-section from any person other than a railway servant or an agent authorised in this behalf, he shall be punishable with imprisonment for a term which may extend to three months and with fine which may extend to five hundred rupees and if the purchaser or holder of any ticket aforesaid travels or attempts to travel therewith, he shall forfeit the ticket which he so purchased or obtained and shall be deemed to be travelling without a proper ticket and shall be liable to be dealt with under section 138:

Provided that in the absence of special and adequate reasons to the contrary to be mentioned in the judgment of the court, the punishment under sub-section (1) or subsection (2) shall not be less than a fine of two hundred and fifty rupees.

143. Penalty for unauthorised carrying on of business of procuring and supplying of railway tickets.--(l) If any person, not being a railway servant or an agent authorised in this behalf,--

(a) carries on the business of procuring and supplying tickets for travel on a railway or for reserved accommodation for journey in a train; or

(b) purchases or sells or attempts to purchase or sell tickets with a view to carrying on any such business either by himself or by any other person, he shall be punishable with imprisonment for a term which may extend to three years or with fine which may extend to ten thousand rupees, or with both, and shall also forfeit the tickets which he so procures, supplies, purchases, sells or attempts to purchase or sell:

Provided that in the absence of special and adequate reasons to the contrary to be mentioned in the judgment of the court, such punishment shall not be less than imprisonment for a term of one month or a fine of five thousand rupees.

(2) Whoever abets any offence punishable under this section shall, whether or not such offence is committed. be punishable with the same punishment as is provided for the offence.

144. Prohibition on hawking, etc., and begging.--(1) If any person convasses for any custom or hawks or exposes for sale any article whatsoever in any railway carriage or upon any part of a railway, except under and in accordance with the terms and conditions of a license granted by the railway administration in this behalf, he shall be punishable with imprisonment for a term which may extend to one year, or with fine which may ex tend to two thousand/rupees, or with both :

Provided that, in the absence of special and adequate reasons to the contrary to be mentioned in the judgment of the court, such punishment shall not be less than a fine of one thousand rupees.

(2) If any person begs in any railway carriage or upon a railway station, he shall be liable for punishment as provided under sub-section (1).

(3) any person referred to in sub-section (1) or sub-section (2) may be removed from the railway carriage or any part of the railway or railway station, as the case may be, by any railway servant authorised in this behalf or by any other person whom such railway servant may call to his aid.

145. Drunkenness or nuisance.--If any person in any railway carriage or upon any part of a railway--

(a) is in a state of intoxication; or
(b) commits any nuisance or act of indecency or uses abusive or obscene language; or
(c) wilfully or without excuse interferes with any amenity provided by the railway administration so as to affect the comfortable travel of any passenger,

he may be removed from the railway by any railway servant and shall, in addition to the forfeiture of his pass or ticket, be punishable with imprisonment which may extend to six months and with fine which may extend to five hundred rupees:

Provided that in the absence-of special and adequate reasons to the contrary to be mentioned in the judgment of the court, such punishment shall not be less than--

(a) a fine of one hundred rupees in the case of conviction for the first offence; and
(b) imprisonment of one month and a fine of two hundred and fifty rupees, in the case of conviction for second or subsequent offence.

146. Obstructing railway servant in his duties.--If any person wilfully obstructs or prevents any railway servant in the discharge of his duties, he shall be punishable with imprisonment for a term which may extend to six months, or with fine which may extend to one thousand rupees, or with both.

147. Trespass and refusal to desist from trespass.--(l) If any person enters upon or into any part of a railway without lawful authority, or having lawfully entered upon or into such part misuses such property or refuses to leave, he shall be punishable with imprisonment for a term which may extend to six months, or with fine which may extend to one thousand rupees, or with both :

Provided that in the absence of special and adequate reasons to the contrary to be mentioned in the judgment of the court, such punishment shall not be less than a fine of five hundred rupees.

(2) Any person referred to in sub-section (1) may be removed from the railway by any railway servant or by any other person whom such railway servant may call to his aid.

148. Penalty for making a false statement in an application for compensation.-If in any application for compensation under section 125, any person makes a statement which is false or which he knows or believes to be false or does not believe to be true, he shall be punishable with imprisonment for a term which may extend to three years, or with fine, or with both.

149. Making a false claim for compensation.-- If any person requiring compensation from a railway administration for loss, destruction, damage, deterioration or non-delivery of any consignment makes a claim which is false or which he knows or believes to be false or does not believe to be true, he shall be punishable with imprisonment for a term which may extend to three years, or with fine, or with both.

150. Maliciously wrecking or attempting to wreck a train.-- (1) Subject to the provisions of sub-section (2), if any person unlawfully.-

- (a) puts or throws upon or across any railways, any wood, stone or other matter or thing; or
- (b) takes up, removes, loosens or displaces any rail, sleeper or other matter or things belonging to any railway; or
- (c) turns, moves, unlocks or diverts any points or other machinery belonging to any railway; or
- (d) makes or shows, or hides or removes, any signal or light upon or near to any railway; or
- (e) does or causes to be done or attempts to do any other act or thing in relation to any railway, with intent or with knowledge that he is likely to endanger the safety of any person travelling on or being upon the railway,

he shall be punishable with imprisonment for life, or with rigorous imprisonment for a term which may extend to ten years:

Provided that in the absence of special and adequate reasons to the contrary to be mentioned in the judgment of the court, where a person is punishable with rigorous imprisonment, such imprisonment shall not be less than-

- (a) three years, in the case of conviction for the first offence; and
- (b) seven years, in the case of conviction for the second or subsequent offence.

(2) If any person unlawfully does any act or thing referred to in any of the clauses of sub-section (1) --

(a) with intent to cause the death of any person and the doing of such act or thing causes the death of any person; or
(b) with knowledge that such act or thing is so imminently dangerous that it muse in all probability cause the death of any person or such bodily injury to any person as is likely to cause the death of such person,

he shall be punishable with death or imprisonment for life.

151. Damage to or destruction of certain railway properties.-- (1) If any person, with intent to cause, or knowing that he is likely to cause damage or destruction to any property of a railway referred to in sub-section (2), causes by fire, explosive substance , or otherwise, damage to such property or destruction of such property, he shall be punishable with imprisonment for a term which may extend to five years, or with fine, or with both.

(2) The properties of a railway referred to in sub-section (1) are railway track, bridges, station buildings, and installations, carriages or wagons, locomotives, signaling, telecommunications, electric traction and block equipments and such other properties as the Central Government being of the opinion that damage thereto or destruction thereof is likely to endanger the operation of a railway, may, by notification, specify.

152. Maliciously hurting or attempting to hurt persons travelling by railway.- If any person unlawfully throws or causes to fall or strike at against, into or upon any rolling stock forming part of a train, any wood, stone or other matter or thing with intent, u or with knowledge that he, is likely to endanger the safety of any person being in or upon such rolling stock or in or upon any other rolling stock forming part of the same train, he shall be punishable with imprisonment for life, or with imprisonment for a term which may extend to ten years.

153. Endangering safety of persons travelling by railway by wilful act or omission.--If any person by any unlawful act or by any wilful omission or neglect, endangers or causes to be endangered the safety of any person travelling on or being upon any railway, or obstructs or causes to be obstructed or attempts to obstruct any rolling stock upon any railway, he shall be punishable with imprisonment for a term which may extend to five years.

154. Endangering safety of persons travelling by railway by rash or negligent act or omission.--If any person in a rash and negligent manner does any act, or omits to do what he is legally bound to do, and the act or omission is likely to endanger the safety of any person travelling or being upon any railway, he shall be punishable with imprisonment for a term which may extend to one year, or with fine, or with both.

155. Entering into a compartment reserved or resisting entry into a compartment not reserved.--(l) if any passenger-

(a) having entered a compartment wherein no berth or seat has been reserved by a railway administration for his use, or
(b) having unauthorisedly occupied a berth or seal reserved by a railway administration for the use of another passenger,

refuses to leave it when required to do so by any railway servant authorised in this behalf, such railway may remove him or cause him to be removed, with the aid of any other person, from the compartment, berth or seat, as the case may be, and he shall also be punishable with fine which may extend to five hundred rupees.

(2) If any passenger resists the lawful entry of another passenger into a compartment not reserved for the use of the passenger resisting, he shall be punishable with fine which may extend to two hundred rupees.

156. Travelling on roof, step or engine of a train.-- If any passenger or any other person, after being warned by a railway servant to desist, persists in travelling on the roof, step or foot-board of any carriage or on an engine, or in any other part of a train not intended for the use of passengers, he shall be punishable with imprisonment for a term which may extend to three months, or with fine which may extend to five hundred rupees, or with both and may be removed from the railway by any railway servant.

157. Altering or defacing pass or ticket.-- If any passenger wilfully alters or defaces his pass or ticket so as to render the date. number or any material portion thereof illegible, he shall be punishable with imprisonment for a term which may extend to three months, or with fine which may extend to five hundred rupees, or with both.

158. Penalty for contravention of any of the provision of Chapter XIV--Any person under whose authority any railway servant is employed in contravention of any of the provisions of Chapter XIV or of the rules made thereunder shall be punishable with fine which may extend to five hundred rupees.

159. Disobedience of drivers or conductors of vehicles to directions of railway servant etc.--If any driver or conductor of any vehicle while upon the premises of a railway disobeys the reasonable directions of any railway servant or police officer, he shall be punishable with imprisonment for a term which may extend to one month, or with fine which may extend to five hundred rupees, or with both.

160. Opening or breaking a level crossing gate.--(l) If any person, other than a railway servant or a person authorised in this behalf, opens any gate or chain or barrier set up on either side of a level crossing which is closed to road traffic, he shall be punishable with imprisonment for a term which may extend to three years.

(2) If any person breaks any gate or chain or barrier set up on either side of a level crossing which is closed to road traffic, he shall be punishable with imprisonment for a term which may extend to five years.

161. Negligently crossing unmanned level crossing.--If any person driving or leading a vehicle is negligent in crossing an unmanned level crossing, he shall be punishable with imprisonment which may extend to one year.

Explanation.--For the purposes of this section, "negligence" in relation to any person driving or leading a vehicle in crossing an unmanned level crossing means the crossing of such level crossing by such person-(a) without stopping or caring to stop the vehicle near such level crossing to observe whether any approaching rolling stock is in sight, or (b) even while an approaching rolling stock is in sight.

162. Entering carriage or other place reserved for females.--If a male person knowing or having reason to believe that a carriage, compartment, berth or seat in a train or room or other place is reserved by a railway administration for the exclusive use of females, without lawful excuse,--

(a) enters such carriage, compartment, room or other place, or having entered such carriage, compartment, room or place, remains therein; or

(b) occupies any such berth or seat having been required by any railway servant to vacate it,

he shall, in addition to being liable to forfeiture of his pass or ticket, be punishable with fine which may extend to five hundred rupees and may also be removed by any railway servant.

163. Giving False account of goods.--If any person required to furnish an account of goods under section 66, gives an account which is materially false, he and, if he is not the owner of the goods, the owner also shall, without prejudice to his liability to pay any freight or other charge under any provision of this Act, be punishable with fink which may extend to five hundred rupees for every quintal or part thereof of such goods.

164. Unlawfully bringing dangerous goods on a railway.--If ally person, in contravention of section 6'7, takes with him any dangerous goods or entrusts such goods for carriage to the railway administration, he shall be punishable with imprisonment for a term which may extend to three years, or with fine which may extend to one thousand rupees or with both and shall also be liable for any loss, injury or damage which may be caused by reason of bringing such goods on the railways.

165. Unlawfully bringing offensive goods on a railway.--If any person, in contravention of section 67, takes with him any offensive goods or entrusts such goods for carriage to the railway administration, he shall be punishable with fine which may extend to five hundred rupees and shall also be liable for any loss, injury or damage which may be caused by reason of bringing such goods on the railway.

166. Defacing public notices.--If any person without lawful authority-

(a) pulls down or wilfully damages any board or document set up or posted by the order of a railway administration on a railway or any rolling stock; or

(b) obliterates or alters any letters of figures upon any such board or document or upon any rolling stock,

he shall be punishable with imprisonment for a term which may extend to one month, or with fine which may extend to five hundred rupees, or with both.

167. Smoking.--(l) No person in any compartment of a train shall, if objected to by any other passenger in that compartment, smoke therein.

(2) Notwithstanding anything contained in sub-section (1), a railway administration may prohibit smoking in any train or part of a train.

(3) Whosoever contravenes the provisions of sub-section (1) or sub-section (2) shall be punishable with fine which may extend to one hundred rupees.

168. Provision with respect to commission of offence by the children of acts endangering safety of person travelling on railway.--(l) If a person under the age of twelve years is guilty of any of the offences under sections 150 to 154, the court convicting him may require the father or guardian of such person to execute, within such time as the court may fix, a bond for such amount and for such period as the court may direct for the good conduct of such person.

(2) The amount of the bond, if forfeited, shall be recoverable by the court as if it were a fine imposed by itself.

(3) If a father or guardian fails to execute a bond under sub-section (1) within the time fixed by the court, he shall be punishable with fine which may extend to fifty rupees.

169. Levy of penalty on non-Government railway.--If a non-Government railway fails to comply with, any requisition made, decision or direction given, by the Central Government, under any of the provisions of this Act, or otherwise contravenes any of the provisions of this Act, it shall be open to the Central Government, by order, to levy a penalty not exceeding two hundred and fifty rupees and a further penalty not exceeding one hundred and fifty rupees for every day during which the contravention continues :

Provided that no such penalty shall be levied except after giving a reasonable opportunity to the non-Government railway to make such representation as it deems fit.

170. Recovery of penalty.-- Any penalty imposed by the Central Government under section 169, shall be recoverable by a suit in the District Court having jurisdiction in the place where the head office of the non-Government railway is situated.

171. Section 169 or 170 not to preclude Central Government from taking any other action.--Nothing in section 169 or 170 shall preclude the Central Government from resorting to any other action to compel a non-Government railway to discharge any obligation imposed upon it by or under this Act.

172. Penalty for intoxication.--If any railway servant is in a state of intoxication while on duty, he shall be punishable with fine which may extend to five hundred rupees and when the performance of any duty in such state is likely to endanger the safety of any person travelling on or being upon a railway, such railway servant shall be punishable with imprisonment for a term which may extend to one year, or with fine, or with both.

173. Abandoning train, etc., without authority.--If any railway servant, when on duty, is entrusted with any responsibility connected with the running of a train, or of any other rolling stock from one station or place to another station or place, and he abandons his duty before reaching such station or place without authority or without properly handing over such train or rolling stock to another authorised railway servant, he shall be punishable with imprisonment-for a term which may extend to two years, or with fine which may extend to one thousand rupees, or with both.

174. Obstructing running of train, etc.--If any railway servant (whether on duty or otherwise) or any other person obstructs or causes to be obstructed or attempts to obstruct any train or other rolling stock upon a railway--

(a) by squatting or picketing or during any rail roko agitation or bandh; or
(b) by keeping without authority any rolling stock on the railway; or
(c) by tampering with, disconnecting or interfering in any other manner with its hose pipe or tampering with signal gear or otherwise, he shall be punishable with imprisonment for a term which may extend to two years, or with fine which may extend to two thousand rupees, or with both.

175. Endangering the safety of persons.--If any railway servant, when on duty, endangers the safety of any person--

(a) by disobeying any rule made under this Act: or
(b) by disobeying any instruction, direction or order under this Act or the rules made thereunder; or
(c) by any rash or negligent act or omission.

he shall be punishable with imprisonment for a term which may extend to two years, or with fine which may extend to one thousand rupees, or with both.

176. Obstructing level crossing.--If any railway servant unnecessarily-

(a) allows any rolling stock to stand across a place where the railway crosses a public road on the level; or
(b) keeps a level crossing closed against the public, he shall be punishable with fine which may extend to one hundred rupees.

177. False returns.-If any railway servant required to furnish a return by or under this Get, signs and furnishes a return which is false in any material particular or which he knows or believes to be false, or does not believe to be true, he shall be punishable with imprisonment which may extend to one year, or with fine which may extend to five hundred rupees, or with both.

178. Making a false report by a railway servant.--If any railway servant who is required by a railway administration to inquire into a claim for loss, destruction, damage, deterioration or non-delivery of any consignment makes a report which is false or which he knows or believes to be false or does not believe to be true, he shall be punishable with imprisonment for a term which may extend to two years, or with fine which may extend to one thousand rupees, or with both.

179. Arrest for offences under certain sections.--(1) If a person commits any offence mentioned in sections 137, 141 to 147, 150, 157, 160 to 162, 164, 166, 168 and 172 to 175, he may be arrested without warrant or other written authority by any railway servant or police officer not below the rank of a head constable.

(2) The railway servant or the police officer may call to his aid any other person to effect the arrest under sub-section (1).

(3) Any person so arrested under this section shall be produced before the nearest Magistrate within a period of twenty-four hours of such arrest excluding the time necessary for the journey from the place of arrest to the court of the Magistrate.

180. Arrest of persons likely to abscond etc.--(1) If any person who commits any offence under this Act, other than an offence mentioned in section 179, or is liable to pay any excess charge or other sum demanded under section 138, fails or refuses to give his name and address or there is reason to believe that the name and address given by him are fictitious or that he will abscond, any railway servant authorised in this behalf or any police officer not below the rank of a head constable may arrest him without warrant or written authority.

(2) The railway servant or the police officer may call to his aid any other person to effect the arrest under sub-section (1).

(3) Any person arrested under this section shall be produced before the nearest Magistrate within a period of twenty-four hours of such arrest excluding the time necessary for the journey from the place of arrest to the court of the Magistrate unless he is released earlier on giving bail or if his true name and address are ascertained on executing a bond without sureties for his appearance before the Magistrate having jurisdiction to try him for the offence.

(4) The provisions of Chapter XXIII of the Code of Criminal Procedure, 1973, [2 of 1974] shall so far as may be, apply to the giving of bail and the execution of bonds under this section.

181. Magistrate having jurisdiction under the Act- Notwithstanding anything contained in the Code of Criminal Procedure, 1973 [2 of 1974], no court inferior to that of a Metropolitan Magistrate or a Judicial Magistrate of the first class shall try an offence under this Act.

182. Place of trial.--(1) Any person committing an offence under this Act or any rule made thereunder shall be tribal for such offence in any place in which he may be or which the State Government may notify in this behalf, as well as in any other place in which he is liable to be tried under any law for the time being in force.

(2) Every notification under sub-section (1) shall be published in the Official Gazette, and a copy thereof shall be exhibited for the information of the public in some conspicuous place at such railway stations as the State Government may direct.

CHAPTER XVI
MISCELLANEOUS

183. Power to provide other transport services.--(l) A railway administration may, for the purpose of facilitating the carriage of passengers or goods or to Provide integrated service for such carriage, provide any other mode of transport.

(2) Notwithstanding anything contained in any other law for the time being in force, the provisions of this Act shall apply to the carriage of passengers or goods by the mode of transport referred to in sub-section (1).

184. Taxation on railways by local authorities.--(l) Notwithstanding anything to contrary contained in any other law, a railway administration shall not be liable to pay any tax in aid of the funds of any local authority unless the Central Government, by notification, declares the railway administration to be liable to pay the tax specified in such notification.

(2) While a notification of the Central Government under sub-section (1) is in force, the railway administration shall be liable to pay to the local authority either the tax specified in the notification or, in lieu thereof, such sum, if any, as an officer appointed in this behalf by the Central Government may, having regard to all the circumstances of the case. from time to time, determine to be fair and reasonable.

(3) The Central Government may at any time revoke or vary a notification issued under sub-section (1).

(4) Nothing in this section shall be construed to prevent any railway administration from entering into a contract with any local authority for the supply of water or light, or for the scavenging of railway premises, or for any other service which the local authority may be rendering or be prepared to render to the railway administration.

185. Taxation on railways for advertisement.-(l) Notwithstanding anything to the contrary contained in any other law, a railway administration shall not be liable to pay any tax to any local authority in respect of any advertisement made on any part of the railway unless the Central Government, by notification, declares the railway administration to be liable to pay the tax specified in such notification.

(2) The Central Government may at any time revoke or vary a notification issued under sub-section (1).

186. Protection of action taken in good faith.--No suit, prosecution or other legal proceeding shall lie against the Central Government, any railway administration, a railway servant or any other person for anything which is in good faith done or intended to be done in pursuance of this Act or any rules or orders made thereunder.

187. Restriction on execution against railway purperty.--(1) No rolling stock, machinery, plant, tools, fittings, materials or effects used or provided by a railway administration for the purpose of traffic on its railway, or of its stations or workshops, shall be liable to be taken in execution of any decree or order of any court or of any local authority or person having: by law the power to attach or distrain property or otherwise to cause property to be taken in execution, without the previous sanction of the Central Government.

(2) Nothing in sub-section (1) shall be construed to affect the authority of any court to attach the earnings of a railway in execution of a decree or order.

188. Railway servants to be public servants for the proposes of Chapter 1X and section 409 of the Indian Penal Code.--(l) Any railway servant, who is not a public servant within the meaning of section 21 of the Indian Penal Code , [45 of 1860] shall be deemed to be a public servant for the purpose of Chapter IX and section 409 Of that Code.

(2) In the definition of "legal remuneration" in section 161 of the Indian Penal Code, [45 of 1860], the word "Government" shall, for the purposes of sub-section (1), be deemed to include any employer of a railway servant as such.

187. Railway servants not to engage in trade.-A railway servant shall not---

(a) purchase or bid for, either in person or by an agent, in his own name or in that of another, or jointly or in shares with others, any property put to auction tinder section 83 or section 84 or section 85 or section 90; or

(b) in contravention of any direction of the railway administration in this behalf, engage in trade.

190. Procedure for delivery to railway administration of property detained by a railway servant.--If a railway servant is discharged from service or is suspended, or dies or absconds or absents himself, and he or his wife or widow or any member of his family or his representative refuses or neglects, after notice in writing for that purpose, to deliver up to the railway administration or to a person appointed by the railway administration, in this behalf, any station, office or other building with its appurtenances, or any books, papers, keys, equipment or other matters, belonging to the railway administration and in the possession or custody of such railway servant at the occurrence of any such event as aforesaid, any Metropolitan Magistrate or Judicial Magistrate of the first class may, on application made by or on behalf of the railway administration, order any police officer, with proper assistance, to enter upon the station, office or other building and remove any person found therein and taken possession thereof, or to take possession of the books, papers of other matters, and to deliver the same to the railway administration or to a person appointed by the railway administration in that behalf.

191. Proof of entries in records and documents.- Entries made in the records or other documents of a railway administration shall be admitted in evidence in all proceedings by or against the railway administration, and all such entries may be proved either by the production of the records of other documents of the railway administration containing such entries or by the production of a copy of the entries certified by the officer having custody of the records or other documents under his signature and stating that it is a true copy of the original entries and that such original entries are contained in the records or other documents of the railway administration in his possession.

192. Service of notice, etc., on railway administration.--Any notice or other document required or authorised by this Act to be served on a railway administration may be served, in the case of a Zonal Railway, on the General Manager or any of the railway servant authorised by the General Manager, and in the case of any other railway, on the owner or lessee of the railway or the person working the railway under an agreement--

(a) by delivering it to him; or
(b) by leaving at his office; or
(c) by registered post to his office address.

193. Service of notice, etc., by railway administration. -- Unless otherwise provided in this Act or the rules framed thereunder, any notice or other document required or authorised by this Act to be served on any person by a railway administration may be served--

(a) by delivering it to the person; or
(b) by leaving it at the usual or last known place of abode of the person; or
(c) by registered post addressed to the person at his usual or last known place of abode.

194. Presumption where notice is served by post.--Where a notice or other document is served by post, it shall be deemed to have been served at the time when the letter containing it would be delivered in the ordinary course of post, and in proving such service, it shall be sufficient to prove that the letter containing the notice or other document was properly addressed and registered.

195. Representation of railway administration.--(1) A railway administration may, by order in writing, authorise any railway servant or other person to act for, or represent, it, as the case may be, in any proceeding before any civil, criminal or other court.

(2) A person authorised by a railway administration to conduct prosecutions on its behalf shall, notwithstanding anything in section 302 of the Code of Criminal Procedure, 1973 [2 of 1974] be entitled to conduct such prosecution without the permission of the Magistrate.

196. Power to exempt railway from Act.--(1) The Central Government may, by notification, exempt any railway from all or any of the provisions of this Act.

(2) Every notification issued under sub-section (1) shall be laid as soon as may be after it is issued before each House of Parliament.

197. Matters supplemental to the definitions of "railways" and "railway servant - (1) For the purposes of sections 67, 113, 121, 123, 147, 151 to 154, 160, 164, 166, 168, 170, 171, 173 to 176, 179, 180, 182, 184, 185, 187 to 190, 192, 193, 195 and of this section, the word "railway" whether it occurs alone or as a prefix to another word, has reference to a railway or portion of a railway under construction and to a railway or portion of a railway not used for the public carriage of passengers, animals or goods as well as to a railway falling within the definition of that word in clause (31) of section 2.

(2) For the purpose of sections 7, 24, 113, 146, 172 to 176 and 188 to 190, the expression "railway servant" includes a person employed under a railway in connection with the service thereof by a person fulfilling a contract with the railway administration.

198. General power to make rules.--Without prejudice to any power to make rules contained elsewhere in this Act, the Central Government may make rules generally to carry out the purposes of this Act.

199. Rules to be laid before Parliament.--Every rule made under this Act shall be laid, as soon as may be after it is made, before each House of Parliament, while it is in session, for a total period of thirty days which may be comprised in one session or in two or more successive sessions, and if, before the expiry of the session immediately following the session or the successive sessions aforesaid, both Houses agree in making any modification in the rule or both Houses agree that the rule should not be made, the rule shall thereafter have effect only such modified form or be of no effect, as the case may be; so, however, that any such modification or annulment shall be without prejudice to the validity of anything previously done under that rule.

200. Repeal and saving.--(1) The India Railways Act, 1890, [9 of 1890] is hereby repealed.

(2) Notwithstanding the repeal of the Indian Railways Act, 1890, [9 of 1890] (hereinafter referred to as the repealed Act) -

- (a) anything done or any action taken or purported to have been done or taken (including any rule, notification inspection, order or notice made or issued, or any appointment or declaration made or any licensee, permission, authorisation or exemption granted or any document or instrument executed or any direction given or any proceedings taken or any penalty or fine imposed) under the repealed Act shall, in so far as it is not inconsistent with the provisions of this Act, be deemed to have been done or taken under the corresponding provisions of this Act;

- (b) any complaint made to the Railway Rates Tribunal under sub-section (1) of section 41 of the repealed Act but not disposed of before the commencement of this Act and any complaint that may be made to the said Tribunal against any act or omission of a railway administration under the repealed Act shall be heard and decided by the Tribunal constituted under this Act in accordance with the provisions of Chapter VII of this Act.

(3) The mention of particular matters in sub-section (2) shall not be held to prejudice or affect the general application of section 6 of the General Clauses Act, 1897, [(10 of 1897] with regard to the effect of repeal.

CHAPTER XVII
AMENDMENTS TO THE RAILWAYS ACT

31. Amendment of section 3,--In section 3 of the Railways Act, alter clause (18), the following clause shall be inserted, namely :--

'(19) "Claims Tribunal" means the Railway Claims Tribunal established under section 3 of the Railway Claims Tribunal Act, 1987.'.

32. Amendment of section 78A.--In section 78A of the Railways Act, for the word "suit", the words "application before the Claims Tribunal" shall be substituted.

33. Substitution of new section for section 80.--For section 80 of the Railways Act, the following section shall be substituted, namely :

"**80. A application for compensation.--**An application to the Claims Tribunal for compensation for loss of the life of, or personal injury to, a passenger or for loss, destruction, damage, deterioration or non-delivery of animals or goods may be made-

(a) if the passenger was, or the animals or goods were, booked from one station to another on the railway of the same railway administration, against that railway administration;

(b) if the passenger was, or the animals or goods were, booked through over the railway of two or more railway administrations, against the railway administration from which the passenger obtained his pass or purchased his ticket or to which the animals or goods were delivered for carriage, as the case may be, or against the railway administration on whose railway the destination station lies, or the loss, injury, destruction, damage or deterioration occurred."

34. Omission of sections 82B, 81D and 8'F.-Section 82B, 82D and 82F of the Railways Act shall be omitted.

35. Amendment of sections 82C.--In section 82C of the Railways Act,-:'

(a) in sub-section (1), for tile words 'Claims Commissioner", the words "Claims Tribunal" shall be substituted;

(b) sub-section(2) and the *Explanation* thereto shall be omitted.

36. Amendment of sections 82E, 82G and 82HH. -In sections 82E, 82G and 82HH of the Railways Act, for the words "Claims Commissioner", wherever they occur, the words "Claims Tribunal" shall be substituted.

37. Amendment of section 82-I.--In section 82-I of the Railways Act, for the words, figures and letters "sections 82A to 82HH", the words, figures and letters "sections 82A, 82C, 82E and 82G to 82HH" shall be substituted.

38. Amendment of section 82J.--In section 82J of the Railways Act,-

(a) in sub-section (1), for the words,, figures and letters "sections 82A to 82I-1 inclusive", the words, figures and letters "sections 82A, 82C, 82E, 82G and 82H" shall be substituted;

(b) in sub-section (2), clause (i) and clauses (iv) to (vi) shall be omitted.

The Railway Claims Tribunal Act, 1987

CHAPTER I
PRELIMINARY

1.	Short title, extent and commencement	59
2.	Definitions	59

CHAPTER II
ESTABLISHMENT OF RAILWAY CLAIMS TRIBUNAL AND BENCHES THEREOF

3.	Establishment of Railway Claims Tribunal	60
4.	Composition of Claims Tribunal and Benches thereof	60
5.	Qualifications for appointment as Chairman, Vice-Chairman or other Member	61
6.	Vice-Chairman to ad as Chairman or to discharge his functions in certain circumstances	61
7.	Term of office	62
8.	Resignation and removal	62
9.	Salaries and allowances and other terms and conditions of service of Chairman, Vice-Chairman and other Members.	62
10.	Provision as to the holding of offices by Chairman, Vice-Chairman etc., on ceasing to be such Chairman or Vice-Chairman, etc.	63
11.	Financial and administrative powers of Chairman	63
12.	Staff of Claims Tribunal	63

CHAPTER III
JURISDICTION, POWERS AND AUTHORITY OF CLAIMS TRIBUNAL

13.	Jurisdiction, powers and authority of Claims Tribunal	63
14.	Distribution of business amongst Benches	64
15.	Bar of jurisdiction	64

CHAPTER IV
PROCEDURE

16.	Application to Claims Tribunal	64
17.	Limitation	65
18.	Procedure and powers of Claims Tribunal	65
19.	Right to legal representation and presenting officers.	66
20.	Power of Chairman to transfer cases from one Bench to another	66
21.	Decision to be by majority	66
22.	Execution of orders of Claims Tribunal	66

CHAPTER V
APPEALS

23.	Appeals	66

CHAPTER VI
MISCELLANEOUS

24.	Transfer of pending cares	67
25.	Proceeding before Claims Tribunal to be judicial proceedings.	67
26.	Members and staff of Claims Tribunal to be public servants	67
27.	Protection of action taken in good faith	67
28.	Act to have overriding effect	67
29.	Power to remove difficulties	68
30.	Power to make rules	68

THE RAILWAY CLAIMS TRIBUNAL ACT, 1987
(54 of 1987)

[23rd December, 1987]

An Act to provide for establishment of a Railway Claims Tribunal for inquiring into and determining claims against a railway administration for loss, destruction, damage, deterioration or non-delivery of animals or goods entrusted to it to be carried by railway or for the refund of fares or freight or for compensation for death or injury to passengers occurring as a result of railway accidents [or untoward incidents] and for matters connected therewith or incidental thereto.

Be it enacted by Parliament in the Thirty-eighth Year of the Republic of India as follows :-

CHAPTER I
PRELIMINARY

1. Short title, extent and commencement.--(i) This Act may be called the Railway Claims Tribunal Act, 1987.

(2) It extends to the whole of India.

(3) It shall come into force on such date as the General Government may, by notification, appoint.

2. Definitions.--In this Act, unless the context otherwise requires;-

(a) "application" means an application made under section 16;
(b) "appointed day" means the date with effect from which the Claims Tribunal is established under section 3;
(c) "Bench" means a Bench of the Claims Tribunal;
(d) "Chairman" means the Chairman of the Claims Tribunal;
(e) "Claims Tribunal" means the Railway Claims Tribunal established under section 3;
(f) "Judicial Member" means a Member of the Claims Tribunal appointed as such under this Act, and includes the Chairman or Vice-Chairman who possesses any of the qualifications specified in sub-section (3) of section 5;
(g) "Member" means a Member (whether Judicial or Technical) of the Claims Tribunal, and includes the Chairman and Vice-Chairman;
(h) "notification" means a notification published in the Official Gazette;
(i) "prescribed" means prescribed by rules;
(j) 'Railways Act" means the Indian Railways Act, 1890 (9 of 1890);
(k) "rules" means rules made under this Act;

1. ins. by Act 28 of 1994, see 7.
2. 8.11.1989, Vide S.O. 783(E), dated 5th October, 1989.
3. 8.1.1989, vide S.O. 784(E), dated 5th October, 1989.

(l) "Technical Member" means a Member of the Claims Tribunal who is not a Judicial Member, and includes the Chairman or a Vice-Chairman who possesses any of the qualifications specified in sub-section (4) of section 5;

(m) "Vice-Chairman" means a Vice-Chairman of the Claims Tribunal. Explanation.-References to the Vice-Chairman in this Act shall be construed as references to each of the Vice-Chairman;

[(n) "untoward incident" shall have the meaning assigned to it in clause (c) of section 123 of the Railways Act, 1989 (24 of 1989)];

(o) words and expressions used and not defined in this Act but defined in the Railways Act or the rules made thereunder shall have the meanings respectively assigned to them in that Act or the said rules.

CHAPTER II

ESTABLISHMENT OF RAILWAY CLAIMS TRIBUNAL AND BENCHES THEREOF

3. Establishment of Railway Claims Tribunal.--The Central Government shall, by notification, establish a Claims Tribunal, to be known as the Railway Claims Tribunal, to exercise the jurisdiction, powers and authority conferred on it by or under this Act.

4. Composition of Claims Tribunal and Benches thereof. - (1) The Claims Tribunal shall consist of a Chairman, four Vice-Chairmen and such number of Judicial Members and Technical Members as the Central Government may deem fit and, subject to the other provisions of this Act, the jurisdiction, powers and authority of the Claims Tribunal may be exercised by Benches thereof.

(2) Subject to the other provisions of this Act, a Bench shall consist of one Judicial Member and one Technical Member.

(3) Notwithstanding anything contained in sub-section (1), the Chairman-

(a) may, in addition to discharging the functions of the Judicial Member or the Technical Member of the Bench to which he is appointed, discharge the functions of the Judicial Member or, as the case may be, the Technical Member, of any other Bench;

(b) may transfer a Vice-Chairman or other Member from one Bench to another Bench;

(c) may authorise the Vice-Chairman or the Judicial Member or the Technical Member appointed to one Bench to discharge also the functions of the Vice Chairman or, as the case may be, the Judicial Member or the Technical Member of another Bench.

(4) Notwithstanding anything contained in the foregoing provisions of this section, it shall be competent for the Chairman or any other Member authorised by the Chairman in this behalf to function as a Bench consisting of a single Member and exercise the jurisdiction, powers and authority of the Claims Tribunal in respect of such classes of cases or such matters pertaining to such classes of cases as the Chairman may, by general or special order, specify,

---

1. Ins. by Act 28 of 1994, Sec. 8.

Provided that if at any stage of the hearing of any such case or matter, it appears to the Chairman or such Member that the case or matter is of such a nature that it ought to be heard by a Bench consisting of two Members, the case or matter may be transferred by the Chairman or, as the case may be, referred to him for transfer, to such Bench as the Chairman may deem fit.

(5) Subject to the other provisions of this Act, the Benches shall sit at such places as the Central Government may, by notification, specify.

5. Qualifications for appointment as Chairman, Vice-Chairman or other Member.---(l) A person shall not be qualified for appointment as the Chairman unless he-

(a) is, or has been, a Judge of a High Court; or

(b) has, for at least two years, held the office of a Vice-Chairman.

(2) A person shall not be qualified for appointment as the Vice-Chairman unless he -

(a) is, or has been, or is qualified to be, a Judge of a High Court; or

(b) has been a member of the Indian Legal Service and has held a post in Grade i of that service or any higher post for at least five years; or

(c) has, for at least five years, held a civil judicial post carrying a scale of pay which is not less than that of a Joint Secretary to the Government of India; or

(d) has, for at least five years, held a post under a railway administration carrying a scale of pay which is not less than that of a Joint Secretary to the Government of India and has adequate knowledge of rules and procedure of, and experience in, claims and commercial matters relating to railways; or

(e) has, for a period of not less than three years, held office as a Judicial Member or a Technical Member.

(3) A person shall not be qualified for appointment as a Judicial Member unless he -

(a) is, or has been, or is qualified to be, a Judge of a High Court; or

(b) has been a Member of the Indian Legal Service and has held a post in Grade I of that service for at least three years; or

(c) has, for at least three years, held a civil judicial post carrying a scale of pay which is not less than of a Joint Secretary to the Government of India.

(4) A person shall not be qualified for appointment as a Technical Member unless he has, for at least three years, held a post under a railway administration carrying a scale of pay which is not less than that of a Joint Secretary to the Government of India and has adequate knowledge of rules and procedure of, and experience in, claims and commercial matters relating to railways.

(5) Subject to the provisions of sub-section (6), the Chairman, Vice-Chairman and every other Member shall be appointed by the President.

(6) No appointment of a person as the Chairman shall be made except after consultation with the Chief Justice of India.

6. Vice-Chairman to act as Chairman or to discharge his functions in certain circumstances.--(1) In the event of the occurrence of any vacancy in the office of the Chairman by reason of his death, resignation or otherwise, such one of the Vice-Chairman as the Central Government may, by notification, authorise in this behalf, shall act as the Chairman until the date on which a new Chairman, appointed in accordance with the provisions of this Act to fill such vacancy, enters upon his office.

(2) When the Chairman is unable to discharge his functions owing to absence, illness or any other cause, such one of the Vice-Chairman as the Central Government may, by notification, authorise in this behalf, shall discharge the functions of the Chairman until the date on which the Chairman resumes his duties.

7. Term of office.- The Chairman, Vice-Chairman or other Member shall hold office as such for a term of five years from the date on which he enters upon his office or until he attains,-(a) in the case of the Chairman, the age of sixty-five years; and (b) in the case of the Vice-Chairman or any other Member, the age of sixty-two years, whichever is earlier.

8. Resignation and removal.--(1) The Chairman, Vice-Chairman or other Member may, by notice in writing under his hand addressed to the President, resign his office:

Provided that the Chairman, Vice-Chairman or other Member shall, unless he is permitted by the President to relinquish his office sooner, continue to hold office until the expiry of three months from the date of receipt of such notice or until a person duly appointed as his successor enters upon his office or until the expiry of his term of office, whichever is the earliest.

(2) The Chairman, Vice-Chairman or any other Member shall not be removed from his office except by an order made by the President on the ground of proved misbehavior or incapacity after an inquiry made by a Judge of the Supreme Court in which such Chairman, Vice-Chairman or other Member had been informed of the charges against him and given a reasonable opportunity of being heard in respect of those charges.

(3) The Central Government may, by rules, regulate the procedure for the investigation of misbehavior or incapacity of the Chairman, Vice-Chairman or other Member referred to in sub-section (2).

9. Salaries and allowances and other terms and conditions of service of Chairman, Vice-Chairman and other Members.--The salaries and allowances payable to, and the other terms and conditions of service (including pension, gratuity and other retirement benefits) of, the Chairman, Vice-Chairman and other Members shall be such as may be prescribed:

Provided that neither the salary and allowances nor the other terms and conditions of service of the Chairman, Vice-Chairman, Vice-Chairman or other Members shall be such as may be prescribed:

Provided that neither the salary and allowances nor the other terms and conditions of service of the Chairman, Vice-Chairman or other Member shall be varied to his disadvantage after his appointment.

10. Provision as to the balding of offices by Chairman, Vice-Chairman etc., on ceasing to be such Chairman or Vice-Chairman, etc.--On ceasing to hold office-

(a) the Chairman of the claims Tribunal shall be ineligible for further employment either under the Government of India or under the Government of a State;

(b) a Vice-Chairman shall, subject to the other provisions of this Act, be eligible for appointment as the Chairman of the Claims Tribunal, or as the Chairman, Vice-Chairman or Member of any other Tribunal established under any law for the time being in force, but rot for any other employment either under the Government of India or under the Government of a State;

(c) a Member (other than the Chairman or Vice-Chairman) shall, subject to the other provisions of this Act, be-eligible for appointment as the Chairman or Vice Chairman or as the Chairman, Vice-Chairman or member of any other Tribunal established under any law for the time being in force, but not for any other employment either under the Government of India or under the Government of a State;

(d) the Chairman, Wee-Chairman or other Member shall not appear, act or plead before the Claims Tribunal.

Explanation.--For the Purposes of this section, employment under the Government of India or under the Government of a State includes employment under any local or other authority within the- territory of India or under the control of the Government of India or under any corporation or society owned or controlled by the Government.

11. Financial and administrative powers of Chairman;--The Chairman shall exercise such financial and administrative powers over the Benches as may be vested in him under the rules:

Provided that the Chairman shall have authority to delegate such of his financial and administrative powers as he may think fit to the Vice-Chairman or any other officer of the Claims Tribunal, subject to the condition that the Vice-Chairman or such officer shall, while exercising such delegated powers, continue to act under the direction, control and supervision of the Chairman.

12. Staff of Claims Tribunal.--(l) The Central Government shall determine the nature and categories of the officers and other employees required to assist the Claims Tribunal in the discharge of its functions and provide the Claims Tribunal with such officers and other employees as it may think fit.

(2) The officers and other employees of the Claims Tribunal shall discharge their functions under the general superintendence of the Chairman.

(3) The salaries and allowances and conditions of service of the officers and other employees of the Claims Tribunal shall be such as may be prescribed.

CHAPTER III
JURISDICTION, POWERS AND AUTHORITY OF CLAIMS TRIBUNAL

13. Jurisdiction, powers and authority of Claims Tribunal.--(l) The Claims Tribunal shall exercise, on and from the appointed day, all such jurisdiction, powers and authority as were exercisable immediately before that day by any civil court or a Claims Commissioner appointed under the provisions of the Railways Act—

(a) relating to the responsibility of the railway administrations as carriers under Chapter-VII of the Railways Act in respect of claims for-

(i) compensation for loss, destruction, damage, deterioration or non-delivery of animals or goods entrusted to a railway administration for carriage by railway;

(ii) compensation payable under section 82A of the Railways Act or the rules made thereunder; and

(b) in respect of the claims for refund of fares or part thereof or for refund of any freight paid in respect of animals or goods entrusted to a railway administration to be carried by railway.

[(1A) The Claims Tribunal shall also exercise, on and from the date of commencement of the provisions of section 12A of the Railways Act, 1989 (24 of 1989), all such jurisdiction, powers and authority as were exercisable immediately before that date by any civil court in respect of claim for compensation now payable by the railway administration under section 124A of the said Act or the rules made thereunder]

(2) The provisions of the [Railways Act 1989 (24 of 1989)]1 and the rules made thereunder shall, so far as may be, be applicable to the inquiring into or determining, any claims by the Claims Tribunal under this Act.

14. Distribution of business amongst Benches.--(l) Where any Benches are constituted, the Central Government may, from time to time, by notification, make provisions as to the distribution of the business of the Claims Tribunal amongst the Benches and specify the matters which may be dealt with by each Bench.

(2) If any question arises as to whether any matter falls within the purview of the business allocated to a Bench, the decision of the Chairman shall be final.

Explanation;--For the removal of doubts, it is hereby declared that the expression "matters" includes an application under section 20.

15. Bar of jurisdiction;--On and from the appointed day no court or other authority shall have, or be entitled to, exercise any jurisdiction, powers or authority in relation to the matters referred to in [sub-sessions (1) and (1A) of section 13.

CHAPTER IV
PROCEDURE

16. Application to Claims Tribunal.--(1) A person seeking any relief in respect of the matters referred to in sub-section (1) [or sub-section (IA)I of section 13 may make an application to the Claims Tribunal.

(2) Every application under sub-section (1) shall be in such from and be accompanied by such documents or other evidence and by such Tee in respect of the filing of such application and by such other fees for the service or execution of processes as may be prescribed:

---

1. Ins. by Act 28 of 1994, Sec. 9.
2. Subs. by Act 28 of 1994, Sec. 9, for "Railway Act".
3. Subs. by Act 28 of 1994, Sec. 10.
4. Ins. by Act 28 of 1994, Sec. 11. for "sub-section (1)".

Provided that no such fee shall be payable in respect of an application under sub clause (ii) of clause (a) of sub-section (1) [or, as the case may be, sub-section (IA)I of section 13.

17. Limitation--(l) The Claims Tribunal shall not admit an application for any claim--

(a) under sub-clause (i) of clause (a) of sub-section (1) of section 13 unless the application is made within three years from the dale on which the goods in question were entrusted to the railway administration for carriage by railway;

(b) under sub-clause (ii) of clause (a) of sub-section (1) [or, as the case may be, subsection (1A)I of section 13 unless the application is made within one year of occurrence of the accident ; (c) under clause (b) sub-section (1) of section 13 unless the application is made within three years from the date on which the fare or freight is paid to the railway administration:

Provided that no application for any claim referred to in sub-clause (i) of clause (a) of sub-section (1) of section 13 shall be preferred to the Claims Tribunal until the expiration of three months next after the date on which the intimation of the claim has been preferred under section 78B of the Railways Act.

(2) Notwithstanding anything contained in sub-section (1). an application may be entertained after the period specified in sub-section (i') if the applicant satisfies the Claims Tribunal that he had sufficient cause for not making the application within such period.

18. Procedure and powers of Claims Tribunal.--(1) The Claims Tribunal shall not be bound by the procedure laid down by the Code of Civil Procedure, 1908, (5 of 1908) but shall be guided by the principles of natural justice and, subject to the other provisions of this Act and of any rules, the Claims Tribunal shall have powers to regulate its own procedure including the fixing of places and Limes of its inquiry.

(2) The Claims Tribunal shall decide every application as expeditiously as possible and ordinarily every application shall be decided on a perusal of documents, written representations and affidavits and after hearing such oral arguments as may be advanced.

COMMENTS

When the Railway Claim Tribunal is approached by an indigent person for compensation on account of the wrong done to him, the tribunal cannot refuse to exercise jurisdiction merely because he does not have the means to pay the fee. In such a situation the ends of justice require that the Tribunal should follow the procedure laid done in Order 33 of the Code of Civil Procedure 1908 (5 of 1908), to do justice for which it came to be established;
A.A. Haja Muniuddin v. Indian Railway, A.I.R. 1993 SC 361.

(3) The Claims Tribunal shall have, for the purposes of discharging its functions under this Act, the same powers as are vested in a civil court under the Code of Civil Procedure, 1908 (5 of 1908), while vying a suit, in respect of the following matters, namely :-

---

1. Ins. by Act 28 of 1994, S. 11 for "sub-section (1)."
2. Ins by Act 28 of 1994, S. 12.

(a) summoning and enforcing the attendance of any person and examining him on oath;
(b) requiring the discovery and production of documents;
(c) receiving evidence on affidavits;
(d) subject to the provisions of sections 123 and 124 of the Indian Evidence Act, 1872 (1 of 1872), requisitioning any public record or document or copy of such record or document from any office;
(e) issuing commissions for the examination of witnesses or documents:
(f) reviewing its decisions;
(g) dismissing an application for default or deciding it ex parte, (h) setting aside any order of dismissal of any application for default or any order passed by it ex parte;
(i) any other matter which may be prescribed.

19. Right to legal representation and presenting officers,--(1) A person making an application to the Claims Tribunal may either appear in person or take the assistance of a legal practitioner of his choice to present his case before the Claims Tribunal.

(2) A railway administration may authorise one or more legal practitioners or any of its officers to act as presenting officers and every person so authorised by it may present its case with respect to any application before the Claims Tribunal.

20. Power of Chairman to transfer cases from one bench to another.---On the application of any of the parties and after notice to the parties, and after hearing such of them as he may desire to be heard, or on his own motion without such notice, the Chairman may transfer any case pending before one Bench, for disposal, to any other Bench.

21. Decision to be by majority.--If the Members of a Bench differ in opinion on any point, they shall state the point or points on which they differ, and make a reference to the Chairman who shall either hear the point or points himself or refer the case for hearing on such point or points by one or more of the other Members and such point or points shall be decided according to the opinion of the majority of the Members who have heard the case, including those who first heard it.

22. Execution of orders of Claims Tribunal.--(1) An order made by the Claims Tribunal under this Act shall be executable by the Claims Tribunal as a decree of civil court, and, for this purpose, the Claims Tribunal shall have all the powers of a civil court.

(2) Notwithstanding anything contained in sub-section (1), the Claims Tribunal may transmit any order made by it to a civil court having local jurisdiction and such civil court shall execute the order as if it were a decree made by that court.

CHAPTER V
APPEALS

23. Appeals.--(1) Save as provided in sub-section (2) and notwithstanding anything contained in the Code of Civil Procedure, 1908 (5 of 1908) or in any other law, an appeal shrill lie from every order, not being an interlocutory order, of the Claims Tribunal, to the High Court having jurisdiction over the place where the Bench is located.

(2) No appeal shall lie from an order passed by the Claims Tribunal with the consent of the parties.

(3) Every appeal under this section shall be preferred within a period of ninety days from the date of the order appealed against.

CHAPTER VI
MISCELLANEOUS

24 Transfer of pending cases.--(1) Every suit, claim or other legal proceeding (other than an appeal) pending before any court, Claims Commissioner or other authority immediately before the appointed day [or, as the case may be, the date of commencement of the provisions of sub-section (IA) of section 13] being a suit, claim or proceeding the cause of action whereon it is based is such that it would have been, if it had arisen after the appointed day, [or, as the case may be, the date of commencement of the provisions of sub-section (IA) of section 13] within the jurisdiction of the Claims Tribunal, shall stand transferred on 2[that day or, as the case may be, date] to the Claims Tribunal.

(2) Where any suit, claim or other legal proceeding stand transferred from any court, Claims Commissioner or other authority to the Claims Tribunal under sub-section (1),--

(a) the court, Claims Commissioner or other authority shall, as soon as may be after such transfer, forward the records of such suit, claim or other legal proceeding to the Claims Tribunal;

(b) the Claims Tribunal may, on receipt of such records, proceed to deal with such suit, claim or other legal proceeding, so far as may be, in the same manner as an application, from the stage which was reached before such transfer or from any earlier stage or de novo as the Claims Tribunal may deem fit.

25. Proceedings before Claims Tribunal to be judicial proceedings.--All proceedings before the Claims Tribunal shall be deemed to be judicial proceedings within the meaning of sections 193, 219 and 228 of the Indian Penal Code, 1860 (45 of 1860).

26. Members and staff of Claims Tribunal to be public servants.--The Chairman, Vice-Chairman and other Members and the officers and other employees of the Claims Tribunal shall be deemed to be public servants within the meaning of section 21 of the Indian Penal Code, 1860 (45 of 1860).

27. Protection of action taken in good faith.--No suit, prosecution or other legal proceeding shall lie against the Central Government or against the Chairman, Vice Chairman or other Member, or any other person authorised by the Chairman, Vice Chairman or other Member for anything which is in good faith done or intended to be done in pursuance of this Act or any rule or order made thereunder.

28. Act to have overriding effect.--The provisions of this Act shall have effect notwithstanding anything inconsistent therewith contained in any other law for the time being in force or in any instrument having effect by virtue of any law other than this Act.

---

1. Ins. by Act 28 of 1994. Sec. 13.

2.   Subs. by Act 28 of 1994, Sec. 13. for "that day".

29. Power to remove difficulties.--(1) If any difficulty arises in giving effect to provisions of this Act, the Central Government may, be order published in the Official Gazette, make such provisions, not inconsistent with the provisions of this Act, as appear to it to be necessary or expedient for removing the difficulty:

Provided that no such order shall be made after the expiry of a period of three years from the appointed day.

(2) Every order made under this section shall, as soon as may be after it is made, be laid before each House of Parliament.

30. Power to make rules.--C1) The Central Government may, be notification, make rules to carry out the provisions of this Act.

(2) Without prejudice of the generality of the foregoing powers, such rules may provide for all or any of the following matters, namely :-

- (a) the procedure under sub-section (3) of section 8 for the investigation of misbehaviour or incapacity of tile Chairman, Vice-Chairman or other Member;
- (b) salaries and allowances payable to, and the other terms and conditions of service (including pension, gratuity and other retirement benefits) of, the Chairman, Vice-Chairman and other Members under section 9;
- (c) the financial and administrative powers which the Chairman may exercise over the Benches under section 11;
- (d) the salaries and allowances and conditions of service of officers and other employees of the Claims Tribunal under sub-section (3) of section 12:
- (e) the form of application, the documents and other evidence to be accompanied with such application and fee in respect of filing of such application and fee for the service or execution of processes under sub-section (2) of section 66;
- (f) the rules subject to which the Claims Tribunal shall have powers to regulate its own procedure under sub-section (1) of section 18 and the additional matters in which the Claims Tribunal may exercise powers of civil court under clause (i) of sub-section (3) of that section;
- (g) any other matter which is required to be, or may be, prescribed.

(3) Every rule made under this Act shall be laid, as soon as may be after it is made, before each House of Parliament, while it is in session, for a total period of thirty days which may be comprised in one session or in two or more successive

sessions, and if, before the expiry of the session immediately following the session or the successive sessions aforesaid, both Houses agree in making any modification in the rule or both Houses agree that the rule should not be made, the rule shall thereafter have effect only in such modified form or be of no effect, as the case may be, so, however, that any such modification or annulment shall be without prejudice to the validity of anything previously done under that rule.

The Railway Companies (Emergency Provisions) Act, 1951

THE RAILWAY COMPANIES (EMERGENCY PROVISIONS) ACT, 1951

ACT NO. 51 OF 1951 [14th September, 1951.]

An Act to make provision for the proper management and administration of railway companies in certain special cases.

1. Short title, extent and application.
    - (1) This Act may be called the Railway Companies (Emergency Provisions) Act, 1951 .
    - (2) It extends to the whole of India except the State of Jammu and Kashmir.
    - (3) It applies to every railway company in respect of which a notified order has been issued under section 3.

2. Definitions. In this Act, unless the context otherwise requires,--
    - (a) " Companies Act" means the Indian Companies Act, 1913 (7 of 1913 .);
    - (b) " directors" means the directors appointed under section 3;
    - (c) " notified order" means an order notified in the Official Gazette;
    - (d) " prescribed" means prescribed by rules made under this Act;
    - (e) " railway company" means any company registered under the Companies Act or any law repealed thereby for the purpose of making and working or making or working a railway, whether alone or in conjunction with other purposes.

3. Power of Central Government to apply Act to any railway company and to appoint directors thereof.
    - (1) Where the Central Government is of opinion that a situation has arisen in the affairs of a railway company which--
        - (a) has prejudicially affected the convenience of persons using the railway administered by the railway company, or
        - (b) has caused serious dislocation in any trade or industry using the railway, or
        - (c) has caused serious unemployment amongst a section of the community, or when, in the opinion of the Central Government, it is necessary in the national interest the Central Government may, by notified The Act comes into force in Pondicherry on 1. 10. 1963 vide Reg. 7 of 1963 , s. 3 and Sch. I.
        - order, apply the provisions of this Act to the railway company and appoint as many persons as it thinks fit to be directors of the railway company for the purpose of taking over its management and administration.
    - (2) The power to appoint directors under this section includes the power to appoint any individual, firm or company to be the managing agent of the railway company on such terms and conditions as to the Central Government may seem fit.

4. Effect of notified order appointing directors or managing agents. On the issue of a notified order under section 3,--
    - (a) all persons holding office as directors of the railway company immediately before the issue of the notified order shall be deemed to have vacated their offices as such;

- (b) any contract of management between the railway company and any managing agent thereof holding office as such immediately before the issue of the notified order shall be deemed to have terminated;
- (c) the managing agent, if any, appointed under this Act shall be deemed to have been duly appointed in pursuance of the Companies Act and the memorandum and articles of association of the railway company, and the provisions of the Companies Act and of the memorandum and articles shall, subject to the other provisions contained in this Act, apply accordingly, but no such managing agent shall be removed from office except with the previous consent of the Central Government;
- (d) the directors shall take such steps as may be necessary to take into their custody or under their control all the property, effects and actionable claims to which the railway company is, or appears to be, entitled, and all the property and effects of the railway company shall be deemed to be in the custody of the directors as from the date of the notified order;
- (e) the directors shall be for all purposes the directors of the railway company duly constituted under the Companies Act, and shall alone be entitled to exercise all the powers of the directors of the railway company, whether such powers are derived from the Companies Act or from the memorandum or articles of association of the railway company or from any other source.

5. Powers and duties of directors.
- (1) Subject to the control of the Central Government, the directors shall take such steps as may be necessary for the purpose of efficiently managing the business of the railway company and, in particular, the directors shall have power, notwithstanding anything contained in the Companies Act or in the memorandum or articles of association of the railway company,--
    - (a) to choose one of their number to be the chairman, and to delegate to him or to any one or more of the directors all or any of their powers;
    - (b) with the previous approval of the Central Government and subject to such conditions as that Government may think fit to impose, to raise funds in such manner and offer such security therefor as they think fit;
    - (c) to carry out such repairs as may be necessary in respect of any machinery, rolling-stock, buildings, works or other property in their custody;
    - (d) to do all acts necessary for making, maintaining, altering or repairing and using the railway of the railway company;
    - (e) to employ such persons as may be necessary for enabling them to efficiently discharge their duties, and define the conditions of service of such employees.
- (2) The directors may, with the previous sanction of the Central Government, cancel or vary, either unconditionally or subject to such conditions as they think fit to impose, any contract or agreement entered into between the railway company and any other person at any time before the issue of the notified order under section 3, if such contract or agreement had been entered into in bad faith and is detrimental to the interests of the railway company.

6. Statement of affairs to be made to directors.
- (1) On the issue of a notified order under section 3, there shall be made out and submitted to the directors a statement as to the affairs of the railway company, verified by affidavit and containing the following particulars, namely:--
    - (a) the assets of the railway company, stating separately the cash balance in hand and at the bank, if any;
    - (b) the debts and liabilities;
    - (c) the names, residences and occupations of the creditors, stating separately the amount of secured debts and unsecured debts and, in the case of secured debts, the particulars of the securities, their value and the dates when they were given;
    - (d) the debts due to the railway company and the names, residences and occupations of the persons from whom they are due and the amount likely to be realised therefrom;

- (e) such other particulars as may be prescribed.
- (2) The statement shall be submitted by one or more of the persons who was or were holding office as a director or as directors of the railway company immediately before the issue of the notified order under section 3 or by the secretary, manager or other chief officer of the railway company who was holding office as such before the issue of the notified order as the directors may require in each case, and the statement shall be submitted within such time as may be so required.
- (3) If any person, without any reasonable excuse, knowingly and wilfully makes default in complying with the requirements of this section, he shall be punishable with imprisonment which may extend to three months, or with fine which may extend to five hundred rupees, or with both.

7. Statements by beneficial owners of shares of railway company. Any person who has any interest in any share of the railway company which stands in the name of another person in the register of shareholders of the railway company shall, within such period as may be specified by the Central Government by notified order, make a declaration in such form as may be prescribed (which shall be countersigned by the person in whose name the share is registered) to the railway company declaring his interest in the share, and notwithstanding anything contained in any other law or in any contract to the contrary, a person who fails to make a declaration as aforesaid in respect of any share shall be deemed to have no right or title whatsoever in or to that share: Provided that nothing in this section shall affect the right of any person who has an interest in any such share to establish in a Court his right thereto if the person in whose name the share is registered refuses to sign that declaration as required by this section.

8. Power of directors to institute proceedings against past directors, etc., for damages.
- (1) The directors may, if they are satisfied that it is necessary in the interests of the railway company or in the public interest so to do, institute in the name of the railway company such proceedings as they think fit for the recovery of damages for any fraud, misfeasance or other misconduct in connection with the management of the affairs of the railway company committed by any person before the issue of the notified order under section 3 or for the recovery of any property of the railway company which has been misapplied or wrongfully retained by any person.
- (2) No director shall be personally liable for any costs or expenses incurred in connection with any proceedings instituted by virtue of this section.

9. Penalties. If any person willfully destroys or fails to deliver to the directors when required any books of account, registers or any other documents
in his custody relating to the business of the railway company or retains any property of the railway company, he shall be punishable with imprisonment which may extend to six months, or with fine which may extend to one thousand rupees, or with both.

10. Filling up of vacancies among directors.
- (1) Casual vacancies occurring in the body of directors, whether caused by death, resignation or otherwise, shall be filled by nomination by the Central Government.
- (2) No act of the directors shall be called in question on the ground merely of the existence of any vacancy among the directors or any defect in the appointment of any of them.

11. No right to compensation for termination of contract of managing agent or any other contract.
- (1) Notwithstanding anything contained in the Companies Act or in any other law for the time being in force, no managing agent shall be entitled to any compensation for the premature termination under this Act of any contract of management entered into by him with the railway company, and no person shall be entitled to compensation in respect of the cancellation or variation under this Act of any other contract or agreement.

- (2) Nothing contained in sub- section (1) shall affect the right of any such managing agent or person to recover from the railway company moneys recoverable otherwise than by way of such compensation.

12. Cancellation of appointment of directors.
    - (1) If at any time it appears to the Central Government that the purpose of the notified order appointing the directors has been fulfilled or that for any other reason it is unnecessary that the notified order should remain in force, the Central Government may, by notified order, cancel the appointment of directors made under this Act.
    - (2) On the cancellation of any such appointment as is referred to in sub- section (1), the Central Government may--
        - (a) direct that all the property, effects and actionable claims of the railway company shall revest in the persons in whom they were vested before the issue of the notified order under section 3; or
        - (b) reconstitute by fresh appointment a new body of persons to take charge of the management and administration of the whole affairs of the railway company, whether as directors or managers or in any other capacity: Provided that no such direction or fresh appointment shall be made except in pursuance of a resolution passed by the shareholders of the railway company at a meeting called for the purpose by the directors appointed under section 3.
    - (3) The Central Government may, at any time before the issue of the notified order under sub- section (1), take such action as may be
    - necessary under clause (b) of sub- section (2) for the purpose of making any fresh appointments.

13. Application of the Companies Act.
    - (1) Notwithstanding anything contained in the Companies Act or in the memorandum or articles of association of the railway company, but subject to the other provisions contained in this Act,--
        - (a) it shall not be lawful for the shareholders of the railway company or any other person to nominate or appoint any person to be a director of the railway company;
        - (b) no resolution passed at any meeting of the shareholders of the railway company shall be given effect to unless approved by the Central Government;
        - (c) no proceeding for the winding- up of the railway company or for the appointment of a receiver in respect thereof shall lie in any Court, unless by or with the sanction of the Central Government.
    - (2) Subject to the provisions contained in sub- section (1) and to the other provisions contained in this Act and subject to such exceptions, restrictions and limitations as the Central Government may by notified order specify, the Companies Act shall continue to apply to the railway company in the same manner as it applied thereto before the issue of the notified order under section 3.

14. Effect of Act on other laws. The provisions of this Act and of any notified order made thereunder shall have effect notwithstanding anything inconsistent therewith in any other law for the time being in force or in the memorandum or articles of association of the railway company or in any other instrument having effect by virtue of any law other than this Act, but save as aforesaid the provisions of this Act shall be in addition to, and not in derogation of, any other law for the time being applicable to the railway company.

15. Directors to be public servants. Every director appointed under section 3 shall be deemed to be a public servant within the meaning of section 21 of the Indian Penal Code. (45 of 1860)

16. Delegation of powers. The Central Government may, by notified order, direct that all or any of the powers exercisable by it under this Act, except the powers given to it under section 3 to apply the provisions of this Act to any railway company or the powers given to it under section 12 or section

18, may be exercised by any State Government, and where any powers are so delegated, they shall be exercised subject to such directions as the Central Government may issue from time to time.

17. Protection of action taken under Act.
- (1) No suit, prosecution or other legal proceeding shall lie against any director in respect of anything which is in good faith done or intended to be done in pursuance of this Act.
- (2) No suit or other legal proceeding shall lie against the Central Government or any State Government or any director for any damage caused or likely to be caused by anything which is in good faith done or intended to be done in pursuance of this Act.

18. Power of Central Government to acquire railway of railway company.
- (1) Where under any instrument, having effect by virtue of any law other than this Act or by virtue of an agreement arrived at between the parties, provision is made for the purchase by a person or local authority or the State Government of a railway which is the property of a railway company on payment of the value thereof calculated in the manner and subject to the conditions specified in the instrument, the Central Government shall also have the same right to purchase the railway on the same terms and subject to the same conditions as the person, local authority or the State Government has under the instrument.
- (2) If in respect of any railway the Central Government exercises its right of purchase under this section, any person, local authority or State Government, in whom or in which a similar right is vested under the instrument, shall be deemed to have become disentitled to exercise the same.

19. Power to make rules.
- (1) The Central Government may by notified order, make rules to carry out the purposes of this Act.
- (2) In particular, and without prejudice to the generality of the foregoing power, any rules made under sub- section (1) may provide for- -
    - (a) the manner in which or the conditions subject to which the directors or managing agents of a railway company may exercise their powers under this Act;
    - (b) the additional particulars which a statement under section 6 should contain;
    - (c) the form in which a declaration under section 7 may be made;
    - (d) the appointment of a Railway Local Advisory Committee;
    - (e) the manner in which books of account shall be maintained by the directors and audited;
    - (f) the submission of specified or periodical returns and reports by the directors to any specified authority in connection with the affairs of the railway company;
    - (g) the conduct of business of the directors appointed by notified order and for the recruitment and employment of officers and staff.
- (3) 1 Every rule made under this Act shall be laid, as soon as may be after it is made, before each House of Parliament, while it is in session, for a total period of thirty days which may be comprised in one session or in two or more successive sessions, and if, before the expiry of the session immediately following the year session or the successive sessions aforesaid, both Houses agree in making any modification in the rule or both Houses agree that the rule should not be made, the rule shall thereafter have effect only in such modified form or be of no effect, as the case may be; so, however, that any such modification or annulment shall be without prejudice to the validity of anything previously done under that rule.]

20. Repeal of Ordinance 2 of 1951 . The Railway Companies (Emergency Provisions) Ordinance, 1951 (2 of 1951 .) is hereby repealed: Provided that the repeal shall not affect--
- (a) the previous operation of the said Ordinance, or
- (b) any penalty, forfeiture or punishment incurred in respect of any offence committed against the said Ordinance, or

- (c) any investigation, legal proceeding or remedy in respect of any such penalty, forfeiture or punishment, and any such investigation, legal proceeding or remedy may be instituted, continued or enforced, and any such penalty, forfeiture, or punishment may be imposed as if this Act had not been passed: Provided further that, subject to the preceding proviso, anything done or any action taken (including any notified order issued, appointment made or direction given under the said Ordinance) shall be deemed to have been done or taken under the corresponding provision of this Act and shall continue in force accordingly, unless and until superseded by anything done or any action taken under this Act.

1. Ins. by Act 4 of 1986, s. 2 and Sch. (w. e. f. 15. 5. 1986).

THE RAILWAYS PROPERTY (Unlawful Possession) Act, 1966

	Description	Page
1.	Short title, extent and commencement	70
2	Definitions	70
3.	Penalty for unlawful possession of Railway Property	70
4.	Punishment for connivance at offence	70
5.	Offences under the Act not to be cognizable	71
6.	Power to arrest without warrant	71
7.	Disposal of persons arrested	71
8.	Inquiry how to be made against arrested persons	71
9.	Power to summon persons to give evidence and produce documents	71
10.	Issue of search warrant	72
11.	Searches and arrests how to be made	72
12	Officers required to assist	72
13.	Power of courts to order forfeiture of vehicles, etc	72
14.	Act to override other laws.	72
15.	Construction of references to laws not in force in Jammu and Kashmir I	72
16.	Repeal and savings	72

THE RAILWAYS PROPERTY
(Unlawful Possession) Act, 1966
(29 of 1966)

[16th September, 1966]

An Act to consolidate and amend the law relating to unlawful possession of railway property.

Be it enacted by Parliament in the seventeenth Year of the Republic of India as follows :-

1. **Short title, extent and commencement**--(1) This Act may be called the Railway Property (Unlawful Possession) Act, 1966. (2) It extends to the whole of India.

(3) It shall come into force on such date as the Central Government may, by notification in the Official Gazette, appoint.

2. **Definitions.**--In this Act unless the context otherwise requires, -

(a) "Force" means the Railway Protection Force constituted under section 3 of the Railway Protection Force Act, 1957 (23 of 1957);

(b) "member of the Force" means a person appointed to the Force, other than a superior officer;

(c) "officer of the Force" means an officer of and above the rank of Assistant Sub Inspector appointed to the Force and includes a superior officer;

(d) "railway property" includes any goods, money or valuable security or animal, belonging to, or in the charge of possession of, a railway administration;

(e) "superior officer" means any of the officers appointed under section 4 of the Railway Protection Force Act, 1957 (23 of 15)57), and includes any other officer appointed by the Central Government as a superior officer of the force;

(f) words and expressions used but not defined in this Act and defined in the Indian Railways Act, 1890 (9 of 1890), shall have the meanings respectively assigned to them under that Act.

3. **Penalty for unlawful possession of railway property.**--Whoever is found, or is proved to have been, in possession of any railway property reasonably suspected of having been stolen or unlawfully obtained shall, unless he proves that the railway property came into his possession lawfully, be punishable -

(a) for the first offence, with imprisonment for a term which may extend to five years, of with fine, or with both and in the absence of special and adequate reasons to be mentioned in the judgment of the court, such imprisonment shall not be less than one year and such fine shall not be less than one thousand rupees;

(b) for the second or a subsequent offence, with imprisonment for a term which may extend to five years and also with fine and in the absence of special and adequate reasons to be mentioned in the judgment of the court, such imprisonment shall not be less than two years and such fine shall not be less than two thousand rupees.

---

1. 1st April. vide S.O. 1228. dated 1.4.1968, Gazette of India. Extraordinary, 1968, Part II, Section 3(ii). Page 413.

4. Punishment for connivance at offences.--Any owner or occupier of land or building, or any agent of such owner or occupier incharge of the management of that land or building, who wilfully connives at an offence against the provisions of this Act, shall be punishable with imprisonment for a term which may extend to live years, or with fine, i or with both.

5. Offences under the Act not to be cognizable.-- Notwithstanding anything contained in the Code of Criminal Procedure, 1898 (5 of 1898)' an offence under this Act shall not be cognizable.

6. Power to arrest without warrant.--Any superior officer or member of the Force may, without an order from a Magistrate and without a warrant,, arrest any person who has been concerned in an offence punishable under this Act or against whom a reasonable suspicion exists of his having been so concerned.

7. Disposal of persons arrested.--Every person arrested for an offence punishable under this Act shall, if the arrest was made by a person other than an officer of the Force, be forwarded without delay to the nearest officer of the Force.

8. Inquiry how to be made against arrested persons.-- (1) When any person is arrested by an officer of the Force for an offence punishable under this Act or is forwarded to him under section 7, he shall proceed to inquiry into the charge against such person.

(2) For this purpose the officer of the Force may exercise the same powers and shall be subject to the same provisions as the officer incharge of a police-station may exercise and is subject to under the Code of Criminal Procedure, 1898 (5 of 1898)', when investigating a cognizable case :

Provided that-

(a) if the officer of the Force is of opinion that there is sufficient evidence or reasonable ground of suspicion against the accused person, he shall either admit him to bail to appear before a Magistrate having jurisdiction in the case, or forward him in custody to such Magistrate;

(b) if it appears to the officer of the Force that there is not sufficient evidence or reasonable ground of suspicion against the accused person, he shall release the accused person on his executing a bond, with or without sureties as the officer of the Force may direct, to appear, if and when so required before the Magistrate having jurisdiction, and shall make a full report of all the particulars of the case to his official superior.

9. Power to summon persons to give evidence and produce documents.--(l) An officer of the Force shall have power to summon any person whose attendance he considers necessary either to give evidence or to produce a document, or any other thing in an inquiry which such officer is making for any of the purposes of this Act.

(2) A summons to produce documents or other things may be for the production of certain specified documents or things or for the production of all documents or things of a certain description in the possession or under the control of the person summoned.

(3) All persons, so summoned, shall be bound to attend either in person or by an authorised agent as such officer may direct; and all persons so summoned shall be bound to state the truth upon any subject respecting which they are examined or make statements and to produce such documents and other things as may be required:

---

1. Now the Code of Criminal Procedure, 1973 (Act 2 of 1974).

Provided that the exemptions under sections 132 and 133 of the Code Civil Procedure, 1908 (5 of 1908), shall be applicable to requisitions for attendance under this section.

(4) Every such inquiry as aforesaid, shall be deemed to be a "judicial proceeding" within the meaning of section 193 and section 228 of the Indian Penal Code (45 of 1860).

10. Issue of search warrant.--(l) If an officer of the Force has reason to believe that any place is used for the deposit or sale of railway property which has been stolen or unlawfully' obtained, he shall make an application to the Magistrate, having jurisdiction over the area in which that place is situate, for issue of a search warrant.

(2) The Magistrate to whom an application is made under sub-section (1), may, after such inquiry as he thinks necessary, by his warrant, authorise any officer of the Force-

(a) to enter, with such assistance as may be required, such place;
(b) to search the same in the manner specified in the warrant;
(c) to take possession of any railway property therein found which he reasonably suspects to be stolen or unlawfully obtained; and
(d) to covey such railway property before a Magistrate, or to guard the same on the spot until the offender is taken before a Magistrate, or otherwise to dispose thereof in some place of safely.

11. Searches and arrests how to be made.--All searches and arrests made under this Act shall be carried our in accordance with the provisions of the Code of Criminal Procedure, 181)8 (5 of 1898), relating respectively to searches and arrests made under that Code.

12. Officers required to assist.--All officers or Government and all village officers are hereby empowered and required to assist the superior officers and members of the Force in the enforcement of this Act.

13. Power of courts to order forfeiture of vehicles, etc.--Any court trying an offence punishable under this Act may order the forfeiture to Government of any property in respect of which the court is satisfied that an offence under this act has been committed & and may also order the forfeiture of any receptacles, packages or coverings in which such property is contained, and the animals, vehicles or other conveyances used in carrying the property.

14. Act to override other laws.--The provisions of this Act shall have effect notwithstanding anything inconsistent therewith contained in any other law for the time being in force.

15. **Construction of references to laws not in force in Jammu and Kashmir**.-- Any reference in this Act to a law which is not in force in the State of Jammu and

Kashmir shall in relation to that State, be construed as a reference to the corresponding law, if any, in force in that State.

16. Repeal and savings.--(1) The Railway Scores (Unlawful Possession) Act, 1955 (51 of 1955) is hereby repealed.

(2) Nothing contained in this Act shall apply to offences punishable under the Act hereby repealed and such offences may be investigated and tried as if this Act had not been passed.

(3) The mention of particular matters in sub-section (2) shall not be held to prejudice or affect the general application of section 6 of the General Clauses Act, 1897 (10 of 1897), with regard to the effect of repeals.

---

1. See now the Code of Criminal procedure, 1973 (Act 2 1974).

The Railway Protection Force Act, 1957

1. Short title, extent and commencement.—
    - (1) This Act may be called The Railway Protection Force Act, 1957.
    - (2) It extends to the whole of India.
    - (3) It shall come into force on such date 1 as the Central Government may, by notification in the Official Gazette, appoint.

2. Definitions.—
    - (1) In this Act, unless the context otherwise requires,—
    - (a) "Force" means the Railway Protection Force constituted under section 3;
    - (b) "Director-General" means the Director-General of the Force appointed under sub-section (1) of section 4;
        - (ba) "enrolled member of the Force" means any subordinate officer, under officer or any other member of the Force of a rank lower than that of under officer;
        - (bb) "Force custody" means the arrest or confinement of a member of the Force in accordance with rules made under this Act;]
    - (c) "member of the Force" means a person appointed to the Force under this Act; 4 [***];
        - (ca) "passenger" shall have the meaning assigned to it in the Railways Act, 1989 (24 of 1989);
        - (cb) "passenger area" shall include railway platform, train, yard and such other area as is frequently visited by passengers;]
    - (d) "prescribed" means prescribed by rules made under this Act;
    - (e) "railway property" includes any goods, money or valuable security, or animal, belonging to, or in the charge or possession of, a railway administration;
        - (ea) "subordinate officer" means a person appointed to the Force as an Inspector, a Sub-Inspector or an Assistant Sub-Inspector;]
    - (f) "superior officer" means any of the officers appointed under section 4 and includes any other officer appointed by the Central Government as a superior officer of the Force;
        - (fa) "under officer" means a person appointed to the Force as a Head Constable or Naik;]
    - (g) words and expressions used but not defined in this Act and defined in the Indian Railways Act, 1890 (9 of 1890), shall have the meanings respectively assigned to them under that Act.
    - (2) Any reference in this Act to a law which is not in force in any area shall, in relation to that area, be construed as a reference to the corresponding law, if any, in force in that area.]

3. Constitution of the Force.—
    - (1) There shall be constituted and maintained by the Central Government 1[an armed force of the Union] to be called the Railway Protection Force for the better protection and security of railway property.
    - (2) The Force shall be constituted in such manner, shall consist of such number of 8 [superior officers, subordinate officers, under officers and other enrolled members] of the Force and shall receive such pay and other remuneration as may prescribed.

4. Appointment and powers of superior officers.—1[
    - (1) The Central Government may appoint a person to be the Director-General of the Force and may appoint other persons to be Inspector-General, Additional Inspectors-General, Deputy Inspectors-General, Assistant Inspectors-General, Senior Commandants, Commandants or Assistant Commandants of the Force.]

- (2) The 9 [Director-General] and every other superior officer so appointed shall possess and exercise such powers and authority over the members of the Force under their respective commands as is provided by or under this Act.

5. [***] ommitted

6. Appointment of members of the Force.—The appointment of enrolled members of the Force shall rest with the Inspector-General, Additional Inspector-General or Deputy Inspector-General, who shall exercise that power in accordance with rules made under this Act: Provided that the power of appointment under this section may also be exercised by other superior officer as the Inspector-General, Additional Inspector-General, or Deputy Inspector-General concerned may, by order, specify in this behalf.]

7. Certificates to members of the Force.—
    - (1) Every member of the Force shall receive on his appointment a certificate in the form specified in the Schedule, under the seal of the 12 [Inspector-General, Additional Inspector-General or Deputy Inspector-General] or such other superior officer as the 12 [Inspector-General, Additional Inspector-General or Deputy Inspector-General] may specify in this behalf, by virtue of which the person holdings such certificate shall be vested with the powers of a member of the Force.
    - (2) Such certificate shall cease to have effect whenever the person named in it ceases for any reason to be a member of the Force 13 [***].

8. Superintendence and administration of the Force.—
    - (1) The superintendence of the Force shall vest in the Central Government, and subject thereto and to the provisions of this Act and of any rules made thereunder, the command, supervision and administration of the Force shall vest in the Director-General.
    - (2) Subject to the provisions of sub-section (1), the administration of the Force, within such local limits in relation to a railway as may be prescribed shall be carried on by an Inspector-General, an Additional Inspector-General or a Deputy Inspector-General in accordance with the provisions of this Act and of any rules made thereunder and they shall, subject to any direction that may be given by the Central Government or the Director-General in this behalf discharge his functions under the general supervision of the General Manager of the Railway.]

9. Dismissal, removal, etc., of members of the Force.—
    - (1) Subject to the provisions of article 311 of the Constitution and to such rules as the Central Government may make under this Act, any superior officer may—
        - (i) dismiss, suspend or reduce in rank any 15 [enrolled member] of the Force whom he shall think remiss or negligent in the discharge of his duty, or unfit for the same; or
        - (ii) award any one or more of the following punishments to any 4[enrolled member] of the Force who discharges his duty in a careless or negligent manner, or who by any act of his own renders himself unfit for the discharge thereof, namely:—
            - (a) fine to any amount not exceeding seven days' pay or reduction in pay scale;
            - (b) confinement to quarters for a period not exceeding fourteen days with or without punishment, drill, extra guard, fatigue or other duty;
            - (c) removal from any office of distinction or deprivation of any special emolument.

10. Officers and members of the force to be deemed to be railway servants.— 16 [Director-General and every member of the Force] shall for all purposes be regarded as railway servants within the meaning of the Indian Railways Act, 1890 (9 of 1890) other than Chapter VIA thereof, and shall be entitled to exercise the powers conferred on railway servants by or under that Act.

11. Duties of members of Force.—It shall be the duty of every superior officer and member of the Force—
    - (a) promptly to execute all orders lawfully issued to him by his superior authority;
    - (b) to protect and safeguard railway property, passenger area and passengers;
    - (c) to remove any obstruction in the movement of railway property or passenger area; and

- (d) to do any other act conducive to the better protection and security of railway property, passenger area and passengers.]
-

12. Power to arrest without warrant.—Any member of the Force may, without an order from a Magistrate and without a warrant, arrest—
- (i) any person who voluntarily causes hurt to, or attempts voluntarily to cause hurt to, or wrongfully restrains or attempts wrongfully to restrain, or assaults, threatens to assault, or uses, or threatens or attempts to use, criminal force to him or any other member of the Force in the execution of his duty as such member, or with intent to prevent or to deter him from discharging his duty as such member, or in consequence of anything done or attempted to be done by him in the lawful discharge of his duty as such member; or
- (ii) any person who has been concerned in, or against whom a reasonable suspicion exists of his having been concerned in, or who is found taking precautions to conceal his presence under circumstances which afford reason to believe that he is taking such precautions with a view to committing a cognizable offence which relates to 19 [railway property, passenger area and passengers]; or
- (iii) any person found taking precautions to conceal his presence within the railway limits under circumstances which afford reason to believe that he is taking such precautions with a view to committing theft of, or damage to, 19 [railway property, passenger area and passengers]; or
- (iv) any person who commits or attempts to commit a cognizable offence which involves or which is likely to involve imminent danger to the life of any person engaged in carrying on any work relating to 19 [railway property, passenger area and passengers].]

13. Power to search without warrant.—
- (1) Whenever 20 [***] any member of the Force, not below the rank of a Senior Rakshak, has reason to believe that any such offence as is referred to in section 12 has been or is being committed and that a search warrant cannot be obtained without affording the offender an opportunity of escaping or of concealing evidence of the offence, he may detain him and search his person and belongings forthwith and, if he thinks proper, arrest any person whom he has reason to believe to have committed the offence.
- (2) The provisions of the 21 [Code of Criminal Procedure, 1973 (2 of 1974)], relating to searches under that Code shall, so far as may be, apply to searches under this section.

14. Procedure to be followed after arrest.—Any 22 [***] member of the Force making an arrest under this Act, shall, without unnecessary delay, make over the person so arrested 23 [to a police officer together with a detailed report of the circumstances leading to the arrest of such person], or, in the absence of a police officer, take such person or cause him to be taken to the nearest police station.

15. Officers and members of the Force to be considered always on duty and liable to be employed in any part of the Railways.— 24 [
- (1) Every member of the Force shall, for the purposes of this Act, be considered to be always on duty, and shall, at any time, be liable to be employed at any place within India].
- (2) No 25 [***] member of the Force shall engage himself in any employment or office other than his duties under this Act.

- 15A. Restrictions respecting right to form association, etc.—
  - (1) No member of the Force shall, without the previous sanction in writing of the Central Government or of the prescribed authority,—
    - (a) be a member of, or be associated in any way with, any trade union, labour union, political association or with any class of trade unions, labour unions or political associations; or
    - (b) be a member of, or be associated in any way with, any other society, institution, association or organisation that is not recognised as part of the Force or is not of a purely social, recreational or religious nature; or

- - (c) communicate with the press or publish or cause to be published any book, letter or other document except where such communication or publication is in the bona fide discharge of his duties or is of a purely literary, artistic or scientific character or is of a prescribed nature. Explanation.—If any question arises as to whether any society, institution, association or organisation is of a purely social, recreational or religious nature under clause (b) of this sub-section, the decision of the Central Government thereon shall be final.
  - (2) No member of the Force shall participate in, or address, any meeting or take part in any demonstration organised by any body of persons for any political purposes or for such other purposes as may be prescribed.]

16. Responsibilities of members of the Force during suspension.—A member of the Force shall not by reason of his suspension from office cease to be a member of the force; and he shall, during that period, be subject to the same responsibilities, discipline and penalties to which he would have been subject if he were on duty.
  - 16A. Surrender of certificate, arms, etc., by persons ceasing to be members of the Force.—
    - (1) Every person who for any reason ceases to be a member of the Force, shall forthwith surrender to any superior officer empowered to receive the same, his certificate of appointment, the arms, accoutrements, clothing and other articles which have been furnished to him for the performance of his duties as a member of the Force.
    - (2) Any person who wilfully neglects or refuses to surrender his certificate of appointment, the arms, accoutrements, clothing and other articles furnished to him, as required by sub-section (1), shall, on conviction, be punished with imprisonment for a term which may extend to one month, or with fine which may extend to two hundred rupees, or with both.
    - (3) Nothing in this section shall be deemed to apply to any article, which, under the orders of the Director-General, has become the property of the person to whom the same was furnished.]

17. Penalties for neglect of duty, etc.—
  - (1) Without prejudice to the provisions contained in section 9, every enrolled member of the Force who shall be guilty of any violation of duty or wilful breach or neglect of any rule or lawful order made by a superior officer, or who shall withdraw from duties of his office without permission, or who, being absent on leave, fails, without reasonable cause, to report himself for duty on the expiration of the leave, or who engages himself without authority for any employment other than his duty as an enrolled member of the Force, or who shall be guilty of cowardice may be taken into Force custody and shall, on conviction, be punished with imprisonment which may extend to one year.
  - (2) Notwithstanding anything contained in the Code of Criminal Procedure, 1973 (2 of 1974), an offence punishable under this section shall be cognizable and non-bailable.
  - (3) Notwithstanding anything contained in the Code of Criminal Procedure, 1973 (2 of 1974), the Central Government may invest Assistant Inspector-General, Senior Commandant or Commandant with the powers of a Magistrate of any class for the purpose of inquiring into or trying any offence committed by an enrolled member of the Force and punishable under this Act, or any offence committed by an enrolled member of the Force against the person or property of another member of the Force: Provided that—
    - (i) when the offender is on leave or absent from duty; or
    - (ii) when the offence is not connected with the offender's duties as an enrolled member of the Force; or
    - (iii) when it is a petty offence even if connected with the offender's duties as an enrolled member of the Force; or
    - (iv) when, for reasons to be recorded in writing, it is not practicable for the Commandant invested with the powers of a Magistrate to inquire into or to try the offence, the offence may, if the prescribed authority within the limits of whose jurisdiction the offence has been

- committed so requires, be inquired into or tried by an ordinary criminal court having jurisdiction in the matter.
- (4) Nothing contained in this section shall be construed to prevent any enrolled member of the Force from being prosecuted under any other law for any offence made punishable by that law, or for being liable under any such law to any other or higher penalty or punishment than is provided for such offence by this section: Provided that no person shall be punished twice for the same offence.]

18. **Application of Act 22 of 1922 to members of the Force.**—The Police (Incitement to Disaffection) Act, 1922 shall apply to members of the Force as it applies to members of a police force.

19. **Certain Acts not to apply to members of the Force.**—Nothing contained in the Payment of Wages Act, 1936 (4 of 1936) or the Industrial Disputes Act, 1947 (14 of 1947) or the Factories Act, 1948 (63 of 1948) or any corresponding law relating to investigation and settlement of industrial dispute in force in a state shall apply to members of the Force.]

20. **Protection of acts of members of the Force.**—
    - (1) In any suit or proceeding against any 30 [***] member of the Force for any act done by him in the discharge of his duties, it shall be lawful for him to plead that such act was done by him under the orders of a competent authority.
    - (2) Any such plea may be proved by the production of the order directing the act, and if it is so proved, the 30 [***] member of the Force shall thereupon be discharged from any liability in respect of that act so done by him, notwithstanding any defect in the jurisdiction of the authority which issued such order.
    - (3) Notwithstanding anything contained in any other law for the time being in force, any legal proceeding, whether civil or criminal, which may lawfully be brought against any 30 [***] member of the Force for anything done or intended to be done under the powers conferred by, or in pursuance of, any provisions of this Act or the rules thereunder shall be commenced within three months after the act complained of shall have been committed and not otherwise; and notice in writing of such proceeding and of the cause thereof shall be given to the person concerned and his superior officer at least one month before the commencement of such proceeding.

21. **Power to make rules.**—
    - (1) The Central Government may, by notification in the Official Gazette, make rules for carrying out the purposes of this Act.
    - (2) In particular, and without prejudice to the generality of the foregoing powers, such rules may provide for—
        - (a) regulating the classes and grades and the pay and remuneration of 31 [***] members of the Force and their conditions of service in the Force;
        - (b) regulating the powers and duties of 31 [***] members of the Force authorised to exercise any functions by or under this Act;
        - (c) fixing the period of service for 32 [***] members of the Force;
        - 33 [(d) prescribing the description and quantity of arms, accoutrements, clothing and other necessary articles to be furnished to the members of the Force;
        - (e) prescribing the places of residence of the member of the force;
        - (f) institution, management and regulation of any fund for any purpose connected with the administration of the force;
        - (g) regulating the punishments and prescribing authorities to whom appeal shall be preferred from orders of punishment, or remission of fines, or other punishments and the procedure to be followed for the disposal of such appeals;
        - (h) regulating matters with respect to Force custody under this Act, including the procedure to be followed for taking persons into such custody;
        - (i) regulating matters with respect to disposal of cases relating to offences under this Act and specifying the places in which persons convicted under this Act may be confined;

- - (j) any other matter which has to be, or may be, imposed, or in respect of which rules are required to be made under this Act.]
- (3) Every rule made under this Act shall be laid, as soon as may be after it is made, before each House of Parliament, while it is in session, for a total period of thirty days which may be comprised in one session or in two or more successive sessions, and if, before the expiry of the session immediately following the session or the successive sessions aforesaid, both Houses agree in making any modification in the rule or both Houses agree that the rule should not be made, the rule shall thereafter have effect only in such modified form or be of no effect, as the case may be; so, however, that any such modification or annulment shall be without prejudice to the validity of anything previously done under that rule.]

RAILWAYS PROTECTION FORCE ACT, 1957 THE SCHEDULE (See Section 7) A. B. has been appointed a member of the Railway Protection Force under the Railway Protection Force Act, 1957, and is vested with the powers, functions and privileges of a member of the Force.

THE RAILWAYS (EMPLOYMENT OF MEMBERS OF THE ARMED FORCES) ACT, 1965

ACT NO. 40 OF 1965 [3rd December, 1965.]

An Act to make certain provisions relating to the employment of members of the Armed Forces of the Union in the working and management of railways.

BE it enacted by Parliament in the Sixteenth Year of the Republic of India as follows:-

1. Short title and extent.
   - (1) This Act may be called the Railways (Employment of Members of the Armed Forces) Act, 1965 .
   - (2) It extends to the whole of India.

2. Interpretation. Words and expressions used in this Act and defined in the Indian Railways Act, 1890 (9 of 1890), shall have the meanings respectively assigned to them in that Act.

3. Employment of members of Armed Forces of the Union to assist a railway administration in connection with the service of a railway.
   - (1) When any member of the Armed Forces of the Union is employed to assist a railway administration in connection with the service of a railway, then, whether such employment was before or is after the commencement of this Act,-
     - (a) any provision of the Indian Railways Act, 1890 (9 of 1890), or of the rules made thereunder, which confers a power, status or immunity, or imposes a duty or liability, upon a railway servant, in connection with the working, use, management and maintenance of railways, shall be construed as conferring the same power, status or immunity or imposing the same duty or liability, as the case may be, upon such member of the Armed Forces of the Union when so employed;
     - (b) the employment of a member of the Armed Forces of the Union, in addition to or in the place of any railway servant, shall not affect any liability that would have attached to the railway administration had such member been a railway servant.
   - (2) Nothing in sub- section (1) shall be construed as making applicable to the members of the Armed Forces of the Union employed to assist a railway administration the provisions of Chapter VIA of the Indian Railways Act, 1890 (9 of 1890), or as derogating from any provision

4. Employment of members of Armed Forces of the Union to replace railway administration in working a railway. If at any time the whole of the working, management and maintenance of a railway or of a specific, portion or section of a railway, is assumed by the Armed Forces of the Union, the Central Government may notify the fact of such assumption in the Official Gazette and thereupon, so long as such assumption continues, the Indian Railways Act, 1890 (9 of 1890), shall cease to be applicable to the Railway or the portion or section of the Railway concerned.

5. Repeal and saving.
   - (1) The Railways (Employment of Members of the Armed Forces) Ordinance, 1965 (4 of 1965) is hereby repealed.

- (2) Notwithstanding such repeal, anything done or any action taken under the said Ordinance shall be deemed to have been done or taken under this Act as if this Act had commenced on the 29th day of September, 1965.

THE TERMINAL TAX ON RAILWAY PASSENGERS ACT, 1956

ACT NO.69 OF 1956

An Act to provide for the levy of a terminal tax on passengers carried by railway from or to certain places of pilgrimage or where fairs, melas or exhibitions are held.

[12th December, 1956]

Be it enacted by Parliament in the Seventh Year of the Republic of India as follows:-

1. Short title, extent and commencement.-

(1) This Act may be called the Terminal Tax on Railway Passengers Act, 1956.

(2) It extends to the whole of India.

(3) It shall come into force on such date {1st April 1957, vide Notification No.S.R.O.867, dated 8-3-57, Gazette of India, pt.II Sec.3, p.492.} as the Central Government may, by notification in the Official Gazette, appoint.

2. Definitions.- In this Act, unless the context otherwise requires,-

(a) "maximum rates" mean the rates of terminal tax specified in the Schedule;

(b) "mela" means a public gathering on the occasion of any religious festival;

(c) "notified place" means a place of pilgrimage or a place where a fair meal or exhibition is being or is likely to be led, which the Central Government has, by notification in the Official Gazette, declared to be a notified place for the purpose of this Act;

(d) "railway administration" has the meaning assigned to it in the Indian Railways Act, 1890 (9 of 1890).

3. Terminal tax on passengers carried by railway from or to notified places.-

(1) Subject to the other provisions contained in this Act, there shall be levied on all passengers carried by railway from or to any notified place a terminal tax in respect of every railway ticket (whether single or return) at such rates not exceeding the maximum rates as the Central Government may, by notification in the Official Gazette, fix; and such notification shall specify the date with effect from which, and may also specify the period for which, the terminal tax shall be liveable:

Provided that where no such period is specified in the notification, the terminal tax shall be leviable for so long as this Act is in force.

(2) Subject to the maximum rates, different rates of terminal tax may be fixed,-

(a) In relation to different notified places; and

(b) in respect of short-distance passengers and long-distance passengers; provided that the rate in respect of short-distance passengers shall be always lower than that in respect of long-distance passengers.

Explanation.-In this sub-section a passenger travelling by railway from or to any notified place to or from a distance of not more than one hundred and fifty miles shall be deemed to be a short-distance passenger and any other passenger travelling by railway shall be deemed to be a long-distance passenger.

4.Terminal tax not to be levied within certain limits.- No terminal tax shall be levied on any passenger travelling by railway from or to any notified place to or from any railway station situated within a radius of forty miles from that notified place or within such shorter distance from that place as the Central Government may, by notification in the Official Gazette, specify.

5.Power of Central Government to vary rates of tax.- The Central Government may, by notification in the Official Gazette, vary from time to time in respect of railway passengers generally or a class of railway passengers the rates of the terminal tax levied in relation to any notified place under section 3.

6.Power of Central Government to discontinue levy.- The Central Government may, by notification in the Official Gazette, declare that with effect from such date as may be specified in the notification, the terminal tax levied in relation to any notified place shall for reasons specified in the notification cease to be levied in relation to that place.

7.Mode of recovery of tax.-

(1) The terminal tax levied under this Act shall be collected by means of a surcharge on fares by the railway administration, and where it is so collected the railway administration shall have all the powers and remedies for the recovery thereof as though the same were a rate or fare which the railway administration is empowered to levy under the Indian Railway Act, 1890 (9 of 1890).

(2) Such portion of the total proceeds of the tax attributable to any notified place as the Central Government may from time to time ascertain shall be deducted to meet the cost of collection of the tax.

8.No other terminal tax on railway passengers when terminal tax under this Act is levied.- Notwithstanding anything contained in any law where a terminal tax in relation to any notified place is levied under this Act on passengers carried by railway, no other terminal tax in relation to such place shall be levied under any other law on such passengers.

9.Exemptions.- Nothing contained in this Act or in any other law shall be deemed to authorise the levy of a terminal tax on the following classes of passengers carried by railway, namely:-

(a) children not over three years of age;

(b) police officers travelling on railway warrants;

(c) persons travelling or military warrants and troops travelling is reserved vehicles at vehicle rate; and

(d) free pass holders.

THE SCHEDULE

MAXIMUM RATES OF TERMINAL TAX

[See section 2 (a)]

	1	2
Class of accommodation	Maximum rates of terminal tax	
	(a) (In respect of every single ticket)	(b) (In respect of every return ticket)
	Rs. A.P.	Rs. A.P.
Air conditioned or first class	1 8 0	3 0 0
Second Class	1 0 0	2 0 0
Third Class	0 8 0	1 0 0

THE CALCUTTA METRO RAILWAY (OPERATION AND MAINTENANCE) TEMPORARY PROVISIONS ACT, 1985

ACT NO.10 OF 1985

[16th February,1985.]

An Act to make temporary provisions for the operation and maintenance of the Calcutta metro railway and for matters connected therewith, pending the making of regular arrangements for such operation and maintenance.

BE it enacted by Parliament in the Thirty-fifth Year of the Republic of India as follows:-

CHAPTER I

PRELIMINARY

1.Short title, commencement and application.-

(1) This Act may be called the Calcutta Metro Railway (Operation and Maintenance) Temporary Provisions Act, 1985.

3. It shall be deemed to have come into force on the 22nd day of October, 1984.

4. It shall apply to the metropolitan city of Calcutta.

2.Definitions.-

(1) In this Act, unless the context otherwise requires,-

(g) "Calcutta metro railway administration" or "metro railway administration" means the General Manager of the metro railway appointed under section 3 of the Construction Act;

(h) "commissioner" means a commissioner of the metro railway appointed under section 27 of the Construction Act;

(i) "Construction Act" means the Metro Railways (Construction of Works) Act, 1978; (33 of 1978.)

(j) "metro railway" means such portion of the metro railway constructed in the metropolitan city of Calcutta under the provisions of the Construction Act as may, for the time being, available for public carriage of passengers, and includes.-

(c) all land within the boundary marks indicating the limits of the land appurtenant to the metro railway;

(d) all lines of rails, sidings, yards or branches worked over for the purposes of, or in connection with the metro railway;

(e) all stations, offices, ventilation shafts and dacts, warehouses, workships, manufactories, fixed plants and machineries, sheds, depots and other works constructed for the purpose of, or in connection with, the metro railway;

(e) "prescribed" means prescribed by rules made under this Act.

(2) All other words and expressions used herein and not defined but defined in the Indian Railway Act, 1890, (9 of 1890.) or the Metro Railways (Construction of Works) Act, 1978, (33 of 1978.) shall have the meanings, respectively, assigned to them in those Acts.

CHAPTER II

THE CALCUTTA METRO RAILWAY ADMINISTRATION

3. Calcutta metro railway administration to be responsible for the operation and maintenance of the metro railway.-

(1) Subject to the other provisions of this Act, the Calcutta metro railway administration shall be responsible for the operation and maintenance of the metro railway.

(2) The Calcutta metro railway administration may, for the efficient performance of its functions under Act, appoint such officers and other employees as it considers necessary on such terms and conditions of service as may be prescribed.

4. Previous sanction of the Central Government required for the opening of metro railway.-

(1) No metro railway shall be opened for the public carriage of passengers except with the previous sanction of the Central Government.

2. Before giving its sanction under sub-section (1), the Central Government shall, after considering the report given (whether before or after the commencement of this Act) by the commissioner under clause (a) of sub-section (2) of section 27 of the Construction Act and other relevant factors, satisfy itself that the metro railway can be opened without changer to the public using it.

3. A section given under this section may be either absolute or subject to such conditions as the Central Government thinks necessary for the safety of the public.

4. Where any sanction for the opening of the metro railway under this section is given subject to any conditions, such railway shall not be worked or used until such conditions are fulfilled to the satisfaction, of the Central Government.

CHAPTER III

SPECIAL PROVISIONS FOR THE RUNNING OF THE METRO RAILWAY

5. Carriage of goods.-

(1) No person shall, while travelling in the metro railway, carry with him any goods other than a small baggage containing personal belongings not exceeding such volume and weight as may be prescribed.

(2) Where any person travels in the metro railway in contravention of the provisions of

> sub-section (1), he shall, notwithstanding that he holds a valid pass or ticket for any travel in such railway, be liable to be removed from the train by any metro railway official authorised by the metro railway administration in this behalf or by any other person whom such metro railway official may call to his aid.

6. Reservation of compartments for females not necessary.- It shall not be necessary for the metro railway administration to reserve any compartment in any train for the exclusive use of females.

7. Dangerous or offensive goods.-

(1) No person shall take or cause to be taken any dangerous or offensive goods upon the metro railway.

(2) If any metro railway official has reason to believe that any such goods are contained in a package in the custody of any passenger, he may cause the package to be opened for the

purpose of ascertaining it contents.

8. Penalty for taking or causing to take offensive or dangerous goods upon the metro railway.-

(1) If, in contravention of sub-section (1) of section 7, a person takes or causes to be taken any offensive goods upon the metro railway, he shall be punishable with fine which may extend to five hundred rupees.

9. if, in contravention of sub-section (1) of section 7, a person takes or causes to be taken any dangerous goods upon the metro railway, he shall be punishable with imprisonment for a term which may extend to four years and with fine which may extend to five thousand rupees.

10. In addition to penalties specified in sub-section (1) or sub-section (2), a person taking or causing to be taken any offensive goods or dangerous goods upon the metro railway shall be responsible also for any loss, injury or damage which may be caused by reason of such goods having been so brought upon the metro railway.

9. Smoking in compartments, etc.-

(1) No person shall smoke in any compartment or carriage of the metro railway or in any underground metro railway station.

(c) Whoever contravenes the provisions of sub-section (1) shall be punishable with fine which may extend to two hundred and fifty rupees.

(d) If any person persists in so smoking after being warned by any metro railway official to desist, he may, in addition to incurring the liability mentioned in sub-section (2), be removed, from the compartment or carriage in which he is travelling or from the underground station at which he may be found smoking by any metro railway official authorised by the metro railway or in any underground metro railway administration in this behalf.

10. Drunkeness or nuisance upon the metro railway.-

(1) If any person-

2. is in a state of intoxication; or

3. commits any nuisance or act of indecency, or uses obscence or abusive language; or

4. Wilfully or without excuse interferes in any way with comfort of any passenger; in any carriage or upon any part of the metro railway, he shall be punishable with fine which may extend to two hundred and fifty rupees and shall also be liable to forfeiture of the fare which he may have paid or any pass or ticket which he may have obtained or purchased, or be removed from such carriage or part by any metro railway official authorised by the metro railway administration in this behalf.

(2) If any metro railway official is in a state of intoxication while on duty he shall be punished with fine which may extend to two hundred and fifty rupees, or where the improper performance of the duty would be likely to endanger the safety of any passenger travelling or being upon the metro

railway, with imprisonment for a term which may extend to two years, or with fine which may extend to five hundred rupees, or with both.

11. Prohibition of demonstrations upon the metro railway.-

(1) No demonstration of any kind whatsoever shall be held on any part of the metro railway or other premises thereof and it shall be open to the metro railway administration to exclude from such premises any person attending such demonstrations whether or not he is in possession of a pass or ticket entitling to be in the said premises.

(2) No person shall paste or put up any poster or write or draw anything or matter in any compartment or carriage of the metro railway, or any premises thereof, without any lawful authority and any person found engaged in doing any such act may be removed from the compartment, carriage or premises by any metro railway official authorised by the metro railway administration in this behalf.

(3) Whoever contravenes any of the provisions of sub-section (1) of sub-section (2) being asked by any railway official to leave any compartment, carriage or premises refuses to do so , shall be punishable with imprisonment for a term which may extend to three months or with fine which may extend to five hundred rupees, or with both.

12. Penalty for travelling on roof, etc., of a train.- If any passenger travels on the roof of a train or persists in travelling in any part of a train not intended for the use of passengers or projects any part of his body out of a train after being warned by any metro railway official to desist, he shall be punishable with imprisonment for a term which may extend to one month, or with fine which may extend to fifty rupees, or with both, and shall also be liable to be removed from the train by any metro railway official authorised by the metro railway administration in this behalf.

13. Penalty for unlawfully entering or remaining upon the metro railway or walking metro railway line.-

(1) If a person enters into or upon the metro railway without any lawful authority of having entered with lawful authority remains there unlawfully and refuses to leave on being requested to do so by any metro railway official, he shall be punishable with imprisonment for a term which may extend to three months, or with fine which may extend to two hundred and fifty rupees, or with both.

(2) If any person walks on the metro railway line without any lawful authority, he shall punishable with imprisonment for term which may extend to six months, or with fine which may extend to five hundred rupees or with both.

14. Endangering the safety of passengers.- If any metro railway official, when on duty, endangers the safety of any passenger:--

b by any rash or negligent act or omission; or

c by disobeying any rule or order which such official was bound by the terms of his employment to obey, and of which he had notice, he shall be punishable with imprisonment for a term which may extend to five years, or with fine which may extend to six thousand rupees, or with both.

15. Abandoning train, etc., without authority.- If any metro railway official, when on duty, is entrusted with any responsibility connected with the running of a train, or any other rolling stock from one station or place to another station or place, and he abandons his duty before reaching such station or place, without authority or without properly handling over such train or rolling stock to another authorised metro railway official, he shall be punishable with imprisonment for a term which may extend to four years, or with fine which may extend to five thousand rupees, or with both.

16. Obstruction running of trains, etc.- If any person obstructs or causes to be obstructed or attempts to obstruct any train or other rolling stock upon the metro railway by squatting, picketing, or keeping without authority any rolling stock on the metro railway or tampering with any signalling installations or by interfering with the working mechanism thereof, or otherwise, he shall be liable to removed by any metro railway official authorised by the metro railway administration in this behalf and shall also be punishable with imprisonment for a term which may extend to four years or with fine which may extend to five thousand rupees, or with both.

17. Offences by companies.-

(1) Where an offence under this Act has been committed by a company, every person who, at the time the offence was committed, was in charge of and was responsible to the company, for the conduct of the business of the company, as well as the company, shall be deemed to be guilty of the offence and shall be liable to be proceeded against and punished accordingly.

Provided that nothing contained in this sub-section shall render any such person liable to any punishment, if he proves that the offence was committed without his knowledge or that he had exercised all due diligence to prevent the commission of such offence.

(2) Notwithstanding any thing contained in sub-section (1), where any offence under this Act has been committed by a company and it is proved that the offence has been committed with the consent or connivance of, or is attributable to any neglect on the part of, any director, manager, secretary, or other officer of the company, such director, manager, secretary or other officer of the company, such director, manager, secretary or other officer shall be deemed to be guilty of that offence and shall be liable to be proceeded against and punished accordingly.

Explanation:--For the purposes of this section:--

(e) "Company" means any body corporate and includes a firm or other association or individuals; and

(f) "director", in relation to a firm, means a partner in the firm.

CHAPTER IV

MISCELLAENOUS

18. Application of Act 9 of 1890 and the rules, etc., made there under to the metro railway.- Save as otherwise expressly provided in this Act, the provisions of the Indian Railways Act, 1890, and the

rules, orders or notifications made or issued thereunder shall, so far as may be, and subject to such modification as may be necessary, apply to the operation and maintenance of the metro railway, as if such metro railway were a railway as defined under that Act, and the references to "railway administration" and "Inspector" in that Act shall be constructed as references to the "metro railway administration" and "commissioner" respectively.

19. Effect of Act and rules, etc., inconsistent with other enactments.- The provisions of this Act or any rule legal proceeding shall lie against the Central Government, the metro railway administration or any officer or other employee of that Government or the metro railway administration for anything which is in good faith done or intended to be done under this Act.

20. Protection of action taken in good faith.-

(1) No suit, prosecution or other legal proceeding shall lie against the Central Government, the metro railway administration or any officer or other employee of that Government or the metro railway administration for anything which is in good faith done or intend to be done under this Act.

(2) No suit, prosecution or other legal proceeding shall lie against the Central Government or the metro railway administration or any officer or other employee of that Government or the metro railway administration for any damage causes or likely to be caused by anything which is in good faith done or intended to be done under this Act.

21. Power to remove difficulties.- If any difficulty arises in giving effect to the provisions of this Act, the Central Government may, by order, do anything not inconsistent with such provisions which appears to it be necessary or expedient for the purpose of removing the difficulty.

22. Power to make rules.-

(1) The Central Government may, by notification in the Official Gazette, make rules to carry out the provisions of this Act.

(2) In particular, and without prejudice to the generality of the foregoing power, such rules may provide for the following matters, namely;-

(a) the terms and conditions of service of the officers and other employees of the metro railway administration under sub-section (2) of section(3);

(b) the cases in which and the extent to which the procedure specified in section 4 for the opening of the metro railway for public carriage of passengers may be dispensed with;

(c) the volume and weight of the baggage containing personal belongings that may be carried by a person while travelling in the metro railway;

(d) any other matter which is required to be, or may be, prescribed.

(3) Every rule made under this section shall be laid, as soon as may be after it is made, before each House of Parliament, while it is in session, for a total period of thirty days which may be comprised in one session or in two or more successive sessions and if, before the expiry of the

session immediately following the session or the successive sessions aforesaid, both Houses agree in making any modification in the rule or both Houses agree that the rule should not be made, the rule shall thereafter have effect only in such modified form or be of no effect, as the case may be; so however, that any such modification or annulment shall be without prejudice to the validity of anything previously done under that rule.

23.Repeal and saving 13 of 1984.- (1) The Calcutta Metro Railway (Operation and Maintenance)

Temporary Provisions Ordinance, 1984, is hereby repealed. (2) Notwithstanding such repeal, anything done or any action taken under this said Ordinance, shall be deemed to have been done or taken under the corresponding provisions of this Act.

THE CHAPARMUKH-SILGHAT RAILWAY LINE AND THE KATAKHAL-LALABAZAR RAILWAY LINE (NATIONALISATION) ACT, 1982

ACT No. 36 OF 1982

[17th August, 1982.]

An Act to provide for the acquisition of the undertakings of the Chaparmukh-Silghat Railway Company Limited in relation to the Chaparmukh-Silghat Railway Line and the undertakings of the Katakhal-Lalabazar Railway Company Limited in relation to the Katakhal-Lalabazar Railway Line with a view to securing the efficient operation of the said Railway lines so as to subserve the needs of the north-eastern areas of India and to protect the links of communication between the said areas and the rest of the country and for matters connected therewith or incidental thereto.

WHEREAS the Chaparmukh-Silghat Railway Line owned by the Chaparmukh-Silghat Railway Company Limited and the Katakhal-Lalabazar Railway Line owned by the Katakhal-Lalabazar Railway Company Limited, are vital communication links between the north-eastern areas of India and the rest of the country;

AND WHEREAS the said Railway Lines are integrated with the metre gauge system of the contiguous North-East Frontier Railway;

AND WHEREAS the condition of assets of the aforesaid companies has reached such a stage that it may not be possible to operate train services for long on the railway lines owned by them;

AND WHEREAS it is necessary to secure the efficient operation of the said Railway lines;

BE it enacted by Parliament in the Thirty-third Year of the Republic of India as follows:—

CHAPTER I

PRELIMINARY

5. **Short title.**—This Act may be called the Chaparmukh-Silghat Railway Line and the Katakhal-Lalabazar Railway Line (Nationalisation) Act, 1982.

6. **Definitions.**—In this Act, unless the context otherwise requires,—

(a) "appointed day" means the day on which this Act comes into force; (b) "notification" means a notification published in the Official Gazette; (c) "specified company" means a company specified in clause (d);

(d) "two specified companies" means,—

(*i*) the Chaparmukh-Silghat Railway Company Limited, being a company as defined in the Companies Act, 1956 (1 of 1956) and having its registered office at 12, Mission Row, Calcutta; and

(*ii*) the Katakhal-Lalabazar Railway Company Limited, being a company as defined in the Companies Act, 1956 (1 of 1956) and having its registered office at Mcleod House, 3, Netaji Subhash Road, Calcutta;

(*e*) "undertakings" means,—

(*i*) in relation to the Chaparmukh-Silghat Railway Company Limited, the Chaparmukh-Silghat Railway Line and all other undertakings of that company relating to that Railway line;

(*ii*) in relation to the Katakhal-Lalabazar Railway Company Limited, the Katakhal-Lalabazar Railway line and all other undertakings of that company relating to that Railway line;

(*f*) words and expressions used herein and not defined but defined in the Companies Act, 1956 (1 of 1956) shall have the meanings respectively assigned to them in that Act.

CHAPTER II

ACQUISITION OF THE UNDERTAKINGS OF THE TWO SPECIFIED COMPANIES

3. Transfer to, and vesting in the Central Government of the undertakings of the two specified companies.—On the appointed day, the undertakings of each of the two specified companies and the right, title and interest of each of the two specified companies in relation to such undertakings shall, by virtue of this Act, stand transferred to, and vest in, the Central Government.

4. General effect of vesting.—(*1*) The undertakings of each specified company shall be deemed to include all assets, rights, lease-holds, powers, authorities and privileges, and all property, movable and immovable, including lands, buildings, workshops, stores, instruments, machinery and equipment, cash balances, cash on hand, cheques, demand drafts, reserve funds, investments, book debts and all other rights and interests in, or arising out of, such property as were immediately before the appointed day in the ownership, possession, power or control of the specified company, whether within or outside India, and all books of account, registers and all other documents of whatever nature relating thereto.

(*2*) All properties as aforesaid which have vested in the Central Government under section 3 shall, by force of such vesting, be freed and discharged from any trust, obligation, mortgage, charge, lien and all other encumbrances affecting them, and any attachment, injunction, decree or order of any court restricting the use of such properties in any manner or appointing any receiver in respect of the whole or any part of such properties shall be deemed to have been withdrawn.

(*3*) For the removal of doubts, it is hereby declared that the mortgagee of any property referred to in sub-section (*2*), or any other person holding any charge, lien or other interest in, or in relation to, any such property shall be entitled to claim, in accordance with his rights and interests, payment of the mortgage money or other dues, in whole or in part, out of the amounts payable under sections 6 and 7 to the specified company owning such property, but no such mortgage, charge, lien or other interest shall be enforceable against any property which has vested in the Central Government.

(*4*) Any licence or other instrument granted to a specified company in relation to any undertaking which has vested in the Central Government under section 3 at any time before the appointed day and in force immediately before that day shall continue to be in force on and after such day in accordance with its tenor in relation to and for the purposes of such undertaking, and, on and from the date of vesting of such undertaking under section 3 in the Central Government, that Government shall be deemed to be substituted in such licence or other instrument as if such licence or other instrument had been granted to that Government and that Government shall hold it for the remainder of the period for which the specified company would have held it under the terms thereof.

5. Owners of the two specified companies to be liable for certain prior liabilities.—(*1*) Every liability of a specified company in respect of any period prior to the appointed day, shall be the liability of the specified company and shall be enforceable against it and not against the Central Government.

(*2*) For the removal of doubts, it is hereby declared that,—

(*a*) no liability of either of the two specified companies in relation to its undertakings in respect of any period prior to the appointed day, shall be enforceable against the Central Government;

(*b*) no award, decree or order of any court, tribunal or other authority in relation to the undertakings of either of the two specified companies passed on or after the appointed day, in respect of any matter, claim or dispute, which arose before that day, shall be enforceable against the Central Government;

(*c*) no liability incurred by a specified company before the appointed day, for the contravention of any provision of law for the time being in force, shall be enforceable against the Central Government.

CHAPTER III

PAYMENT OF AMOUNT

6. Payment of amount.—(*1*) For the transfer to, and vesting in, the Central Government, under section 3, of the right, title and interest of each of the two specified companies in relation to its undertakings, there shall be paid in cash by the Central Government, before the expiry of a period of three months from the appointed day,—

(*i*) to the Chaparmukh-Silghat Railway Company Limited, an aggregate amount of rupees ten lakhs and fifty thousand; and

(*ii*) to the Katakhal-Lalabazar Railway Company Limited, an aggregate amount of rupees nine lakhs.

(*2*) Notwithstanding anything contained in sub-section (*1*), out of the amount referred to in clause (*i*) of that sub-section, the Central Government shall deduct, in the first instance, any amount due from the Chaparmukh-Silghat Railway Company Limited to that Government and the liability of that company shall, to the extent of such deduction, stand discharged and such deduction shall have priority over all other debts, secured or unsecured.

(*3*) Notwithstanding anything contained in sub-section (*1*), out of the amount referred to in clause (*ii*) of that sub-section, the Central Government shall deduct, in the first instance, the amount due from the Katakhal-Lalabazar Railway Company Limited in respect of the secured debentures issued by that company and shall pay the sums so deducted for the redemption of such debentures and the liability of that company in relation to the said debentures shall, to the extent of such deduction, stand discharged and such deduction shall have priority over all other debts, secured or unsecured.

7. Interest.—The amount referred to in clause (*i*) or clause (*ii*) of sub-section (*1*) of section 6 as reduced by the deduction under that section, shall, if not paid to the company concerned before the expiry of the period specified in the said sub-section, carry simple interest at the rate of four per cent. per annum for the period commencing on the appointed day and ending on the date on which payment of such amount as so reduced is made by the Central Government to that company:

Provided that if the amount as so reduced is tendered to the specified company but not accepted by it, no interest shall run from the date of such tender.

CHAPTER IV

DUTY OF PERSONS IN CHARGE OF MANAGEMENT OF THE UNDERTAKINGS OF THE TWO SPECIFIED COMPANIES TO DELIVER ALL ASSETS, ETC.

(k) **Duty of persons in charge of management of the undertakings of the two specified companies to deliver all assets, etc.**—On the vesting of the undertakings of the two specified companies in the Central Government, all persons in charge of the management of the undertakings immediately before such vesting, shall be bound to deliver to the Central Government all assets, books of account, registers or other documents in their custody relating to the undertakings.

(l) **Duty of persons to account for assets, etc., in their possession.**—(*1*) Any person who has, on the appointed day, in his possession or under his control any assets, books, documents or other papers relating to any undertaking owned by a specified company which have vested in the Central Government and which belong to the specified company, or would have so belonged, if the undertakings owned by the specified company had not vested in the Central Government, shall be liable to account for the said assets, books, documents and other papers to the Central Government and shall deliver them up to the Central Government or to such person or persons as the Central Government may specify in this behalf.

(*2*) The Central Government may take or cause to be taken all necessary steps for securing possession of the undertakings of the two specified companies which have vested in the Central Government under this Act.

(*3*) The two specified companies shall within such period as the Central Government may allow in this behalf, furnish to that Government a complete inventory of all their properties and assets, as on the appointed day, pertaining to the undertakings which have vested in the Central Government under section 3 and, for this purpose, the Central Government shall afford to the two specified companies all reasonable facilities.

CHAPTER V

MISCELLANEOUS

(f) **Act to have overriding effect.**—The provisions of this Act shall have effect notwithstanding anything inconsistent therewith contained in any other law for the time being in force or any instrument having effect by virtue of any law, other than this Act, or in any decree or order of any court, tribunal or other authority.

(g) **Penalties.**—Any person who,—

(*a*) having in his possession, custody or control any property forming part of any undertaking of either of the two specified companies, wrongfully withholds such property from the Central Government; or

(*b*) wrongfully obtains possession of, or retains any property forming part of any undertaking of either of the two specified companies; or

(*c*) wilfully withholds or fails to furnish to the Central Government or any person or persons specified by that Government any document relating to such undertaking, which may be in his possession, custody or control; or

(*d*) fails to deliver to the Central Government or any person or persons specified by that Government, any assets, books of account, registers or other documents in his possession, custody or control, relating to the undertakings of either of the two specified companies; or

(*e*) wrongfully removes or destroys any property forming part of any undertaking of either of the two specified companies or prefers any claim which he knows or has reason to believe to be false or grossly inaccurate,

shall be punishable with imprisonment for a term which may extend to two years, or with fine which may extend to ten thousand rupees, or with both.

12. Offences by companies.—(*1*) Where an offence under this Act has been committed by a company, every person who, at the time of the offence was committed, was in charge of, and was responsible to, the company for the conduct of the business of the company, as well as the company, shall be deemed to be guilty of the offence and shall be liable to be proceeded against and punished accordingly:

Provided that nothing contained in this sub-section shall render any such person liable to any punishment, if he proves that the offence was committed without his knowledge or that he had exercised all due diligence to prevent the commission of such offence.

(*2*) Notwithstanding anything contained in sub-section (*1*), where any offence under this Act has been committed by a company and it is proved that the offence has been committed with the consent or connivance of, or is attributable to any neglect on the part of, any director, manager, secretary or other officer of the company, such director, manager, secretary or other officer shall be deemed to be guilty of that offence and shall be liable to be proceeded against and punished accordingly.

Explanation.—For the purposes of this section,—

(*a*) "company" means any body corporate and includes a firm or other association of individuals;
and

(*b*) "director", in relation to a firm, means a partner in the firm.

13. Protection of action taken in good faith.—(*1*) No suit, prosecution or other legal proceeding shall lie against the Central Government or any officer or other employee of that Government or any officer or other person authorised by that Government for anything which is in good faith done or intended to be done under this Act.

(*2*) No suit or other legal proceeding shall lie against the Central Government or any officer or other employee of that Government or any officer or other person authorised by that Government for any damage caused or likely to be caused by anything which is in good faith done or intended to be done under this Act.

14. Delegation of powers.—(*1*) The Central Government may, by notification, direct that all or any of the powers exercisable by it under this Act, other than the powers conferred by this section and sections 15 and 16 may also be exercised by such person or persons as may be specified in the said notification.

(*2*) Whenever any delegation of power is made under sub-section (*1*), the person to whom such power has been delegated shall act under the direction, control and supervision of the Central Government.

15. Power to make rules.—(*1*) The Central Government may, by notification, make rules for carrying out the provisions of this Act.

(*2*) Every rule made by the Central Government under this Act shall be laid, as soon as may be after it is made, before each House of Parliament, while it is in session, for a total period of thirty days which may be comprised in one session or in two or more successive sessions, and if, before the expiry of the session immediately following the session or the successive sessions aforesaid, both Houses agree in making any modification in the rule or both Houses agree that the rule should not be made, the rule shall thereafter have effect only in such modified form or be of no effect, as the case may be; so, however, that any such modification or annulment shall be without prejudice to the validity of anything previously done under that rule.

16. Power to remove difficulties.—If any difficulty arises in giving effect to the provisions of this Act, the Central Government may, by order, not inconsistent with the provisions of this Act, remove the difficulty:

Provided that no such order shall be made after the expiry of a period of two years from the appointed day.

THE METRO RAILWAYS (CONSTRUCTION OF WORKS) ACT, 1978

1 Short title, commencement and application.
- (1) This Act may be called the Metro Railways (Construction of Works) Act, 1978.
- (2) It shall come into force on such date 1 as the Central Government may, by notification in the Official Gazette, appoint.
- (3) It applies in the first instance to the metropolitan city of Calcutta; and the Central Government may, by notification in the Official Gazette, declare that this Act shall also apply to 2 [the National Capital Region, such other metropolitan city and metropolitan area, after consultation with the State Government, and with effect from such date as may be specified in that notification and thereupon the provisions of this Act shall apply to the National Capital Region, such metropolitan city or metropolitan area accordingly]. Name of region or metropolitan area Name of State (1) (2) National Capital Region National Capital Territory—Delhi, Haryana, Rajasthan and Uttar Pradesh Bangalore Karnataka Mumbai Maharashtra Chennai Tamil Nadu

2. Definitions.
- (1) In this Act, unless the context otherwise requires,
    - (a) Advisory Board means the Advisory Board constituted under section 4;
    - (b) 1[appellate authority] means the 1[appellate authority] appointed under section 16;
    - (c) building means a house, outhouse, stable, latrine, urinal, shed, hut or wall or any other structure or erection, whether of masonry bricks, wood, mud, metal or any other material or any part of a building, but does not include a plant or machinery installed in a building or any part thereof or any portable shelter;
    - (d) commissioner means a commissioner of metro railway appointed under section 27; 2[(e) competent authority means the competent authority appointed under section 16;]
    - (f) development with its grammatical variations means the carrying out of building, engineering, mining or other operations in, on, over or under land or the making of any material change in any building or land or planting of any tree on land and includes redevelopment;
    - (g) land includes any right or interest in land;
    - (h) metro alignment , in relation to any metropolitan city, means such alignment of the metro railway as is specified in the Schedule under that city and includes the metro railway;
    - (i) metro railway means a metro railway or any portion thereof for the public carriage of passengers, animals or goods and includes,
    - (a) all land within the boundary marks indicating the limits of the land appurtenant to a metro railway,
    - (b) all lines of rails, sidings, yards or branches worked over for the purposes of, or in connection with, a metro railway,
    - (c) all stations, offices, ventilation shafts and ducts, ware-houses, workshops, manufactories, fixed plants and machineries, sheds, depots and other works constructed for the purpose of, or in connection with, a metro railway;
    - (j) metro railway administration , in relation to any metro railway, means the General Manager of that metro railway;
    - (k) metropolitan city means the metropolitan city of Bombay, Calcutta, Delhi or Madras;
    - (l) metropolitan city of Bombay means the area covered by Greater Bombay as defined in the Bombay Municipal Corporation Act, 1888 (Bombay Act III of 1888);
    - (m) metropolitan city of Calcutta means the area described under the heading 1. Calcutta Metropolitan District in the Schedule to the Calcutta Metropolitan Planning Area (Use and Development of Land) Control Act, 1965 (West Bengal Act XIV of 1965);
    - (n) metropolitan city of Delhi means the entire area of the Union territory of Delhi*;

- (o) metropolitan city of Madras means the area covered by the City of Madras as defined in the Madras City Municipal Act, 1919 (Madras Act IV of 1919);
- (p) prescribed means prescribed by rules made under this Act;
- (q) rolling stock includes locomotives, engines, carriages (whether powered or not), wagons, trollies and vehicles of all kinds moving or intended to move on rails;
- (r) to erect , in relation to any building, includes
    - (i) any material alteration or enlargement of such building,
    - (ii) conversion, by structural alteration, into a place for human habitation of such building not originally constructed for human habitation,
    - (iii) conversion into more than one place for human habitation of such building originally constructed as one such place,
    - (iv) conversion of two or more places of human habitation in such building into a greater number of such places,
    - (v) such alteration of such building as would alter the drainage or sanitary arrangements therein or would materially affect its security, and
    - (vi) the addition of any rooms in such building.

- (2) All other words and expressions used herein and not defined but defined in the *Indian Railways Act, 1890 (9 of 1890), shall have the meanings, respectively, assigned to them in that Act.

3. General Manager.The Central Government may, for the purposes of this Act, appoint a General Manager for every metro railway.

4. Constitution of Advisory Board.
- (1) The Central Government may constitute an Advisory Board for every metro railway for the purpose of assisting or advising that Government on
    - (a) the formulation and co-ordination of plans for the development of metro railway and its expansion;
    - (b) the financing and execution of any project for the construction of the metro railway;
    - (c) such other matters as may be referred to it for carrying out the purposes of this Act and in particular for the purpose of ensuring that the functions of the metro railway administration are exercised with due regard to the circumstances or conditions prevailing in, and requirements of, the metropolitan city.

- (2) The Advisory Board shall consist of such number of members (being officers of the Government) not exceeding nine as may be appointed to it by the Central Government.
- (3) The Central Government shall appoint one of the members of the Advisory Board as its Chairman.
- (4) The Central Government shall publish in the Official Gazette the names of all the members of the Advisory Board and the Chairman thereof.
- (5) The Advisory Board shall meet at such times and places and shall observe such procedure in regard to the transaction of its business as may be prescribed.
- (6) The members of the Advisory Board shall hold office for such term as may be prescribed.

5. Committees.
    - (1) The Advisory Board may constitute as many committees as it deems necessary consisting wholly of members of such Board or wholly of other persons or partly of members of the Board and partly of other persons for such purposes as it may think fit.
    - (2) Every committee constituted under sub-section (1) shall meet at such times and places and shall observe such procedure in regard to the transaction of its business as may be prescribed.
    - (3) There shall be paid to the members of the committee who are not members of the Advisory Board, such fees and allowances for attendance at the meetings of the committee and such travelling allowances as may be prescribed.

6. Power to acquire land, etc. Where it appears to a metro railway administration that for the construction of any metro railway or any other work connected therewith
    - (a) any land, building, street, road or passage, or
    - (b) any right of user, or any right in the nature of easement, therein, is required for such construction or work, it shall apply to the Central Government in such form as may be prescribed for acquiring such land, building, street, road or passage or such right of user or easement.

7. Publication of notification for acquisition.
    - (1) On receipt of an application under section 6, the Central Government, after being satisfied that the requirement mentioned therein is for a public purpose, may, by notification in the Official Gazette, declare its intention to acquire the land, building, street, road or passage, or the right of user, or the right in the nature of easement, therein referred to in the application.
    - (2) Every notification under sub-section (1) shall give a brief description of the land, building, street, road or passage.
    - (3) The competent authority shall cause the substance of the notification to be published in such places and in such manner as may be prescribed.

8. Power to enter for survey, etc. On the issue of a notification under sub-section
    - (1) of section 7, it shall be lawful for the metro railway administration or any officer or other employee of the metro railway
        - (a) to enter upon and survey and take level of the land, building, street, road or passage specified in the notification;
        - (b) to dig or bore into the sub-soil;
        - (c) to set out the intended work;
        - (d) to mark such levels, boundaries or lines by placing marks and cutting trenches;
        - (e) to do all other acts necessary to ascertain whether the metro railway can be laid upon or under the land, building, street, road or passage, as the case may be: Provided that while exercising any power under this section the metro railway administration or such officer or other employee shall cause as little damage or injury as possible to such land, building, street, road or passage, as the case may be.

9. Hearing of objection.
    - (1) Any person interested in the land, building, street, road or passage may, within twenty-one days from the 1[date of publication under sub-section (3) of section 7 of the substance of the

notification under sub-section (1) of that section] object to the construction of the metro railway or any other work connected therewith upon or under the land, building, street, road or passage, as the case may be. 2[Explanation.For the purposes of this sub-section, where the substance of the notification under sub-section (1) of section 7 is published on different dates at different places, the last of such dates shall be deemed to be the date on which substance of the notification has been published.]

- (2) Every objection under sub-section (1) shall be made to the competent authority in writing and shall set out the grounds thereof and the competent authority shall give the objector an opportunity of being heard, either in person or 2[by an agent or] by a legal practitioner, and may, after hearing all such objections and after making such further enquiry, if any, as the competent authority thinks necessary, by order, either allow or disallow the objections. Explanation.For the purposes of this sub-section legal practitioner has the same meaning as in clause (i) of sub-section (1) of section 2 of the Advocates Act, 1961 (25 of 1961).
- (3) Any order made by the competent authority under sub-section (2) shall be final.

10. Declaration of acquisition.
    - (1) Where no objection under sub-section (1) of section 9 has been made to the competent authority within the period specified therein or where the competent authority has disallowed the objection under sub-section (2) of that section, the competent authority shall, as soon as may be, submit a report accordingly to the Central Government and on receipt of such report, the Central Government shall declare, by notification in the Official Gazette, that the land, building, street, road or passage, or the right of user, or the right in the nature of easement, therein for laying the metro railway should be acquired.
    - (2) On the publication of the declaration under sub-section (1), the land, building, street, road or passage, or the right of user, or the right in the nature of easement, therein shall vest absolutely in the Central Government free from all encumbrances.
    - (3) Where in respect of any land, building, street, road or passage, a notification has been published under sub-section (1) of section 7 either for its acquisition or for the acquisition of the right of user, or any right in the nature of easement, therein, but no declaration under this section has been published within a period of one year from the date of publication of that notification, the said notification shall cease to have any effect: 1[Provided that in computing the said period of one year, the period or periods during which any action or proceeding to be taken in pursuance of the notification issued under sub-section (1) of section 7 [including any such action or proceeding pending immediately before the commencement of the Metro Railways (Construction of Works) Amendment Act, 1987] is stayed by an order of a court, whether granted before or after such commencement, shall be excluded.]
    - (4) A declaration made by the Central Government under sub-section (1) shall not be called in question in any court or by any other authority.

11. Power to take possession.
    - (1) 1[Where any land, building, street, road or passage has vested under sub-section (2) of section 10 and the amount determined by the competent authority under section 13 with respect to such land, building, street, road or passage has been deposited under sub-section (1) of section 14, with the Competent Authority by the Central Government], the competent authority may by notice in writing direct the owner as well as any other person who may be in possession of such land, building, street, road or passage to surrender or deliver possession thereof to the competent authority or any person duly authorised by it in this behalf within sixty days of the service of the notice.
    - (2) If any person refuses or fails to comply with any direction made under sub-section (1), the competent authority shall apply,
    - (a) in the case of any land, building, street, road or passage situated in any area falling within the Presidency-town of Bombay, Calcutta or Madras, to the Commissioner of Police;
    - (b) in the case of any land, building, street, road or passage situated in any area other than the area referred to in clause (a), to the Executive Magistrate, and such Commissioner or Magistrate, as the

case may be, shall enforce the surrender of the land, building, street, road or passage to the competent authority or to the person duly authorised by it.

12. Right to enter into the land where right of user, etc., is vested in the Central Government. Where the right of user in, or any right in the nature of easement on, any land, building, street, road or passage has vested in the Central Government under section 10, it shall be lawful for the metro railway administration or any officer or other employee of the Central Government to enter and do any other act necessary upon the land, building, street, road or passage for carrying out the construction of the metro railway or any other work connected therewith.

13. Determination of amount payable for acquisition.
    - (1) Where any land, building, street, road or passage is acquired under this Act, there shall be paid an amount which shall be determined 1[by an order of the competent authority].
    - (2) Where the right of user in, or any right in the nature of an easement on, any land, building, street, road or passage is acquired under this Act, there shall be paid an amount to the owner and any other person whose right of enjoyment in that land, building, street, road or passage has been affected in any manner whatsoever by reason of such acquisition an amount calculated at ten per cent. of the amount determined under sub-section (1) for that land, building, street, road or passage. 2[(2A) Before proceeding to determine the amount under sub-section (1) or sub-section (2), the competent authority shall give a public notice published in the prescribed manner inviting claims from all persons interested in the land, building, street, road or passage, or the right of user or the right in the nature of easement therein to be acquired.
    - (2B) Such notice shall state the particulars of the land, building, street, road or passage acquired, or the right of user or the right in the nature of easement therein acquired and shall require all persons interested in such land, building, street, road or passage or right of user or right in the nature of easement therein, to appear in person, or by an agent or by a legal practitioner referred to in sub-section (2) of section 9, before the competent authority, at a time and place therein mentioned (such time not being earlier than fifteen days after the date of the publication of the notice) and to state the nature of their respective interests in such land, building, street, road or passage or right of user or right in the nature of easement therein.]
    - (3) If the amount determined by the competent authority under sub-section (1) or sub-section (2) is not acceptable to either of the parties the amount shall, 3[on an appeal preferred by either of the parties to the appellate authority, within a period of sixty days from the date of the order appealed against, be determined by an order of the appellate authority].
    - (4) The competent authority or the 4[appellate authority] while determining the amount under sub-section (1) or sub-section (3), as the case may be, shall take into consideration
    - (a) the market value of the land, building, street, road or passage on the date of publication of the notification under section 7;
    - (b) the damage, if any, sustained by the person interested at the time of taking possession of the land, by reason of the severing or such land from other land;
    - (c) the damage, if any, sustained by the person interested at the time of taking possession of the land, building, street, road or passage by reason of the acquisition injuriously affecting his other immovable property in any other manner, or his earnings;
    - (d) if, in consequence of the acquisition of the land, building, street, road or passage, the person interested is compelled to change his residence or place of business, the reasonable expenses, if any, incidental to such change.

14. Deposit and payment of amount.
    - (1) The amount determined 1[***] under section 13 shall be deposited by the Central Government in such manner as may be prescribed with the competent authority 2[within such time as may be fixed by that authority].
    - (2) As soon as may be after the amount has been deposited under sub-section (1), the competent authority shall on behalf of the Central Government pay the amount to the person or persons entitled thereto: 3[Provided that where an appeal has been or is likely to be preferred under section 13 against the order by which such amount was determined and the competent authority is

satisfied for reasons to be recorded in writing that it is necessary or expedient so to do, he may by order in writing

- (a) require the person claiming payment of such amount to furnish as a condition of receiving such payment, such security as may be specified in the order; or
- (b) if such person fails to furnish such security, withhold the payment of the whole or any part of such amount for such period as may be specified in the order.]
- (3) Where several persons claim to be interested in the amount deposited under sub-section (1) the competent authority shall determine the persons who in its opinion are entitled to receive the amount payable to each of them.
- (4) If any dispute arises as to the apportionment of the amount or any part thereof or to any person to whom the same or any part thereof is payable, the competent authority shall refer the dispute to the decision of the principal civil court of original jurisdiction within the limits of whose jurisdiction the land, building, street, road or passage is situated.
- (5) Where the amount determined under section 13 by the 4[appellate authority] is in excess of the amount determined by the competent authority, the 4[appellate authority] may award interest at six per cent. per annum on such excess amount from the date of taking possession under section 11 till the date of the actual deposit thereof.
- (6) Where the amount determined by the 4[appellate authority] is in excess of the amount determined by the competent authority, the excess amount together with interest, if any, awarded under sub-section (5) shall be deposited by the Central Government in such manner as may be prescribed with the competent authority and the provisions of sub-sections (2) to (4) shall apply to such deposit.

15. Competent authority to have certain powers of civil court.The competent authority shall have, for the purposes of this Act, all the powers of a civil court while trying a suit under the Code of Civil Procedure, 1908 (5 of 1908), in respect of the following matters, namely:

- (a) summoning and enforcing the attendance of any person and examining him on oath;
- (b) requiring the discovery and production of any document;
- (c) reception of evidence on affidavits;
- (d) requisitioning any public record from any court or office;
- (e) issuing commission for examination of witnesses.
    - 15A. Power to inspect property under acquisition.The competent authority may, with or without assistants or workmen, enter into or upon any land, building, street, road or passage, for the purpose of performing his functions under this Act and make such enquiry, inspection, measurement and take such photographs and prepare such memorandum thereof as he may consider necessary: Provided that
    - (i) no such entry shall be made except between the hours of sunrise and sunset and without giving reasonable notice to
        - (a) the owner of or the person interested in, the land, building, street, road or passage; or
        - (b) the person whose right of user in or right in the nature of easement on the land, building, street, road or passage is acquired; or
        - (c) the person who sustains any loss or damage to the land, building, street, road or passage in consequence of any direction given by the Central Government or any power exercised by the metro railway administration under this Act;
    - (ii) sufficient opportunity shall in every instance be given to enable women, if any, to withdraw from such land, building, street, road or passage;
    - (iii) due regard shall always be had, so far as may be compatible with the exigencies of the purpose for which the entry is made, to the social and religious usage of the person to whom notice as aforesaid is given;
    - (iv) the competent authority making the entry shall cause a little damage or injury as possible, to the land, building, street, road or passage.]

16. Competent authority and appellate authority.

- (1) For every metro railway, the Central Government shall, for the purposes of this Act, by notification in the Official Gazette, appoint
  - (i) a competent authority; and
  - (ii) an appellate authority, for such area as may be specified in the notification.
- (2) A person shall not be qualified for appointment as a competent authority unless he is holding, or has held, a judicial office, not lower in rank than that of a subordinate judge.
- (3) A person shall not be qualified for appointment as an appellate authority unless he is holding, or has held, a judicial office, not lower in rank than that of a subordinate judge. Explanation.For the purpose of this section,
  - (a) district judge includes an additional district judge;
  - (b) subordinate judge means subordinate judge in the judicial service of West Bengal, and includes any judicial officer (by whatever name called) of an equivalent rank in the judicial service of any other State.]
- 16A. Powers of the appellate authority.
  - (1) The appellate authority may admit an appeal filed after the expiry of the period referred to in section 13 or section 22 or section 25, as the case may be, if he is satisfied that there was sufficient cause for not presenting it within that period.
  - (2) For the disposal of an appeal under this Act, the appellate authority shall have the same powers (including the powers under sections 15 and 15A), and shall, subject to the provisions of this section, perform as nearly as may be the same duties as are conferred or imposed by this Act on the competent authority in respect of the matters under Chapter III and Chapter IV.
  - (3) The appellate authority may, if he thinks it expedient so to do, call in his aid one or more assessors and hear the appeal wholly or partly with the aid of such assessors.
  - (4) for the purpose of determining the amount under any appeal before him, the appellate authority may, after making such further enquiry or after taking such additional evidence, as may be necessary, pass such order as he thinks fit, determining the amount, by confirming, modifying or annulling the order appealed against.
  - (5) An order of the appellate authority determining the amount under this Act shall be final.]
- 16B. Competent authority, etc., to have certain inherent powers.The competent authority and the appellate authority may exercise powers of the nature referred to in section 151 of the Code of Civil Procedure, 1908 (5 of 1908) to the same extent and for the same purposes as such powers are exercisable by civil courts.]
- 16C. Enforcement of the orders of the competent authority and appellate authority.
  - (1) Any order made by the competent authority or the appellate authority determining any amount payable under this Act may be enforced in the same manner as if such order were a decree made by a civil court in a suit pending therein, and it shall be lawful for such authority to send, in the case of his inability to execute, such order, to the principal civil court of original jurisdiction within the local limits of whose jurisdiction the order was made.
  - (2) Where any order under sub-section (1) is required to be enforced by the principal civil court of original jurisdiction, a certified copy of the order shall be produced to the proper officer of the court required to enforce the order.
  - (3) The production of such certified copy shall be sufficient evidence of the order.
  - (4) Upon the production of such certified copy, the principal civil court of original jurisdiction shall take the requisite steps for enforcing the order, in the same manner as if it had been a decree made by itself.]

17. Land Acquisition Act 1 of 1894 not to apply.Nothing in the Land Acquisition Act, 1894, shall apply to an acquisition under this Act.

18. Functions of metro railway administration.Subject to the control of the Central Government, the metro railway administration shall, for the purpose of constructing any metro railway or any other work connected therewith,

- (a) make or construct in, upon, across, under or over any lands, buildings, streets, roads, railways or tramways or any rivers, canals, brooks, streams or other waters or any drains, water-pipes, gas-pipes, electric lines or telegraph lines, such temporary or permanent inclined planes, arches, tunnels, culverts, embankments, aqueducts, bridges, ways or passages, as the metro railway administration thinks proper;
- (b) alter the course of any rivers, canals, brooks, streams or water-courses for the purpose of constructing tunnels, passages or other works over or under them and divert or alter as well temporarily as permanently, the course of any rivers, cannals, brooks, streams or water-courses or any drains, water-pipes, gas-pipes, electric lines or telegraph lines or raise or sink the level thereof in order the more conveniently to carry them over or under, as the metro railway administration thinks proper;
- (c) make drains or conduits into, through or under, any lands adjoining the metro railway for the purpose of conveying water from or to the metro railway;
- (d) erect or construct such houses, warehouses, offices and other buildings and such yards, stations, engines, machinery, apparatus and other works and conveniences, as the metro railway administration thinks proper;
- (e) alter, repair or discontinue such buildings, works and conveniences as aforesaid or any of them, and substitute others in their stead;
- (f) draw, make or conduct such maps, plans, surveys or tests, as the metro railway administration thinks property;
- (g) do all other acts necessary for making, maintaining, altering or repairing and using the metro railway.

19. Powers of metro railway administration.
    - (1) The metro railway administration shall, for the purpose of 1[performing its functions under section 18], have power
        - (a) to enter into contracts and leases and to execute all instruments necessary therefor;
        - (b) to make such number of rail tracks as the Central Government may think necessary upon, under, along or across any land, canal, river, street or road on or in the metro alignment and all other works and conveniences in connection therewith;
        - (c) 2[to open, divert or temporarily close], as the case may be, any street, road, cable, trench, drain (including a sewer), channel, ditch, culvert or any other device (whether for carrying of sullage, sewage, offensive matter, polluted water, trade effluent, rain water, sub-soil water or any other object), electric or gas supply line or tele-communication line, or telegraph installation, over, across or under any land, building, street, road, railway or tramway;
        - (d) to burrow tunnels;
        - (e) to lay down signalling and other communication facilities, electric sub-stations, supply lines and other works;
        - (f) to regulate drilling of tubewells or sinking of wells, public or private, in the proximate vicinity of the metro alignment;
        - (g) to do all other things necessary or expedient for the exercise of any of the aforesaid powers.
    - (2) While exercising any powers under sub-section (1), the metro railway administration shall take such precautionary measures as are necessary, shall do as little damage as possible and shall be liable only for the damage or cost actually suffered or incurred by any person as a result of the exercise of such powers.

20. Development over metro alignment.
    - (1) Any person who proposes to develop any land or building along or on the metro alignment shall, before commencing such development and without in any way limiting his obligation under any other Act to obtain any approval or consent, submit to the metro railway administration details of the proposed development and shall comply with any conditions imposed by the metro railway administration in respect thereof.

- (2) The metro railway administration shall, while imposing any condition under sub-section (1), have regard to
    - (a) the safety of the metro railway;
    - (b) such other matters as may be prescribed.

21. Power to prohibit or regulate construction of buildings and excavation.
    - (1) If the Central Government is of opinion that it is necessary or expedient so to do for facilitating the construction of any metro railway or for ensuring the safety of any metro railway, it may, by notification in the Official Gazette,
        - (a) direct that no building or any such development as may be specified in the notification shall be constructed or made above the metro alignment or on any land within such distance, not exceeding 1[twenty metres] on either side of the metro alignment, as may be specified in the notification and where there is any building on such land also direct the owner of, or the person having control over, such building to demolish such building or to make such additions or alterations to such building as may be specified in the notification or to desist from making any such development and within such period as may be specified in the notification;
        - (b) direct temporary evacuation of all persons together with any movable property or animal that may be in the custody, control or possession of such persons from any building situated above the metro alignment or in any area within a distance not exceeding twenty metres on either side of such alignment and within such period as may be specified in the notification: Provided that before issuing any notification under this clause, the Central Government shall provide every such person temporarily with alternative accommodation, which in its opinion is suitable, free of cost, or an amount, which in its opinion is sufficient, to procure a temporary alternative accommodation.
    - (2) Where any property is needed or likely to be needed for providing any alternative accommodation under the proviso to clause (b) of sub-section (1), such property shall be deemed to be needed for a public purpose under section 3 of the Requisitioning and Acquisition of Immovable Property Act, 1952 (30 of 1952), and the competent authority under that Act shall requisition the property in accordance with the provisions of that Act and such provisions shall, in relation to such requisition, apply accordingly.
    - (3) In specifying the distance under clause (a) of sub-section (1), the Central Government shall have regard to
        - (a) the nature and the requirement of the metro railway;
        - (b) the safety of the building;
        - (c) such other matters as may be prescribed.
    - (4) Where any notification has been issued under sub-section (1) directing the owner or the person having control over any building to demolish such building or to make additions or alterations to such building or to desist from making any development specified in such notification, a copy of the notification containing such direction shall be served on the owner of, or the person having control over, such building, as the case may be,
        - (i) by delivering or tendering it to such owner or person; or
        - (ii) if it cannot be delivered or tendered, by delivering or tendering it to the agent of such owner or person or any adult male member of the family of such owner or person or by affixing a copy thereof on the outer door or on some conspicuous part of the premises in which such owner or person is known to have last resided or carried on business or personally worked for gain; or failing service by these means;
        - (iii) by post.
    - (5) Every person shall be bound to comply with any direction contained in any notification issued under sub-section (1).

22. Payment of amount for prohibition of construction, etc.
    - (1) If in consequence of any direction contained in any notification issued under sub-section (1) of section 21 any person sustains any loss or damage, such person shall be paid an amount which shall be determined 1[by an order of the competent authority] in the first instance.

- (2) If the amount determined by the competent authority is not acceptable to either of the parties, the amount shall, 2[on an appeal preferred by either of the parties, within sixty days from the date of the order of the competent authority, to the appellate authority, be determined by an order of the appellate authority].
- (3) The competent authority or the 3[appellate authority], while determining the amount under sub-section (1) or sub-section (2), as the case may be, shall take into consideration
    - (i) the loss or damage sustained by such person in his earnings;
    - (ii) the diminution, if any, of the market value of the land or building immediately after the date of publication of such notification;
    - (iii) where in pursuance of any direction any building has been demolished or any additions or alterations to such building have been made or any development has been desisted by such person, the damage sustained by him in consequence of such demolition or the making of such additions or alterations or the desisting from making such development and the expenses incurred by such person for such demolition or additions or alterations: Provided that the expenses incurred for such demolition or additions or alterations shall not be taken into consideration if such demolition or additions or alterations has or have been done by the metro railway administration under sub-section (2) of section 36;
    - (iv) if any such person is compelled to change his residence or place of business the reasonable expenses, if any, that may have to be incurred by him incidental to such change.

23. Power to underpin building or otherwise strengthen it.
    - (1) If the metro railway administration is of opinion that it is necessary or expedient so to do for facilitating the construction of any metro railway or for ensuring the safety of any metro railway, it may, underpin or otherwise strengthen any building within such radius not exceeding, fifty metres from the metro alignment.
    - (2) The metro railway administration shall give to the owner or occupier of such building at least ten days notice in writing before undertaking the work of underpinning or otherwise strengthening the building: Provided that where the metro railway administration is satisfied that an emergency exists, no such notice shall be necessary.
    - (3) Where the underpinning or strengthening was executed in connection with
        - (a) the carrying out of the works upon the land where any building is situated, or
        - (b) the construction or operation of any metro railway, the metro railway administration may, at any time after the underpinning or strengthening of such building is completed and before the expiration of a period of twelve months,
            - (i) in a case referred to in clause (a), from the completion of such works; and
            - (ii) in a case referred to in clause (b), from the date on which traffic was opened in the metro railway, enter upon and survey such building and do such further underpinning or strengthening thereon as it may deem necessary.

24. Power to enter, etc.
    - (1) With a view to making survey, or to ascertaining the nature or condition, of any land or building for the purpose of construction of any metro railway or any other work connected therewith, the metro railway administration or any person authorised by that administration may, at any reasonable hour in the day time and after giving reasonable notice to the owner or occupier of such land or building, enter upon or into such land or building in, along, over or near the alignment to
        - (a) inspect the same;
        - (b) make measurements and drawings and take photographs thereof and such other suitable measures as may be necessary to explore and check-up, by digging trial pits or otherwise, the foundation of any building in the vicinity of the metro alignment;
        - (c) take such other measures as the said administration deems necessary and proper.
    - (2) Without prejudice to the powers conferred on it under section 19, the metro railway administration may, by writing, request any person or body of persons controlling any sewer, storm water drain, pipe, wire or cable to carry out at the expense of the metro railway

administration any alterations thereto which that administration is authorised or may be required to carry out to meet any particular situation for carrying out the purposes of this Act.

- (3) If any difference or dispute arises between the metro railway administration and the person or body of persons referred to in sub-section (2) in relation to any such alterations or the cost thereof, such difference or dispute shall be determined by the Central Government in consultation (wherever necessary) with the State Government and the decision of the Central Government in this regard shall not be called in question in any court.

25. Amount payable for damage, loss or injury.
    - (1) Where the metro railway administration exercises any power conferred on it by or under this Act and in consequence thereof any damage, loss or injury is sustained by any person interested in any land, building, street, road or passage, the metro railway administration shall be liable to pay to such person for such damage, loss or injury such amount as may be determined by the competent authority.
    - (2) If the amount determined by the competent authority under sub-section (1) is not acceptable to either of the parties, the amount payable shall, 1[on an appeal preferred by either of the parties, within sixty days from the date of the order of the competent authority, to the appellate authority, be determined by an order of the appellate authority].
    - (3) The competent authority or the 2[appellate authority] while determining the amount under sub-section (1) or sub-section (2), as the case may be, shall have due regard to the damage, loss or injury sustained by any person interested in the land, building, street, road or passage by reason of
        - (i) the removal of trees or standing crops, if any;
        - (ii) the temporary severance of the land, building, street, road or passage;
        - (iii) any injury to any other property whether movable or immovable. 3[(4) The procedure and the manner of deposit and payment of the amount payable for acquiring any land, building, street, road or passage or any right of user in or any right in the nature of easement on any land, building, street, road or passage shall be followed in the case of the procedure and the manner of deposit and payment of the amount determined by the competent authority or the appellate authority under this section.]

26. Right to claim for damages.No claim in respect of any damage, loss or injury alleged to have been caused as a consequence of construction of any metro railway or any other work connected therewith under this Act shall lie against the metro railway administration unless such claim is made within a period of twelve months from the date of completion of the construction of such metro railway or other work in the area in which such damage, loss or injury is caused.

27. Appointment and duties of commissioner.
    - (1) The Central Government may appoint as many persons as it thinks fit by name or by virtue of their office to be commissioners of metro railway.
    - (2) Every commissioner shall
        - (a) inspect the metro railway with a view to determining whether it is fit to be opened for public carriage of passengers and report thereon to the Central Government;
        - (b) make such periodical or other inspections of any metro railway or of any rolling stock used thereon as the Central Government may direct;
        - (c) perform such other duties as may be imposed on him by or under this Act or any other enactment for the time being in force relating to railways or required by the Central Government.

28. Powers of Commissioners.Subject to the control of the Central Government every commissioner shall have the power
    - (a) to enter upon and inspect any metro railway or any rolling stock used thereon;
    - (b) to make any enquiry or to take any measurement as he thinks fit for the performance of his duties under this Act;
    - (c) by an order in writing under his hand and official seal addressed to any metro railway administration, to require the attendance before him of any officer or other employee of the metro

railway and to require answers or returns, to such enquiries as he thinks fit to make, from such officer or other employee or from the said administration;
- (d) to require the production of any book or other documents belonging to, or in the possession or control of, any metro railway administration which it appears to him to be necessary to inspect for the performance of his duties by or under this Act.

29. Facilities to be afforded to commissioner.Every metro railway administration shall afford to every commissioner all reasonable facilities for performing the duties or exercising the powers imposed or conferred upon him by or under this Act.

30. Surplus land to be sold or otherwise disposed of.Every metro railway administration may, with the previous approval of the Central Government, sell or otherwise dispose of any land vested in the Central Government under the provisions of this Act when such land is no longer required for the purposes of the metro railway.

31. Notice of accidents and enquiries.
- (1) If any accident occurs during the construction of any metro railway or at any stage subsequent thereto as a consequence of such construction and the accident results in, or is likely to have resulted in, loss of human being or animal or damage to any property, it shall be the duty of the metro railway administration to give notice to the Central Government of the occurrence of any such loss or damage in such form and within such time as may be prescribed.
- (2) On receipt of a notice under sub-section (1), the Central Government may, if it thinks fit, appoint a commission to enquire into the accident and report as to
  - (a) the cause of such accident;
  - (b) the manner in which and the extent to which the provisions of this Act or any other Act for the time being in force in so far as those provisions regulate and govern the safety of any person, animal or property, have been complied with.
- (3) The commission appointed under sub-section (2), while holding an enquiry, shall have all the powers of a civil court while trying a suit under the Code of Civil Procedure, 1908 (5 of 1908), in respect of the following matters, namely:
  - (a) summoning and enforcing the attendance of any person and examining him on oath;
  - (b) requiring the discovery or production of any document;
  - (c) reception of evidence on affidavits;
  - (d) requisitioning any public record from any court or office;
  - (e) issuing commission for examination of witnesses.

32. Power to alter the entries in the Schedule.
- (1) The Central Government may, by notification in the Official Gazette,
  - (a) add to the Schedule the metro alignment in respect of a metropolitan city to which this Act is made applicable under sub-section (3) of section 1;
  - (b) alter any metro alignment specified in the Schedule if it is of opinion that such alteration is necessary for the construction and maintenance of the metro railway to which such alignment relates.
- (2) Every notification issued under sub-section (1) shall, as soon as may be after it is issued, be laid before each House of Parliament.

33. Prohibition of obstruction.No person shall, without any reasonable cause or excuse, obstruct any person with whom the metro railway administration has entered into a contract, in the performance or execution by such person of such contract.

34. Local authorities to assist.Every local authority shall render such help and assistance and furnish such information to the metro railway administration as that administration may require for discharging its functions and shall make available to the said administration for inspection and examination such records, maps, plans and other documents as may be necessary for the discharge of such functions.

35. Prohibition of removal of marks. No person shall remove any marks placed or fill up any trench cut for the purpose of marking levels, boundaries or lines by the metro railway administration.

36. Penalty for failure to comply with directions issued under section 21.
    - (1) If any person wilfully fails to comply with any direction contained in any notification issued under section 21, he shall be punished with imprisonment for a term which may extend to six months, or with fine which may extend to one thousand rupees, or with both.
    - (2) Without prejudice to the provisions of sub-section (1), if any person fails to demolish any building or make additions or alterations thereto in pursuance of any direction contained in any notification issued under section 21 within the period specified in the notification, then, subject to such rules as the Central Government may make in this behalf, it shall be competent for any officer authorised by the metro railway administration in this behalf to demolish such building or make necessary additions or alterations thereto. 1[(2A) Without prejudice to the provisions of sub-section (2), if any person fails to vacate temporarily any building together with any movable property or animal that may be in his custody, control or possession in pursuance of any direction contained in any notification issued under section 2 within the period specified in the notification, the competent authority may enforce the direction of temporary evacuation physically by taking such police help, as may be considered by him necessary, and for this purpose the provisions of sub-section (2) of section 11 shall, as far as may be, apply.]

37. General provision for punishment of offences. Whoever contravenes any provision of this Act or of any rule made thereunder shall, if no other penalty is provided for such contravention elsewhere in this Act or the rules, be punishable with imprisonment for a term which may extend to three months, or with fine which may extend to five hundred rupees, or with both.

38. Offences by companies.
    - (1) Where an offence under this Act has been committed by a company, every person who at the time the offence was committed was in charge of, and was responsible to, the company for the conduct of the business of the company as well as the company, shall be deemed to be guilty of the offence and shall be liable to be proceeded against and punished accordingly: Provided that nothing contained in this sub-section shall render any such person liable to any punishment, if he proves that the offence was committed without his knowledge or that he had exercised all due diligence to prevent the commission of such offence.
    - (2) Notwithstanding anything contained in sub-section (1), where any offence under this Act has been committed by a company and it is proved that the offence has been committed with the consent or connivance of, or is attributable to any neglect on the part of, any director, manager, secretary or other officer of the company, such director, manager, secretary or other officer shall be deemed to be guilty of that offence and shall be liable to be proceeded against and punished accordingly. Explanation. For the purposes of this section,
        - (a) company means any body corporate and includes a firm or other association of individuals; and
        - (b) director , in relation to a firm, means a partner in the firm.

39. Bar of jurisdiction. No suit or application for injunction shall lie in any court against the Central Government or the metro railway administration or any officer or other employee of that Government or the metro railway or any person working for or on behalf of the metro railway administration, in respect of any work done or purported to have been done or intended to be done by it or the said administration or such officer or other employee or such person in connection with the construction of any metro railway or any other work connected therewith.

40. Effect of Act and rules, etc., inconsistent with other enactments. The provisions of this Act or any rule made or any notification issued thereunder shall have effect notwithstanding anything inconsistent therewith contained in any enactment other than this Act or in any instrument having effect by virtue of any enactment other than this Act.

41. Protection of action taken in good faith.
- (1) No suit, prosecution or other legal proceeding shall lie against the Central Government, the metro railway administration or any officer or other employee of that Government or the metro railway for anything which is in good faith done or intended to be done under this Act.
- (2) No suit, prosecution or other legal proceeding shall lie against the Central Government or the metro railway administration or any officer or other employee of that Government or the metro railway for any damage caused or likely to be caused by anything which is in good faith done or intended to be done under this Act.

42. Power to remove difficulties. If any difficulty arises in giving effect to the provisions of this Act, the Central Government may, by order, do anything not inconsistent with such provisions, which appears to it to be necessary or expedient for the purpose of removing the difficulty: Provided that no such order shall, in relation to any metropolitan city, be made after the expiry of a period of two years from the date on which this Act applies or is made applicable to such metropolitan city under sub-section (3) of section 1.

43. Application of the *Indian Railways Act, 1890.Save as otherwise provided in this Act, the provisions of this Act shall be in addition to, and not in derogation of, the *Indian Railways Act, 1890 (9 of 1890).

44. Power to make rules.
- (1) The Central Government may, by notification in the Official Gazette, make rules to carry out the purposes of this Act.
- (2) In particular and without prejudice to the generality of the foregoing power, such rules may provide for the following matters, namely:
    - (a) the times and places at which the Advisory Board shall meet and the procedure in regard to transaction of business by the Advisory Board under sub-section (5) of section 4;
    - (b) the term of office of the members of the Advisory Board under sub-section (6) of section 4;
    - (c) the times and places at which the committees shall meet and the procedure in regard to transaction of business by the committees under sub-section (2) of section 5;
    - (d) the payment of fees, allowances and travelling allowances to the members of the committee under sub-section (3) of section 5;
    - (e) the form in which an application for acquisition shall be made under section 6;
    - (f) the places at which and the manner in which the substance of the notification shall be published under sub-section (3) of section 7;
    - (g) the manner in which the amount shall be deposited with the competent authority under sub-sections (1) and (6) of section 14;
    - (h) the matters to be specified under clause (b) of sub-section (2) of section 20;
    - (i) the matters to be specified under clause (c) of sub-section (3) of section 21;
    - (j) the form in which and the time within which a notice shall be given under sub-section (1) of section 31;
    - (k) any other matter which is required to be or may be prescribed.
- (3) Every rule made under this section shall be laid, as soon as may be after it is made, before each House of Parliament, while it is in session for a total period of thirty days which may be comprised in one session or in two or more successive sessions, and if, before the expiry of the session immediately following the session or the successive sessions aforesaid, both Houses agree in making any modification in the rule or both Houses agree that the rule should not be made, the rule shall thereafter have effect only in such modified form or be of no effect, as the case may be; so, however, that any such modification or annulment shall be without prejudice to the validity of anything previously done under that rule.

45. Saving. Notwithstanding anything contained in this Act any proceeding, for the acquisition of any land, under the Land Acquisition Act, 1894 (1 of 1894), for the purpose of any metro railway, pending immediately before the commencement of this Act before any court or other authority shall be continued and be disposed of under that Act as if this Act had not come into force.

The Indian Railway Companies Act, 1895

THE INDIAN RAILWAY COMPANIES ACT, 1895

ACT NO. 10 OF 1895 [7th March, 1895.] WH

An Act to provide for the payment by Railway Companies registered under the Indian Companies Act, 1882, of interest out of capital during construction.

1. Title and extent.
    - (1) This Act may be called the Indian Railway Companies Act, 1895 .
    - (2) It extends to the whole of India except 2 the territories which, immediately before the 1st November, 1956 , were comprised in Part B States]. 3 3

2. Definitions. In this Act, unless there is something repugnant in the subject or context,--
    - (1) " railway" means a railway as defined in section 3, clause (4), of the Indian Railways Act, 1890 (9 of 1890 .):
    - (2) " the railway" means the railway in relation to the construction of which interest out of capital is permitted to be paid as hereinafter provided: and
    - (3) " Railway Company" means a Company registered under the 4 Indian Companies Act, 1882 (6 of 1882 .), and formed for the purpose of making and working, or making or working, a railway in India, whether alone or in conjunction with other purposes.

3. Payment of interest out of capital. A Railway Company may pay interest on its paid- up share capital out of capital, for the period, and subject to the conditions and restrictions, in this section mentioned, and may charge the same to capital as part of the cost of construction of the railway:--
    - (1) Such interest shall be paid only for such period as shall be determined by the Central Government; and such period The Act comes into force in Pondicherry on 1. 10. 1963 vide Reg. 7 of 1963 , s. 3 and Sch. I. Extonded to and brought into force in Dadra and Nagar Haveli (w. e. f. 1- 7- 65) by Reg. 6 of 1963 , s. 2 and Sch. I.
    - -------------------------------

- 1. This Act has been rep. by the Indian Companies Act, 1913 (7 of 1913), which has also been rep. by the Companies Act, 1956 (1 of 1956). 2 Subs. by the Adaptation of Laws (No. 2) Order, 1956, for" Part B States". 3 The word" and" at the end of sub- section (2) and sub- section (3) rep. by Act 10 of 1914, s. 3 and Sch. II. 4 See now the Companies Act, 1956 (1 of 1956).
- -------------------------------
- shall in no case extend beyond the close of the half- year next after the half- year during which the railway shall be actually completed and opened for traffic.
- (2) No such payment shall be made unless the same is authorised by the Company' s memorandum of association or by a special resolution of the Company.
- (3) No such payment, whether authorised by the Company' s memorandum of association or by special resolution as aforesaid, shall be made without the previous sanction of the Central Government.
- (4) The amount so paid out of capital by way of interest, in respect of any period, shall in no case exceed a sum which shall, together with the net earnings of the railway during such period, make up the rate of four per cent. per annum.
- (5) No such payment of interest shall be made until such Railway Company has satisfied the Central Government that two- thirds at least of its share capital, in respect whereof interest is to be so paid, has been actually issued and accepted, and is held by shareholders who, or whose representatives, are legally liable for the same.
- (6) No such interest shall accrue in favour of any shareholder for any time during which any call on any of his shares is in arrear.
- (7) The payment of such interest shall not operate as a reduction of the amount paid up on the shares in respect of which it is paid.

4. Provisions of section 3 applicable to additional share capital for extensions. A railway in course of construction and intended to be made or worked by a Railway Company in addition to or way of extentsion of any railway owned or worked by such Company shall be deemed to be the railway of such Company for the purposes of this Act, and all the provisions of the last preceding section shall apply to such railway and to the share capital issued for the purpose of its construction.

5. Notice in prospectus and other documents. When a Railway Company has power to pay interest under this Act, notice to that effect shall be given in every prospectus, advertisement or other document inviting subscriptions for shares therein, and in every certificate of such shares.

6. Accounts. When any interest has been paid by a Railway Company under this Act, the annual or other accounts of such company shall show the amount on which, and the rate at which, interest has been so paid.

7. Construction of borrowing powers. If by any memorandum of association, articles of association or other document any power of borrowing money is conferred on a Railway Company, or on its Directors, with or without the sanction of any meeting, and if such power of borrowing is limited to an amount bearing any proportion to the capital of such Company, the amount of capital applied or to be applied in payment of interest under this Act shall, for the purpose of ascertaining the extent of such power of borrowing, be deducted from the capital of such Company.

The Indian Tramways Act, 1902

THE INDIAN TRAMWAYS ACT, 1902

ACT NO. 4 OF 1902 [14th February, 1902.]

An Act to apply the provisions of the Indian Railway Companies Act, 1895, to certain Tramway Companies.

1. Short title and extent.
    - (1) This Act may be called the Indian Tramways Act, 1902 ; and
    - (2) It extends to the whole of India except 1 the territories which, immediately before the 1st November, 1956 , were comprised in Part B States].

2. Application of Act 10, 1895 , to Tramway Companies. The Central Government may, by notification in the Official Gazette, direct that the provisions of the Indian Railway Companies Act, 1895 (10 of 1895), in so far as the same are applicable, shall apply to any Company formed for the construction of a tramway under the Bengal Tramways Act, 1883 (Ben. 3 of 1883), or the Indian Tramways Act, 1886 (11 of 1886), and thereupon it shall be lawful for the Tramway Company mentioned in the notification to pay interest upon its paid- up share capital out of capital in the manner and subject to the conditions prescribed by the said Indian Railway Companies Act, 1895 .

---

1. Subs. by the Adaptation of Laws (No. 2) Order, 1956, for" Part B States". The Act comes into force in Pondicherry on 1. 10. 1963 vide Reg. 7 of 1963, s. 3 and Sch. I.

The Indian Railway Board Act, 1905

THE INDIAN RAILWAY BOARD ACT, 1905

ACT NO. 4 OF 1905 1 [22nd March, 1905.] W

An Act to provide for investing the Railway Board with certain powers or functions under the Indian Railways Act, 1890.

1. Short title and construction.
    - (1) This Act may be called the Indian Railway Board Act, 1905 ; and
    - (2) It shall be read with, and taken as part of, the Indian Railways Act, 1890 (9 of 1890 .).

2. Investment of Railway Board with powers under Indian Railways Act, 1890 . The Central Government may, by notification 2 in the Official Gazette, invest the Railway Board, either absolutely or subject to conditions,--
    - (a) with all or any of the powers or functions of the Central Government under the Indian Railways Act, 1890 (9 of 1890), with respect to all or any railways, and
    - (b) with the power of the officer referred to in section 47 of the said Act to make general rules for railways administered by the Government.

3. Mode of signifying communications from the Railway Board. Any notice, determination, direction, requisition, appointment, expression of opinion, approval or sanction, to be given or signified on the part of the Railway Board, for any of the purposes of, or in relation to, any powers or functions with which it may be invested by notification under section 2, shall be sufficient and binding if in writing signed by the Secretary to the Railway Board, or by any other person authorized by the said Railway Board to act in its behalf in respect of the matters to which such authorization may relate; and the said Railway Board shall not in any case be bound in respect of any of the

----

1. This Act has been extended to Berar by the Berar by the Berar Laws Act, 1941 (4 of 1941) and has been declared to be in force in the Sonthal Parganas by notification under s. 3 (3) (a) of the Sonthal Parganas Settlement Regulation (3 of 1872), see Calcutta Gazette, 1906, Pt. I, p. 334, and in the Angul District by the Angul Laws Regulation, 1936 (5 of 1936), s. 3 and Sch. The Act comes into force in Pondicherry on 1. 10. 1963 vide Reg. 7 of 1963, s. 3 and Sch. I. Extended to Goa, Daman and Diu with modifications, by Reg. 12 of 1962, s. 3 and Sch. Extended to and brought into force in dara and nagar Haveli (w. e. f. 1- 7- 65) by Reg. 6 of 1963, s. 2 and Sch. I.

2. For notifications see Gazette of India, 1905, Pt. I. p. 232; 1906, Pt. I, p. 927, and 1908, Pt. I, p. 169.

----

matters aforesaid unless by some writing signed in manner aforesaid.

4. 1 [Cessation of Railway Board on establishment of Federal Railway Authority.] Rep. by the A. O. 1948 .

1. Ins. by the A. O. 1937.

The Railways (Local Authorities' Taxation) Act, 1941

THE RAILWAYS (LOCAL AUTHORITIES' TAXATION) ACT, 1941

ACT NO. 25 OF 1941 [26th November, 1941.]

An Act to regulate the extent to which railway property shall be liable to taxation imposed by an authority within a 1 State].

1. Short title and extent.
    - (1) This Act may be called the Railways (Local Authorities' Taxation) Act, 1941 .
    - (2) It extends to the whole of India 3 except the State of Jammu and Kashmir].

2. Definitions. In this Act,--
    - (a) " local authority" means a local authority as defined in the General Clauses Act, 1897 (10 of 1897), and includes any authority legally entitled to or entrusted with the control or management of any fund for the maintenance of watchmen or for the conservancy of a river;
    - (b) " railway administration" has the meaning assigned to the expression in clause (6) of section 3 of the Indian Railways Act, 1890 (9 of 1890).

3. Liability of railways to taxation by local authorities.
    - (1) In respect of property vested in 2 the Central Government, being property of a railway, a railway administration shall be liable to pay and tax in aid of the funds of any local authority, if the Central Government, by notification in the Official Gazette, declares it to be so liable.
    - (2) While a notification under sub- section (1) is in force, the railway administration shall be liable to pay to the local authority either the tax mentioned in the notification or in lieu thereof such sum, if any, as a person appointed in this behalf by the Central Government

----

1. Subs. by Act 3 of 1951, s. 3 and Sch., for" Part A State", which had been subs. for" Province" by the A. O. 1950. 2 The words" His Majesty for the purposes of" omitted by the A. O. 1950. 3 Subs. by Act 3 of 1951, s. 3 and Sch., for" except Part B States".

----

may, having regard to the services rendered to the railway and all the relevant circumstances of the case, from time to time determine to be fair and reasonable. The person so appointed shall be a person who is or has been a Judge of a High Court or a District Judge.

4. Modification of existing liability to taxation. The Central Government may, by notification in the Official Gazette, revoke or vary any notification issued under clause 1 of section 135 of the Indian Railways Act, 1890 (9 of 1890); and where a notification is so revoked any liability arising out of the notification to pay any tax to any local authority shall cease, and where a notification is so varied the liability arising out of the notification shall be varied accordingly.

5. Saving. Nothing in this Act shall be construed as debarring any railway administration administering a railway from entering into a contract with any local authority for the supply of water or light or for the scavenging of railway premises, or for any other service which the local authority may be rendering or be prepared to render within any part of the local area under its control.

The Railway Companies (Substitution Of Parties In Civil Proceedings) Act, 1946

THE RAILWAY COMPANIES (SUBSTITUTION OF PARTIES IN CIVIL PROCEEDINGS) ACT, 1946

ACT NO. 14 OF 1946 [18th april, 1946.]

An Act to provide forr the substitution of the Governor- General in Counicil for certain RAilway Companies in certain civil proceedings.

WHEREAS under certain arrangements madeby the Central Government with the Bengal- Nagpur Railway Company, Limited, the Bombay, Baroda and Central India Railway Company, the Bengal and North Western Railway Company, Limited, and the Rohilkhand and Kumaon Railway Company, limited, certain rights and liabilitties of the said Companies have been assumed by the Central Government;

AND WHEREAS it is expedient to provide for the substitution of the governor- General in Council in the place and stead of the said Companies in all pending civil proceedings founded on any right of libility so assumed by the Central Government:

It is hereby enacted as follows:-

1. Short title. This Act may be called the Railway Companies (Substitution of Parties in Civil Proceedings) Act, 1946 .

2. Interpretation. In this Act," civil proceeding" includes and appeal or execution proceeding.

3. Substitution of Governor- General in Council in certain civil proceedings.

- (1) In every civil proceeding pending at the commencement of this Act to which the Bengal-Nagpur Railway Company, Limited, or the Bombay, Baroda and Central India Railway Company, or the Bengal and North Western Railway Company, Limited, or the Rohilkhand and Kumaon Railway Company, Limited, is a party, and which is founded on any right 5 or liability assumed by the Central Government undercertain arrangements made by the Central Government with the said Companies, the Governor- General in Council shall, notwithstanding anything to the contrary in the Code of Civil Procedure, 1908 (5 of 1908), be deemed to be substituted in the place and stead of the Company; and every such proceeding may be continued by or against the Governor-General in Concil accordingly, and the Company shall be discharged from all liability in connection with the proceeding.
- (2) References in sub- section (1) to any Company shall be construed as including references to the liquidators of that Company.

The Cotton Transport Act, 1923

THE COTTON TRANSPORT ACT, 1923

ACT NO. 3 OF 1923 1 [23rd February, 1923.]

An Act to provide for the restriction and control of the transport of cotton in certain circumstances.

WHEREAS it is expedient for the purpose of maintaining the quality and reputation of the cotton grown in certain areas 2 to enable the restriction and control of the transport by rail and the import of cotton into those areas; It is hereby enacted as follows:--

1. Short title and extent.
    - (1) This Act may be called the Cotton Transport Act, 1923 .
    - (2) 3 It extends to the whole of India except the State of Jammu and Kashmir.]

2. Definitions. In this Act, unless there is anything repugnant in the subject or context,--
    - (a) " certified copy," in relation to a licence, means a copy of the licence certified in the manner described in section 76 of the Indian Evidence Act, 1872 (1 of 1872), by the authority by which the licence was granted;
    - (b) " cotton" means every kind of unmanufactured cotton, that is to say, ginned and unginned cotton, cotton waste and cotton seed;
    - (c) " cotton waste" means droppings, strippings, fly and other waste products of a cotton- mill other than yarn waste;
    - (d) " licence" means a licence granted under this Act;
    - (e) " notified station" means a railway station specified in a notification under section 3;
    - (f) " prescribed" means prescribed by rules made under this Act; and

---

- 1. This Act was partially extended to Berar by the Berar Laws Act, 1941 (4 of 1941). It was extended to Shahda, Nandurbar and Taloda Talukas of the West Khandesh District, the Dohad Taluka and the Jhalod Mahal of the Panch Mahal District of the State of Bombay by Schedule II of the Absorbed Areas (Laws) Act, 1954 (20 of 1954). The Act comes into force in Pondicherry on 1. 10. 1963 vide Reg. 7 of 1963, s. 3 and Sch. I.
- 2. The words" in the Provinces" omitted by the A. O. 1950. 3 Subs. by Act 22 of 1960, s. 2, for sub- section (2).

- (g) " protected area" means an area into which the import of cotton or of any kind of cotton has been prohibited 1 wholly or partly] by a notification under section 3.

3. Power to issue notification prohibiting import of cotton into protected area.
- (1) The State Government may, for the purpose of maintaining the quality or reputation of the cotton grown in any area in the State, by notification in the Official Gazette, prohibit the import of cotton or of any specified kind of cotton into that area 2 by rail, road, river and sea, or by any one or more of such routes] save under, and in accordance with the conditions of, a licence: Provided that no such notification shall be deemed to prohibit the import into any protected area of packages containing any kind of cotton and not exceeding ten pounds avoirdupois weight.
- (2) Any such notification may prohibit the delivery to, and the taking of delivery by, any person, at any specified railway station situated in the protected area, of any cotton, the import of which 2 by rail] into that area is prohibited when such cotton has been consigned from a railway station not situated in that area, unless such person holds a licence for the import 2 by rail] of the cotton into that area.

4. Refusal to carry unlicensed cotton.
- (1) Notwithstanding anything contained in the Indian Railways Act, 1890 (9 of 1890), or any other law for the time being in force, the station master of any railway station or any other railway servant responsible for the booking of goods or parcels at that station may refuse to receive for carriage at, or to forward or allow to be carried on the railway from, that station any cotton consigned to a notified station, being cotton of a kind of which the delivery at such notified station has been prohibited unless both stations are in the same protected area, or unless the consignor produces a certified copy of a licence for the import of the cotton 3 by rail] into the protected area in which such notified station is situated.
- (2) Every certified copy of a licence when so produced shall be attached to the invoice or way- bill, as the case may be, and shall accompany the consignment to its destination, and shall there be dealt with in the prescribed manner.
- (3) Where by or under any law in force in the territories of any State in India the import 3 by rail] into any area, or the delivery

---

1. Ins. by Act 34 of 1925, s. 2. 2 Ins. by s. 3, ibid. 3 Ins. by s. 4, ibid.

---

at any railway station, of cotton or of any kind of cotton has been prohibited, the Central Government may, by notification 1 in the Official Gazette, declare that the provisions of sub- section (1) shall apply in respect of cotton consigned to any such station as if such area and such station were respectively a protected area and a notified station, and as if any licence granted under such law were a licence granted under this Act.

5. Procedure where cotton arrives at notified station.
- (1) Where any cotton, the import of which 2 by rail] into any protected area has been prohibited, has been consigned to and arrives at a notified station in any such protected area, the station master or other railway servant responsible for the receipt and delivery to the consignee of goods or parcels, as the case may be, at that station shall, unless both the notified station and the railway station from which the cotton has been consigned are situated in the same protected area, refuse to deliver the cotton until he is satisfied that the consignee holds a licence for the import of the cotton 2 by rail] into the protected area in which such notified station is situated; and, if he is not so

satified, or if within fourteen days the consignee or some person acting on his behalf does not appear in order to take delivery, shall return the cotton to the railway station from which it was consigned, together with an intimation that delivery of the cotton has been refused or has not been taken, as the case may be.

- (2) Any station master or other railway servant receiving any cotton returned under sub- section (1), or returned with a like intimation from a railway station specified in a notification under sub- section (3) of section 4, shall cause to be served on the consignor in any manner authorised by section 141 of the Indian Railways Act, 1890 (9 of 1890), a notice stating that the cotton has been so returned and requiring the consignor to pay any rate, terminal or other charges due in respect of the carriage of the cotton to and from the railway station to which it was consigned, and such charges shall be deemed to be due from the consignor for all the purposes of section 55 of that Act.

6. Penalties. Any person who, in contravention of the provisions of this Act or of any notification or rule made hereunder, knowingly takes delivery of any cotton from a notified station or imports, or attempts to import, any cotton into a protected area, and any station master or other railway servant who, in contravention of the provisions of

---

1. For such notifications see Gen. R. and O. Vol. V, p. 90; ibid., Supplementary Vol. II, p. 998; and ibid., Supplementary Vol. VI, p. 457. 2 Ins. by Act 34 of 1925, s. 5.

---

sub- section (1) of section 5, without reasonable excuse, the burden of proving which shall lie upon him, delivers any cotton to a consignee or other person, shall be liable to a fine not exceeding one thousand rupees, and upon any subsequent conviction to imprisonment which may extend to three months, or to fine which may extend to five thousand rupees, or to both.

7. Power to make rules.
    - (1) The State Government may, by notification in the Official Gazette, make rules to provide for any of the following matters, namely:--
        - (a) the prevention of the import into a protected area by road, river or sea, save under and in accordance with the conditions of a licence, of cotton the import of which into that area has been prohibited 1 wholly or partly] by a notification under section 3;
        - (b) 2 the terms and conditions to be contained in licences, the authorities by which they may be granted and the fees which may be levied in respect thereof; and]
        - (c) the manner in which licences and certified copies thereof shall be dealt with on and after the delivery of the cotton to which they relate.
    - (2) Any such rules may provide that any contravention thereof or of the conditions of any licence, not otherwise made punishable by this Act, shall be punishable with fine which may extend to five hundred rupees.

8. Previous approval of State Legislature to issue of notifications and rules. No notification under section 3 or rule under section 7 shall be issued by the State Government 3 , unless it has been laid in draft before 4 the Legislative Assembly of the State], and has been approved by a Resolution 5 of that Assembly], either with or without modification or addition, but upon such approval being given the notification or rule, as the case may be, may be issued in the form in which it has been so approved:

---

1. Ins. by Act 34 of 1925, s. 6. 2 Subs. by Act 22 of 1960, s. 3, for cl. (b). 3 The words" of any Part A State" omitted by the Adaptation of Laws (No. 3) Order, 1956. 4 Subs. by the A. O. 1937 for" the Legislative Council of the Province". 5 Subs., ibid., for" of the Legislative Council".

1] Provided that if the State Legislature has two 2 Houses], the notification must be laid in draft before, and be approved by Resolutions of, both 2 Houses], either without modifications or additions, or with modifications or additions approved by both 2 Houses].]

9. Protection for acts done under Act. No suit or other legal proceeding shall be instituted against any person in respect of anything which is in good faith done or intended to be done under this Act.

1.] Ins. by the A. O. 1937. 2 Subs. by the A. O. 1950 for" Chambers".

Other References:

THE PUBLIC GAMBLING ACT, 1867

Section 2: State government powers to extends "THE PUBLIC GAMBLING ACT, 1867" laws to railway stations.

THE COURT-FEES ACT, 1870

Section 19 (xi)(xviii) Complaint of a public servant (as defined in the Indian Penal Code), a municipal officer, or an officer or servant of a Railway Company.

THE POLICE ACT, 1861

Section 14. Appointment of additional force in the neighbourhood of rail- way and other works.-- Whenever any railway, canal or other public work, or any manufactory or commercial concern shall be carried on, or be in operation in any part of the country, and it shall appear to the Inspector- General that the employment of an additional police- force in such place is rendered necessary by the behaviour or reasonable apprehension of the behaviour of the persons employed upon such work, manufactory or concern, it shall be lawful for the Inspector- General, with the consent of the State Government, to depute such additional force to such place, and to employ the same so long as such necessity shall continue, and to make orders, from time to time, upon the person having the control or custody of the funds used in carrying on such work, manufactory or concern, for the payment of the extra force so rendered necessary, and such person shall thereupon cause payment to be made accordingly.

The Indian Evidence Act, 1872

Section 106 (b) Burden of proving fact especially within knowledge:- When 'A' is charged with travelling on a railway without a ticket. The burden of proving that he had a ticket is on him.

The Indian Contract Act, 1872

Section 72(b) Liability of person to whom money is paid, or thing delivered, by mistake or under coercion:- A railway company refuses to deliver up certain goods to the consignee except upon the payment of an illegal charge for carriage. The consignee pays the sum charged in order to obtain the goods. He is entitled to recover so much of the charge as was illegal and excessive. (b) A railway company refuses to deliver up certain goods to the consignee except upon the payment of an illegal charge for carriage. The consignee pays the sum charged in order to obtain the goods. He is entitled to recover so much of the charge as was illegal and excessive."

The Indian Forest Act, 1927

Section 35(1)(c)(iv). Protection of forests for special purposes. The [State Government] may, by notification in the [Official Gazette], regulate or prohibit in any forest or waste-land the firing or clearing of the vegetation; when such regulation or prohibition appears necessary for the protection of roads, bridges, railways and other lines of communication

The Elephants Preservation Act, 1879

Section 3(b). Killing and capture of wild elephant prohibited.—No person shall kill, injure or capture, or attempt to kill, injure or capture, any wild elephant unless— when such elephant is found injuring houses or cultivation, or upon, or in the immediate vicinity of, any main public road or any railway or canal

The Hackney- Carriage Act, 1879

Section 5. Power to extent operation of rules beyond limits of municipality or cantonment.- The authority making any rules under this Act may'[with the sanction of the Commissioner] extend their operation to any railway station, or specified part of a road, not more than six miles from the local limits of the municipality concerned.

THE LEGAL PRACTITIONERS ACT, 1879

Section 3(b) Interpretation clause. In this Act, unless there be something repugnant in the subject or context, Judge means the presiding judicial officer in every Civil and Criminal Court, by whatever title he is designated: subordinate Court means all Courts subordinate to the High Court, including Courts of Small Causes established under Act No. 9 of 1850 [3] or Act No. 11 of 1865 [4] : revenue-office includes all Courts (other than Civil Courts) trying suits under any Act for the time being in force relating to land-holders and their tenants or agents: the legal practitioner means an advocate, vakil or attorney of any High Court, a pleader, mukhtar or revenue-agent: [5] [tout means a person who for the purposes of such procurement frequents the precincts of Civil or Criminal Courts or of revenue-offices, or railway stations, landing stages, lodging places or other places of public resort]

The Indian Trusts Act, 1882

Section 20. Investment of trust-money.—Where the trust property consists of money and cannot be applied immediately or at an early date to the purposes of the trust, the trustee is bound (subject to any direction contained in the instrument of trust) to invest the money on the following securities and on no others in stock or debentures of, or shares in, railway or other companies the interest whereon shall have been guaranteed by the Secretary of State for India in Council; [or by the Central Government] [or in debentures of the Bombay [Provincial] Co-operative Bank Limited, the interest whereon shall have been guaranteed, by the Secretary of State for India in Council] [or the State Government of Bombay]; [(d) in debentures or other securities for money issued, under the authority of [any Central Act or Provincial Act or State Act], by or on behalf of any municipal body, port trust, or city improvement trust in any Presidency-town or in Rangoon Town, or by or on behalf of the trustees of the port of Karachi:] [Provided that after the 31st day of March, 1948, no money shall be invested in any securities issued by or on behalf of a municipal body, port trust or city improvement trust in Rangoon Town, or by or on behalf of the trustees of the port of Karachi;]

THE TRANSFER OF PROPERTY ACT, 1882

Section 67(C). **Right to fore-closure or sale.**—In the absence of a contract to the contrary, the mortgagee has, at any time after the mortgage-money has become 1[due] to him, and before a decree has been made for the redemption of the mortgaged property, or the mortgage-money has been paid or deposited as hereinafter provided, a right to obtain from the Court 2[a decree] that the mortgagor shall be absolutely debarred of his right to redeem the property, or 2[a decree] that the property be sold. A suit to obtain 2[a decree] that a mortgagor shall be absolutely debarred of his right to redeem the mortgaged property is called a suit for foreclosure. Nothing in this section shall be deemed to authorise the mortgagee of a railway, canal, or other work in the maintenance of which the public are interested, to institute a suit for foreclosure or sale

Section 137. **Saving of negotiable instruments, etc.**—Nothing in the foregoing sections of this Chapter applies to stocks, shares or debentures, or to instruments which are for the time being, by law or custom, negotiable, or to any mercantile document of title to goods. Explanation.—The expression "mercantile document of title to goods" includes a bill of lading, dock-warrant, warehouse-keeper's certificate, railway receipt, warrant or order for the delivery of goods, and any other document used in the ordinary course of business as proof of the possession or control of goods, or authorising or purporting to authorise, either by endorsement or by delivery, the possessor of the document to transfer or receive goods thereby represented.

THE EXPLOSIVES ACT, 1884

Section 13. **Power to arrest without warrant persons committing dangerous offences.**—Whoever is found committing any act for which he is punishable under this Act or the rules under this Act, and which tends to cause explosion or fire in or about any place where an explosive is manufactured or stored, or any railway or port, or any carriage,

1[aircraft or vessel], may be apprehended without a warrant by a police officer, or by the occupier of, or the agent or servant of, or other person authorised by the occupier of, that place, or by any agent or servant of, or other person authorised by, the railway administration or 2[conservator of the port or officer in charge of the airport], and be removed from the place where he is arrested and conveyed as soon as conveniently may be before a Magistrate.—Whoever is found committing any act for which he is punishable under this Act or the rules under this Act, and which tends to cause explosion or fire in or about any place where an explosive is manufactured or stored, or any railway or port, or any carriage, 2[aircraft or vessel], may be apprehended without a warrant by a police officer, or by the occupier of, or the agent or servant of, or other person authorised by the occupier of, that place, or by any agent or servant of, or other person authorised by, the railway administration or 3[conservator of the port or officer in charge of the airport], and be removed from the place where he is arrested and conveyed as soon as conveniently may be before a Magistrate."

THE INDIAN TELEGRAPH ACT, 1885

6. **Power to establish telegraph on land of Railway Company.**—Any Railway Company, on being required so to do by the Central Government, shall permit the Government to establish and maintain a telegraph upon any part of the land of the Company, and shall give every reasonable facility for working the same

22. **Opposing establishment of telegraphs on railway land.**—If a Railway Company, or an officer of a Railway Company, neglects or refuses to comply with the provisions of section 6, it or he shall be punished with fine which may extend to one thousand rupees for every day during which the neglect or refusal continues

THE POLICE ACT, 1888

Section

4. Consent of State Government to exercise of powers and jurisdiction. Nothing in this Act shall be deemed to enable the police of one State to exercise powers and jurisdiction in any area within another State, not being a railway area, without the consent of the Government of that other State.]

THE METAL TOKENS ACT, 1889

Section 8. (1) No piece of metal which is not coin as defined in the Indian Penal Code shall be received as money by or on behalf of any railway administration or local authority.

(2) If any person on behalf of a railway administration, or on behalf of a local authority, or onbehalf of the lessee of the collection of any toll or other impost leviable by a railway-administration or local authority, receives as money any piece of metal which is not such coin as aforesaid, he shall be punished with fine which may extend to ten rupees.

THE LAND ACQUISITION ACT, 1894

Section 17 (2) Special powers in cases of urgency. Whenever owing to any sudden change in the channel of any navigable river or other unforeseen emergency, it becomes necessary for any Railway administration to acquire the immediate possession of any land for the maintenance of their traffic or for the purpose of making thereon a river-side or ghat station, or of providing convenient connection with or access to any such station, [47] [or the appropriate Government considers it necessary to acquire the immediate possession of any land for the purpose of maintaining any structure or system pertaining to irrigation, water supply, drainage, road communication or electricity,] the Collector may, immediately after the publication of the notice mentioned in sub-section (1) and with the previous sanction of the [47] [appropriate Government], enter upon and take possession of such land, which shall thereupon [49] [vest absolutely in the [50] [Government]] free from all encumbrances: Provided that the Collector shall not take possession of any building or part of a building under this sub-section without giving to the occupier thereof at least forty-eight hours' notice of his intention so to do, or such longer notice as may be reasonably sufficient to enable such occupier to remove his movable property from such building without unnecessary inconvenience.

Section 43 Sections 39 to 42 not to apply where Government bound by agreement to provide land for Companies. The provisions of sections 39 to 42, both inclusive, shall not apply and the corresponding sections of the [108] Land Acquisition Act, 1870 (10 of 1870), shall be deemed never to have applied, to the acquisition of land of any Railway or other Company, for the purposes of which, [109] [under any agreement with such Company, the Secretary of State for India in Council, the Secretary of State, [110] [The Central Government or any State Government] is or was bound to provide land.]

Section 44 How agreement with railway Company may be proved. In the case of the acquisition of land for the purposes of a Railway Company, the existence of such an agreement as is mentioned in section 43 may be proved by the production of a printed copy thereof purporting to be printed by order of Government.

Section 17 (4)(2)(a)In the case of any land to which, in the opinion of the [53] [appropriate Government], the provisions of sub-section (1) or sub-section (2) are applicable, the [53] [appropriate Government] may direct that the provisions of section 5A shall not apply, and, if it does so direct, a declaration may be made under section 6 in respect of the land at any time [54] [after the date of the publication of the notification] under section 4, sub-section (1).] State AmendmentS Andhra Pradesh. ☐(1) Same as that made by Madras Act 21 of 1948, sec. 2 reproduced In the following cases, that is to say Whenever owing to any sudden change in the channel of any navigable river or other unforeseen emergency, it becomes necessary for any Railway Administration to acquire the immediate possession of any land for the maintenance of their traffic or for the purpose of making thereon a river-side or ghat station, or of providing a convenient connection with or access to any such station

Whenever it becomes necessary for the purpose of protection life or property from flood, erosion or other natural calamities or for the maintenance of communication other than a railway communication or it becomes necessary for any Railway Administration (other than Railway Administration of the Union), owing to any sudden change in a channel of any navigable river or other unforeseen emergency for the maintenance of their traffic or for the purpose of making thereon a river-side or ghat station, or providing convenient connection with or access to any such station to acquire the immediate possession of any land, the Collector may, immediately after the publication of the declaration mentioned in section 6, or, with the consent in writing of the person interested, given in the presence of headman of the village or Mukhiya and Sarpanch as defined in the Bihar Panchayat Raj Act, 1947 (Bihar Act 7 of 1948), at any time after the publication of the notification under section 4 in the village in which the land is situated and with the previous sanction of the appropriate Government, enter upon and take possession of such land which shall thereon vest absolutely in the government free from encumbrances: Provided that the Collector shall not take possession of any building or part of a building under this sub-section without giving to the occupier thereof at least forty-eight hours' notice of his intention to do so, or such longer notice as may be reasonably sufficient to enable such occupier to remove his movable property from such building without unnecessary inconvenience.

The Indian Tolls (Army and Air Force) Act, 1901

Section 6(1) If any owner or lessee, or any Company, railway administration or local authority claims compensation for any loss alleged to have been incurred to the operation of this Act, the claim shall be submitted to the [31] [Central Government]

Section 2(C) "ferry" includes every bridge and other thing which is a ferry within the meaning of any enactment authorising the levy of tolls on ferries, but does not include any ferry or other thing which is included in the definition of "railway" in section 3 of the Indian Railways Act, 1890)

Section 2(i) "public authority" means the Central Government [11] [***] or a State Government or a local authority; and, so far as regards tolls levied by a railway company under section 4 of the Indian Guaranteed Railways Act, 1879 [12] or section 51 of the Indian Railways Act, 1890, includes such a railway company; and

THE INDIAN ELECTRICITY ACT, 1910

Section 2(a)"appropriate Government" means in relation to any works or electric installations belonging to, or under the control of, the Central Government or in relation to any mines, oilfields, railways, aerodromes, telegraphs, broadcasting stations and any works of defence, the Central Government, and in any other case, the State Government.

Section 12
Provision as to the opening and breaking up of streets, railways and tramways.—
(1) Any licensee may, from time to time but subject always to the terms and conditions of his license, within the area of supply, or, when permitted by the terms of his license to lay down or place electric supply-lines without the area of supply, without that area—
(a) open and break up the soil and pavement of any street, railway or tramway;
(b) open and break up any sewer, drain or tunnel in or under any street, railway or tramway

Nothing contained in sub-section (1) shall be deemed to authorise or empower any licensee to open or break up any street not repairable by 5[the Central Government or the State Government] or a local authority, or any railway or tramway, except such streets, railways or tramways (if any), or such parts thereof, as he is specially authorised to break up by his license, without the written consent of the person by whom the street is repairable or of the person for the time being entitled to work the railway or tramway, unless with the written consent of the State Government: Provided that the State Government shall not give any such consent as aforesaid, until the licensee has given notice by advertisement or otherwise as the State Government may direct, and within such period as the State Government may fix in this behalf, to the person above referred to, and until all representations or objections received in accordance with the notice have been considered by the State Government. 6[(6) In this section, "occupier" of any building or land means a person in lawful occupation of that building or land.]

Section 13 Notice of new works
Where the exercise of any of the powers of a licensee in relation to the execution of any works involves the placing of any works, in, under, over, along or across any street, part of a street, railway, tramway, canal or waterway, the following provisions shall have effect, namely:—
(a) not less than one month before commencing the execution of the works 1[***] the licensee shall serve upon the person responsible for the repair of the street or part of a street (hereinafter in this section referred to as "the repairing authority") or upon the person for the time being entitled to work the railway, tramway, canal or waterway (hereinafter in this section referred to as "the owner"), as the case may be, a notice in writing describing the proposed works together with a section and plan thereof on a scale sufficiently large to show clearly the details of the proposed works, and not in any case smaller than one inch to eight feet vertically and sixteen inches to the mile horizontally, and intimating the manner in which, and the time at which, it is proposed to interfere with or alter any existing works, and shall, upon being required to do so by the repairing authority or owner, as the case may be, from time to time give such further information in relation thereto as may be desired
(e) where no requisition has been served by the owner upon the licensee under clause (d), within the time named, the owner shall be deemed to have approved of the works, section and plan, and in that case, or where after a requisition for arbitration the matter has been determined by arbitration, the works may, upon payment or securing of compensation, be executed according to the notice and the section and plan, subject to such modifications as may have been determined by arbitration or agreed upon between the parties.

Section 16. Streets, railways, tramways, sewers, drains or tunnels broken up to be reinstated without delay.
—

- (1) Where any person, in exercise of any of the powers conferred by or under this Act, opens or breaks up the soil or pavement of any street, railway or tramway or any sewer, drain or tunnel, he shall—
    - (a) immediately cause the part opened or broken up to be fenced and guarded;
    - (b) before sunset cause a light or lights, sufficient for the warning of passengers, to be set up and maintained until sunrise against or near the part opened or broken up;
    - (c) with all reasonable speed fill in the ground and reinstate and make good the soil or pavement, or the sewer, drain or tunnel, opened or broken up, and carry away the rubbish occasioned by such openings or breaking up; and
    - (d) after reinstating and making good the soil or pavement, or the sewer, drain or tunnel, broken or opened up, keep the same in good repair for three months and for any further period, not exceeding nine months, during which subsidence continues.
- (2) Where any person fails to comply with any of the provisions of sub-section (1), the person having the control or management of the street, railway, tramway, sewer, drain or tunnel in respect of which the default has occurred, may cause to be executed the work which the defaulter has delayed or omitted to execute, and may recover from him the expenses incurred in such execution

Section 18 (1) Save as provided in section 13, sub-section (3), nothing in this Part shall be deemed to authorise or empower a licensee to place any 1[overhead line] along or across any street, railway, tramway, canal or waterway unless and until the State Government has communicated to him a general approval in writing of the methods of construction which he proposes to adopt: Provided that the communication of such approval shall in no way relieve the licensee of his obligations with respect to any other consent required by or under this Act.

Section 27 Supply of energy outside area of supply.—Notwithstanding anything in this Act, the 1[State Government] may, by order in writing, and subject to such conditions and restrictions, if any, as it thinks fit to impose, authorise any licensee to supply energy to any person outside the area of supply, and to lay down or place electric supply-lines for that purpose: Provided, first, that no such authority shall be conferred on the licensee within the area of supply of another licensee without that licensee's consent, unless the State Government considers that his consent has been unreasonably withheld: Provided, secondly, that such authority shall not be conferred unless the person to whom the supply is to be given has entered into a specific agreement with the licensee for the taking of such supply: Provided, thirdly, that a licensee on whom such authority has been conferred shall not be deemed to be empowered outside the area of supply to open or break up any street, or any sewer, drain or tunnel in or under any street, railway or tramway; or to interfere with any telegraph-line, without the written consent of the local authority or person by whom such street, sewer, drain or tunnel is repairable, or of the telegraph-authority, as the case may be, 2[unless the State Government, after such inquiry as it thinks fit, considers that such consent has been unreasonably withheld]: Provided, fourthly, that, save as aforesaid, the provisions of this Act shall apply in the case of any supply authorised under this section as if the said supply were made within the area of supply.

Section 29(a) Application of section 18 to over-head lines maintained by railways.—The provisions of sub-sections (3) and (4) of section 18 and of the Explanation thereto shall apply in the case of any 2[overhead line] placed by any railway administration as defined 3[in clause (32) of section 2 of the Railways Act, 1989 (24 of 1989),] as if references therein to the licensee were references to the railway administration.]

Section 30 (1)(b)(iii)Control of transmission and use of energy [Save as otherwise exempted under this Act, no person other than Central Transmission Utility, State Transmission Utility, a transmission licensee, a licensee or a person to whom sanction is granted under section 28, duly authorised under the terms of his license or sanction, as the case may be, shall transmit or use energy at a rate exceeding two hundred and fifty watts and one hundred volts—] in any place, to which the State Government, by general or special order, declares the provisions of this sub-section to apply, without giving, before the commencement of transmission or use of energy, not less than seven days' notice in writing of his intention to the Electrical

Inspector and to the District Magistrate, or in a presidency-town to the Commissioner of Police, containing particulars of the electrical installation and plant, if any, the nature and the purpose of supply, and complying with such of the provisions of Part IV, and of the rules made thereunder, as may be applicable:] Provided that nothing in this section shall apply to energy used for the public carriage of passengers, animals or goods, on, or for the lighting or ventilation of the rolling stock of, any railway or tramway subject to the provisions of 2[the Railways Act, 1989 (24 of 1989)]: Provided, also, that the 3[State Government] may, by general or special order and subject to such conditions and restrictions as may be specified therein, exempt from the application of this section or of any such provision or rule as aforesaid any person or class of persons using energy on premises upon or in connection with which it is generated, or using energy supplied under Part II in any place specified in clause (b).

Section 31 Protection of railways, aerodromes, and canals, docks, wharfs and piers.—No person shall, in the generation, transmission, supply or use of energy, in any way injure any railway, 1[aerodrome,] tramway, canal or water-way or any dock, wharf or pier vested in or controlled by a local authority, or obstruct or interfere with the traffic on any railway, 1[airway,] tramway, canal or water-way.
THE INDIAN ELECTRICITY ACT, 1910

Section 36 (A)(1)(g) Central Electricity Board. A Board to be called the Central Electricity Board shall be constituted to exercise the powers conferred by section 37. 2[(2)] The Central Electricity Board shall consist of the following members, namely one member to be nominated by the Railway Board .

THE DESTRUCTIVE INSECTS AND PESTS ACT, 1914

Section 4 [B][a] Refusal to carry article of which transport is prohibited. When a notification has been issued under section 4A, then, notwithstanding any other law for the time being in force, the person responsible for the booking of goods or parcels at any railway station or inland steam vessel station where the notification prohibits export or transport, shall refuse to receive for carriage at, or to forward or knowingly allow to be carried on, the railway or inland steam vessel from that station anything, of which import or transport is prohibited, consigned to any place in a State other than the State in which such station is situate

Section 5 [A] Penalties. Any person who knowingly exports any article or insect from a State or transports any article or insect from one State to another [2] in contravention of a notification issued under section 4A, or attempts so to export or transport any article or insect [3] and any person responsible for the booking of goods or parcels at a railway or inland steam vessel station who knowingly contravenes the provisions of section 4B shall be punishable with fine which may extend to two hundred and fifty rupees and, upon any subsequent conviction, with fine which may extend to two thousand rupees.]

THE INDIAN BOILERS ACT, 1923

Section 3[2] Limitation of application The Central Government may, by notification [5] in the Official Gazette, declare that the provisions of this Act shall not apply in the case of boilers or steam- pipes, or of any specified class of boilers or steam- pipes, belonging to or under the control of any railways administered [6] by the [7] Central Government] or by any State Government] or by any railway company as defined in clause (5) of section 3 of the Indian Railways Act, 1890 (9 of 1890)

Secttion 27 [A](2)(a) Central Boilers Board. The Board shall consist of the following members, namely such number of members, including the Chairman, not exceeding fifteen, as the Central Government may nominate, in the prescribed manner to represent that Government, the Union territories, the railways, the coal industry, the Indian Standards Institution, the boiler manufacturing industry, the users of boilers and, any other interests which, in the opinion of the Central Government, ought to be represented on the Board.

THE CANTONMENTS (HOUSE-ACCOMMODATION) ACT, 1923

Section 9 Sanction to be obtained before a house is occupied as a hospital, etc. No house in any cantonment or part of a cantonment in which this Act is operative shall, unless it was so occupied at the date of the issue of the notification declaring this Act or the [1] Cantonments (House- Accommodation) Act, 1902 (2 of 1902), as the case may be, to be operative, be occupied for the purposes of a hospital, school, school hostel, bank, hotel, or shop, or by a railway administration, a company or firm engaged in trade or business or a club, without the previous sanction of the Officer Commanding the District given with the concurrence of the Commissioner or, in a State where there are no Commissioners, of the Collector.

Section 10 [B] Houses not to be appropriated in certain cases.- No notice shall be issued under section 7 if the house was, at the date of such a notification as is referred to in clause (a), or is, with such sanction as aforesaid, occupied by a railway administration or by a company or firm engaged in trade or business or by a club

THE WORKMEN' S COMPENSATION ACT, 1923

Section 2[n][i] " workman" means any person (other than a person whose employment is of a casual nature and who is employed otherwise than for the purposes of the employer' s trade or business) who is a railway servant as defined in section 3 of the Indian Railways Act, 1890 (9 of 1890), not permanently employed in any administrative, district or sub- divisional office of a railway and not employed in any such capacity as is specified in Schedule II

THE OFFICIAL SECRETS ACT, 1923

Section 8[d] "prohibited place" means any railway, road, way or channel, or other means of communication by land or water (including any works or structures being part thereof or connected therewith) or any place used for gas, water or electricity works or other works for purposes of a public character, or any place where any munitions of war or any sketches, models, plans or documents relating thereto, are being made, repaired, or stored otherwise than on behalf of [3] [Government], which is for the time being declared by the [5] [Central Government], by notification in the Official Gazette, to be a prohibited place for the purposes of this Act on the ground that information with respect thereto, or the destruction or obstruction thereof, or interference therewith, would be useful to an enemy, and to which a copy of the notification in respect thereof has been affixed in English and in the vernacular of the locality

THE PROVIDENT FUNDS ACT, 1925

Section 2[D] " Government Provident Fund" means a Provident Fund, other than a Railway Provident Fund, constituted by the authority of [3] the Secretary of State, the Central Government, the Crown Representative or any State Government] for any class or classes of [4] persons in the service of the Government] or [5] of persons employed in educational institutions or employed by bodies existing solely for educational purposes], [6] and references in this Act to the Government shall be construed accordingly]

Section 2[f] " Railway administration" means--
- (i) any company administering a railway or tramway in [9] any part of India] either under a special Act of Parliament of the United Kingdom] or an Indian law, or under contract with the Government, or
- (ii) the manager of any railway or tramway administered by the [2] Central Government] of by a State Government, and includes, in any case referred to in sub- clause (ii), the [2] Central Government] or the State Government, as the case may be']

Section 2[g] " Railway Provident Fund" means a Provident Fund constituted by the authority of a railway administration for any class or classes of its employees

Section 3[1] A compulsory deposit in any Government or Railway Provident Fund shall not in any way be capable of being assigned or charged and shall not be liable to attachment under any decree or order of any Civil, Revenue or Criminal Court in respect of any debt or liability incurred by the subscriber or depositor, and neither the Official Assignee nor any receiver appointed under the Provincial Insolvency Act, 1920 , (5 of 1920 .) shall be entitled to, or have nay claim on, any such compulsory deposit .

Section 4 Provisions regarding re- payments.
- (1) When under the rules of any Government or Railway Provident Fund the sum standing to the credit of any subscriber or depositor, or the balance thereof after the making of any deduction authorized by this Act, has become payable, the officer whose duty it is to make the payment shall pay the or balance, as the case may be, to the subscriber or depositor, or, if he is dead, shall--
    - (a) if the sum or balance, or any part thereof, vests in a dependent under the provisions of section 3, pay the same to the dependent or to such person as may be authorized by law to receive payment on his behalf; or
    - 1. Ins. by the A. O. 1950. 2. Subs. by the A. O. 1948, for" Federal Railway Authority".
    - (b) if the whole sum or balance, as the case may be, does not exceed five thousand rupees, pay the same, or any part thereof, which is not payable under clause (a), to any person nominated to receive it under the rules of the Funds, or, if no person is so nominated, to any person appearing to him to be otherwise entitled to receive it; or

- - (c) in the case of any sum or balance, or any part thereof, which is not payable to any person under clause (a) or clause (b) pay the same,--
    - (i) to any person nominated to receive it under the rules of the Fund on production by such person of probate of letters of administration evidencing the grant to him of administration to the estate of the deceased or a certificate granted under the Succession Certificate Act, 1889 [1], (7 of 1889 .) or under the Bombay Regulation VIII of 1827, entitling the holder thereof to receive payment of such sum, balance or part, or
    - (ii) where no person is so nominated, to any person who produces such probate, letters or certificate: Provided that, where the whole or any part of any sum standing to the credit of the subscriber or depositor has been assigned to any other person before the commencement of this Act, and notice in writing of the assignment has been received by the officer from the assignee, the officer shall after making any deduction authorised by this Act and any payment due under clause (a) to or on behalf of the widow or children of the subscriber or depositor--
      - (i) if the subscriber or depositor or, if he is dead, the person to whom in the absence of any valid assignment the sum or balance would be payable under this sub- section gives his consent in writing, pay the sum or part or the balance thereof, as the case may be, to the assignee, or
      - (ii) if such consent is not forthcoming, withhold payment of the sum, part or balance, as the case may be, pending a decision of a competent Civil Court as to the person entitled to receive it.
  - (2) The making of any payment authorised by sub- section (1) shall be a full discharge to the Government or the railway administration, as the case may be, from all liability in respect of so much of the sum standing to the credit of the subscriber or depositor as is equivalent to the amount so paid.

Section 5 Rights of nominees. [1]
- (1) Notwithstanding anything contained in any law for the time being in force or in any disposition, whether testamentary or otherwise, by a subscriber to, or depositor in, a Government or Railway Provident Fund of the sum standing to his credit in the Fund, or of any part thereof, where any nomination, duly made in accordance with the rules of the Fund, purports to confer upon any person the right to receive the whole or any part of such sum on the death of the subscriber or depositor occurring before the sum has become payable or before the sum, having become payable, has been paid, the said person shall, on the death as aforesaid of the subscriber or depositor, become entitled, to the exclusion of all other persons, to receive such sum or part thereof, as the case may be, unless--
  - (a) such nomination is at any time varied by another nomination made in like manner or expressly cancelled by notice given in the manner and to the authority prescribed by those rules, or
  - (b) such nomination at any time becomes invalid by reason of the happening of some contingency specified therein,-- and if the said person predeceases the subscriber or depositor, the nomination shall, so far as it relates to the right conferred upon the said person, become void and of no effect: Provided that where provision has been duly made in the nomination in accordance with the rules of the Fund, conferring upon some other person such right in the stead of the person deceased, such right shall, upon the decease as aforesaid of the said person, pass to such other person.]

Section 6 Power to make deductions. When the sum standing to the credit of any subscriber or depositor in any Government or Railway Provident Fund which is a contributory Provident Fund becomes payable, there may, if the authority [1] specified in this behalf in the rules of the Fund] so directs, be deducted therefrom and paid to [2] Government or the Railway administration, as the case may be,]--

- (a) any amount due under a liability incurred by the subscriber or depositor to [2] Government or the Railway administration], but not exceeding in any case the total amount of any contributions credited to the account of the subscriber or depositor and of any interest or increment which has accrued on such contributions; or
- (b) where the subscriber or depositor has been dismissed from [3] his employment] for any reasons specified in this behalf in the rules of the Fund, or where he has resigned such employment within five years of the commencement thereof, the whole or any part of the amount of any such contributions, interest and increment.

THE INDIAN SUCCESSION ACT, 1925

Section 143 Bequest of certain sum where stocks, etc., in which invested are described.—Where a certain sum is bequeathed, the legacy is not specific merely because the stock, funds or securities in which it is invested are described in the will. Illustration A bequeaths to B— "10,000 rupees of my funded property"; "10,000 rupees of my property now invested in shares of the East Indian Railway Company"; "10,000 rupees, at present secured by mortgage of Rampur factory". None of these legacies is specific.

Section 170 Exoneration of specific legatee's stock in joint stock company.—In the absence of any direction in the Will, where there is a specific bequest of stock in a joint-stock company, if any call or other payment is due from the testator at the time of his death in respect of the stock, such call or payment shall, as between the testator's estate and the legatee, be borne by the estate; but, if any call or other payment becomes due in respect of such stock after the testator's death, the same shall, as between the testator's estate and the legatee, be borne by the legatee if he accepts the bequest. Illustrations
(i) A bequeaths to B his share in a certain railway. At A's death there was due from him the sum of 100 rupees in respect of each share, being the amount of a call which had been duly made and the sum of five rupees in respect of each share, being the amount of interest which had accrued due in respect of the call. These payments must be borne by A's estate
(iii) A bequeaths to B his shares in a certain railway. B accepts the legacy. After A's death a call is made in respect of the shares. B must pay the call
(v) A is the owner of ten shares in a railway company. At a meeting held during his lifetime a call is made of fifty rupees per share, payable by three instalments. A bequeaths his shares to B, and dies between the day fixed for the payment of the first and the day fixed for the payment of the second instalment, and without having paid the first instalment. A's estate must pay the first instalment, and B, if he accepts the legacy, must pay the remaining instalments.

Section 306 Demands and rights of action of or against deceased survive to and against executor or administrator.—All demands whatsoever and all rights to prosecute or defend any action or special proceeding existing in favour of or against a person at the time of his decease, survive to and against his executors or administrators; except causes of action for defamation, assault, as defined in the Indian Penal Code, 1860 (45 of 1860) or other personal injuries not causing the death of the party; and except also cases where, after the death of the party, the relief sought could not be enjoyed or granting it would be nugatory. Illustrations

(i) A collision takes place on a railway in consequence of some neglect or default of an official, and a passenger is severely hurt, but not so as to cause death. He afterwards dies without having brought any action. The cause of action does not survive.

The Sale of Goods Act, 1930

"document of title to goods" includes a bill of lading, dock-warrant, warehouse keeper's certificate, wharfingers' certificate, railway receipt, 1[multimodal transport document,] warrant or order for the delivery of goods and any other document used in the ordinary course of business as proof of the possession or control of goods, or authorising or purporting to authorise, either by endorsement or by delivery, the possessor of the document to transfer or receive goods thereby represented

Section 25 Reservation of right of disposal.—
- (1) Where there is a contract for the sale of specific goods or where goods are subsequently appropriated to the contract, the seller may, by the terms of the contract or appropriation, reserve the right of disposal of the goods until certain conditions are fulfilled. In such case, notwithstanding the delivery of the goods to a buyer, or to a carrier or other bailee for the purpose of transmission to the buyer, the property in the goods does not pass to the buyer until the conditions imposed by the seller are fulfilled. 1[(2) Where goods are shipped or delivered to a railway administration for carriage by railway and by the bill of lading or railway receipts, as the case may be, the goods are deliverable to the order of the seller or his agent, the seller is prima facie deemed to reserve the right of disposal.
- (3) Where the seller of goods draws on the buyer for the price and transmits to the buyer the bill of exchange together with the bill of lading or, as the case may be, the railway receipt, to secure acceptance or payment of the bill of exchange, the buyer is bound to return the bill of lading or the railway receipt if he does not honour the bill of exchange; and, if he wrongfully retains the bill of lading or the railway receipt, the property in the goods does not pass to him. Explanation.—In this section, the expressions "railway" and "railway administra-tion" shall have the meanings respectively assigned to them under the 2Indian Railways Act, 1890 (9 of 1890).]

The Petroleum Act, 1934

Section 10 No licence needed by railway administration acting as carrier.—Notwithstanding anything contained in this Chapter, a railway administration as defined in section 3 of the Indian Railways Act, 1890 (9 of 1890) [26] need not obtain any licence for the import or transport of any petroleum in its possession in its capacity as carrier

PAYMENT OF WAGES ACT 1936

Section 1(4) It applies to the payment of wages to persons employed in any factory [industrial establishment or commercial establishment] and to persons employed (otherwise
than in a factory) upon any railway by a railway administration or, either directly or through a
sub-contractor, by a person fulfilling a contract with a railway administration.

Section 3(c) Responsibility for payment of wages Every employer 23 [including a contractor,]
shall be responsible for the payment to persons employed by him of all wages required to be
paid under this Act upon railways(otherwise than in factories), if the employer is the railway
administration and the railway administration has nominated a person in this behalf for the local area concerned, the person so named, the person so responsible to the employer, or the person so nominated, as the case may be, shall be responsible for such payment.

Section 5[a] Time of payment of wages The wages of every person employed upon or in any railway, factory or industrial establishment [or commercial establishment] upon or in which less than one thousand persons are employed, shall be paid before the expiry of the seventh day

Section 5[b][3]The [Government] may, by general or special order, exempt, to such extent and
subject to such conditions as may be specified in the order, the person responsible for the
payment of wages to persons employed upon any railway (otherwise than in a factory) from
the operation of this section in respect of the wages of any such persons or class of such
persons

Section 7 Deductions which may be made from wages (1) Notwithstanding the provisions of
sub-section (2) of section 47 of the Indian Railways Act, 1890 28, the wages of an employed
person shall be paid to him without deductions of any kind except those authorised by or under this Act.

Section 8 [2] A notice specifying such acts and omissions shall be exhibited in the prescribed
manner on the premises in which the employment is carried on or in the case of persons

employed upon a railway (otherwise than in a factory), at the prescribed place or places.

Section 14[2] The [Government] may appoint Inspectors for the purposes of this Act in
respect of all persons employed upon a railway (otherwise than in a factory) to whom this Act
applies.

The Insurance Act, 1938

Section 118[d](iii) Exemptions.—Nothing in insurance Act 1938 shall apply if the 2[Authority] so orders in any case, and to such extent or subject to such conditions or modifications as may be specified in the order, to any mutual or provident insurance society composed wholly of Government servants or of railway servants which has been exempted from any or all of the provisions of the Provident Insurance Societies Act, 1912 (5 of 1912).]

The Motor Vehicles Act, 1988

Section 131 Duty of the driver to take certain precautions at unguarded railway level crossings.—Every driver of a motor vehicle at the approach of any unguarded railway level crossing shall cause the vehicle to stop and the driver of the vehicle shall cause the conductor or cleaner or attendant or any other person in the vehicle to walk up to the level crossing and ensure that no train or trolley is approaching from either side and then pilot the motor vehicle across such level crossing, and where no conductor or cleaner or attendant or any other person is available in the vehicle, the driver of the vehicle shall get down from the vehicle himself to ensure that no train or trolley is approaching from either side before the railway track is crossed .

THE WAR INJURIES (COMPENSATION INSURANCE) ACT, 1943

Section 9 Compulsory insurance.
- (1)Every employer of workmen to whom this Act applies or is subsequently made applicable [2] except an employer whose total wages bill for any quarter after the commencement of this Act has never exceeded fifteen hundred rupees] shall, before such date as may be prescribed, or before the expiry of such period as may be prescribed after his having first become such an employer, take out a policy of insurance issued in accordance with the Scheme, whereby he is insured until the termination of the present hostilities or until the date, if any, prior to the termination of the present

hostilities at which he ceases to be an employer to whom this section applies, against all liabilities imposed on him by this Act.

- (2) Whoever contravenes the provisions of sub- section (1) or, having taken out a policy of insurance as required by that sub- section, fails to make any payment by way of premium thereon which is subsequently due from him in accordance with the provisions of the Scheme shall be punishable with fine which may extend to one thousand rupees and shall also be punishable with a further fine which may extend to five hundred rupees for every day after having been so convicted on which the contravention or failure continues.
- (3) This section shall not bind the Government nor, unless the Central Government by notification in the Official Gazette otherwise orders, any [1] Railway Administration].

THE INDUSTRIAL EMPLOYMENT (STANDING ORDERS) ACT, 1946

Section 13B. Act not to apply to certain industrial establishments.—Nothing in this Act shall apply to an industrial establishment in so far as the workmen employed therein are persons to whom the Fundamental and Supplementary Rules, Civil Services (Classification, Control and Appeal) Rules, Civil Services (Temporary Services) Rules, Revised Leave Rules, Civil Service Regulations, Civilians in Defence Service (Classification, Control and Appeal) Rules or the Indian Railway Establishment Code or any other rules or regulations as may be notified in this behalf by the appropriate Government in the Official Gazette, apply.]

THE DELHI SPECIAL POLICE ESTABLISHMENT ACT, 1946

Section 5. Extension of powers and jurisdiction of special police establishment to other areas.—
(1) The Central Government may by order extend to any area (including Railway areas), 1[in 2[a State, not being a Union territory]] the powers and jurisdiction of members of the Delhi Special Police Establishment for the investigation of any offences or classes of offences specified in a notification under section

Section 6 Consent of State Government to exercise of powers and jurisdiction.—Nothing contained in section 5 shall be deemed to enable any member of the Delhi Special Police Establishment to exercise powers and jurisdiction in any area in 2[a State, not being a Union territory or railway area], without the consent of the Government of that State.]

THE DAMODAR VALLEY CORPORATION ACT, 1948

Section 25. Co- operation with other authorities to minimise inconvenience caused by submersion. The Corporation shall co- operate with the participating Governments, railway authorities and local authorities and bodies, with a view to minimising the inconvenience likely to be caused by the submersion of roads and communications and shall bear the cost of any realignment thereof or resettlement of any population rendered necessary by such submersion.

THE JUNAGADH ADMINISTRATION (PROPERTY) ACT, 1948

Section 3[1] Vesting and disposal of property and powers of Administrator. Notwithstanding anything contained in any law for the time being in force, the property described in the Schedule, whether in the name of His Highness the Nawab of Junagadh, or the Dewan or the Private Secretary to His Highness the Nawab of Junagadh, or the Manager and Engineer- in- Chief, Junagadh State Railway, or the Chief Accounts Officer, Junagadh State, or any other person whatsoever or in the name of more than one of them, shall be deemed on and from the 9th day of November 1947 to have vested in the Administrator, and the Administrator shall, as from that date, hold and be entitled to and have the power to deal with and dispose of the said property as such Administrator.

THE EMPLOYEES' STATE INSURANCE ACT, 1948

Section 12 factory means any premises including the precincts thereof whereon ten or more persons are employed or were employed on any day of the preceding twelve months, and in any part of which a manufacturing process is being carried on or is ordinarily so carried on, but does not include a mine subject to the operation of the Mines Act, 1952 (35 of 1952) or a railway running shed;]

Section 24 all other words and expressions used but not defined in this Act and defined in the Industrial Disputes Act, 1947 (14 of 1947), shall have the meanings respectively assigned to them in that Act.] (i) a widow, a minor legitimate or adopted son, an unmarried legitimate or adopted daughter;. (v) dependant parents. (12) factory means any premises including the precincts thereof whereon twenty or more persons are employed or were employed for wages on any day of the preceding twelve months, and in any part of which a manufacturing process is being carried on without the aid of power or is ordinarily so carried on, but does not include a mine subject to the operation of the Mines Act, 1952 (35 of 1952) or a railway running shed.

THE CENSUS ACT, 1948

Section 6[1][e] Discharge of duties of census- officers in certain cases Where the District Magistrate, or such authority as the State Government may appoint in this behalf, by a written order so directs every manager or officer of a railway or any commercial or industrial establishment .

The Factories Act, 1948

Section 2 [m][ii]"factory" means any premises including the precincts thereof whereon twenty or more workers are working, or were working on any day of the preceding twelve months, and in any part of which a manufacturing process is being carried on without the aid of power, or is ordinarily so carried on,— but does not include a mine subject to the operation of [6] [the Mines Act, 1952 (35 of 1952)], or [7] [a mobile unit belonging to the armed forces of the Union, railway running shed or a hotel, restaurant or eating place]. [4] [Explanation [8] [I].—For computing the number of workers for the purposes of this clause all the workers in [9] [different groups and relays] in a day shall be taken into account;] [10] [Explanation II.—For the purposes of this clause, the mere fact that an Electronic Data Processing Unit or a Computer Unit is installed in any premises or part thereof, shall not be construed to make it a factory if no manufacturing process is being carried on in such premises or part thereof;]

Section 64 [2][j]Power to make exempting rules. The [99] [State Government] may make rules in respect of adult workers in factories providing for the exemption, to such extent and subject to such conditions as may be prescribed of workers engaged in the loading or unloading of railway wagons, [104] [or lorries or trucks] from the provisions of sections 51, 52, 54, 55 and 56]

Section 78[2] The provisions of this Chapter shall not apply to workers 3[in any factory] of any railway administered by the Government, who are governed by leave rules approved by the Central Government.

BANKING REGULATION ACT,1949

Sectrion 6[1][a]In addition to the business of banking, a banking company may engage in any one or more of the following forms of business, namely the borrowing, raising, or taking up of money; the lending or advancing of money either upon or without security; the drawing, making, accepting, discounting, buying, selling, collecting and dealing in bills of exchange, hoondees, promissory notes, coupons, drafts, bills of lading, railway receipts, warrants, debentures, certificates, scrips and other instruments and securities whether transferable or negotiable or not; the granting and issuing of letters of credit, traveller's cheques and circular notes; the buying, selling and dealing in bullion and specie; the buying and selling of foreign exchange including foreign bank notes; the acquiring, holding, issuing on commission, underwriting and dealing in stock, funds, shares, debentures, debenture stock, bonds, obligations, securities and investments of all kinds; the purchasing and selling of bonds, scrips or other forms of securities on behalf of constituents or others, the negotiating of loans and advances; the receiving of all kinds of bonds, scrips or valuables on deposit or for safe custody or otherwise; the providing of safe deposit vaults; the collecting and transmitting of money and securities

THE REPRESENTATION OF THE PEOPLE ACT, 1951

Section 123[5]Corrupt practices.—The following shall be deemed to be corrupt practices for the purposes of this Act . The hiring or procuring, whether on payment or otherwise, of any vehicle or vessel by a candidate or his agent or by any other person 11[with the consent of a candidate or his election agent] 12[or the use of such vehicle or vessel for the free conveyance] of any elector (other than the candidate himself the members of his family or his agent) to or from any polling station provided under section 25 or a place fixed under sub-section (1) of section 29 for the poll: Provided that the hiring of a vehicle or vessel by an elector or by several electors at their joint costs for the purpose of conveying him or them to and from any such polling station or place fixed for the poll shall not be deemed to be a corrupt practice under this clause if the vehicle or vessel so hired is a vehicle or vessel not propelled by mechanical power: Provided further that the use of any public transport vehicle or vessel or any tramcar or railway carriage by any elector at his own cost for the purpose of going to or coming from any such polling station or place fixed for the poll shall not be deemed to be a corrupt practice under this clause. Explanation.—In this clause, the expression "vehicle" means any vehicle used or capable of being used for the purpose of road transport, whether propelled by mechanical power or otherwise and whether used for drawing other vehicles or otherwise.

The Forward Contracts (Regulation) Act, 1952

Section 2[f] "non-transferable specific delivery contract" means a specific delivery contract, the rights or liabilities under which or under any delivery order, railway receipt, bill of lading, warehouse receipt or any other document of title relating thereto are not transferable; tc" (f) "non-transferable specific delivery contract" means a specific delivery contract, the rights or liabilities under which or under any delivery order, railway receipt, bill of lading, warehouse receipt or any other document of title relating thereto are not transferable;"

The Collection of Statistics Act, 1953

Section 2[b][vi]"commercial concern" means a public limited company or a co-operative society or a firm or any other person or body of persons engaged in trade or commerce, and includes— a light railway .

THE [SALARY, ALLOWANCES AND PENSION] OF MEMBERS OF PARLIAMENT ACT, 1954

Section 6 Free transit by railway.
- (1) Every member shall be provided with one free non- transferable[air conditioned two tier] 7 pass which shall entitle him to travel at any time by any railway in India. Explanation.- 4 For the purposes of this sub- section and section 6A and 6B], a member shall include a Minister as defined in the Salaries and Allowances of Ministers Act, 1952 (58 of 1952) 5 a Leaders of Opposition as defined in the Salary and Allowances of Leaders of Opposition in Parliament Act, 1977 33 of 1977 . and an officer of Parliament as defined in the Salaries and Allowances of Officers of Parliament Act, 1953 20 of 1953 . other than the Chairman of the Council of States.
-
- (2) A free railway pass issued to a member under sub- section (1) shall be valid for the term of his office and on the expiration of such term, the pass shall be surrendered to the Secretary of the House of the People or the Council of States, as the case may be: Provided that where any such pass is issued to a new member before he takes his seat in either House of Parliament, he shall be entitled to use the pass for attending a session of that House for taking his seat therein.
- (3) Until a member is provided with a free railway pass under sub- section (1), he shall be, and shall be deemed always to have been entitled to an amount equal to one 3 air conditioned two tier] fare for any journey of the nature referred to in sub- section (1) of section 4 performed by him by rail.
- (4) A member who on ceasing to be a member surrenders his pass shall, if he performs any return journey by rail of the nature referred to in sub- section (1) of section 4, be entitled and be deemed always to have been entitled in respect of that journey to an amount equal to one[air conditioned two- tier] 3 fare.
- (5) Nothing in this section shall be construed as disentailing a member to any travelling allowances to which he is otherwise entitled under the provisions of this Act.]

6A. Without prejudice to the provisions of section 6, every member representing the Union territory of the Andaman and Nicobar Islands or the Union territory of Lakshadweep shall-
(a) be provided with one free non- transferable pass which shall entitle him to travel at any time by the highest class by steamer to and from any part of his constituency and any other part of his constituency or the nearest part in the main land of India; and
(b) be entitled to an amount equal to the fare by air from his usual place of residence to the nearest airport the main land of India 5 and back] Provided that nothing in this sub- section shall be construed as absolving the member from payment of any diet charges payable by him during such travel.
(2) A free steamer pass issued to a member under sub- section (1) shall be valid for the term of his office and on the expiration of his term, the pass shall be surrendered to the Secretary of the House of the People: Provided that where any such pass is issued to a new member before he takes his seat in the House of the People, he shall be entitled to use the pass for attending a session of that House for taking his seat therein.

(3) Until a member is provided with a free steamer pass under sub- section (1), he shall be entitled to an amount equal to one fare (without diet) for the highest class for any journey of the nature referred to in sub- section (1) of section 4 performed by him by steamer.

(4) A member who on ceasing to be a member surrenders the steamer pass issued to him under sub- section (1) shall, if he performs any return journey by steamer of the nature referred to in sub- section (1) of section 4, be entitled in respect of that journey to an amount equal to one fare (without diet) for the highest class.
(5) Nothing in this section shall be construed as disentitling a member to any travelling allowances to which he is otherwise entitled under the provisions of this Act.
(6) In addition to[the facilities provided to a member] 4 under sub- section (1), he also be entitled-
(i) to one free pass for one person to accompany the member and travel by the[highest class] 4 by steamer to and fro any part of the constituency of the member and any other part of his constituency or the nearest port in the mainland of India; 4 or]
(ii) to one free- non- transferable pass for the spouse, if any of the member to travel by the highest class by steamer to and the usual place of residence of the member in his constituency and the nearest port in the mainland of India,
(iii) 4 To an amount equal to the fare by air either for the spouse, if any, of the member or for one person to accompany the member from the usual place of residence in the Island to the nearest airport of the main land of India[and back.] 7 Provided that nothing in this sub- section shall be constructions absolving the person accompanying the member or the spouse of the member from payment of any diet charges payable by such person or spouse during such travel.]
6AA. 5 Special facility to members from Ladakh.
(1) Without prejudice to the provisions of section 6, every member who has his ordinary place of residence in the Ladakh area of the State of Jammu and Kashmir shall be entitled to an amount equal to the fare by air for each single journey by air performed by him from any airport in Ladakh to the airport in Delhi and back at any time.
(2) In addition to the air travel provided to a member under sub- section (1), he shall also be entitled to an amount equal to the fare by air for each single journey by air- performed by the spouse, if any, of the member or one person to accompany such member, from any- airport in Ladakh area to the airport in Delhi and back at any time.] 1 2 6B.] Travel facilities to members. Without prejudice to the other provisions of this Act the member shall be entitled-
(i) to travel by any railway in India at any time in first class air- conditioned on payment of the difference between the railway fares for first class air- conditioned[and air conditioned two- tier.] 6
(ii) to one free air[conditioned two- tier] 6 railway pass for one person to accompany the member when he travels by rail; and
(iii) to one free non- transferable[air conditioned two- tier] 6 railway pass for the spouse, if any, of the member to travel from the usual place of residence of the member to Delhi and back once during every session.
8 and if such journey or any part thereof is performed by air from any place other than the usual place of residence of the member, to Delhi and back to an amount equal to the fare by air for such journey or part thereof. Provided that where such journey or part thereof by such spouse is performed by air from any other place, the expenditure on such journey or part thereof shall not exceed the amount payable if the journey had been performed from the usual place of residence of the member to Delhi and back:] 8 Provided further that where a member travels by rail in first class air- conditioned and no person accompanies that member in that journey in air- conditioned two- tier by virtue of the free air- conditioned two- tier railway pass referred to in clause (ii) then in determining the amount payable by the member under clause (i) the amount of air- conditioned two- tier fare for such journey shall be adjusted against the difference referred to in that clause; so however, that the member shall not be entitled to claim the balance of such air- conditioned two- tier fare left after such adjustment."]

Section 582[a][i] Managing of" unregistered company". For the purposes of this Part, the expression" unregistered company"- shall not include- a railway company incorporated by any Act of Parliament or other Indian law or any Act of Parliament of the United Kingdom

THE ARMS ACT, 1959

Section 21 Arrest of persons conveying arms, etc., under suspicious circumstances.- Where any person is found carrying or conveying any arms or ammunition whether covered by a licence or not, in such manner or under such circumstances as to afford just grounds of suspicion that the same are or is being carried by him with intent to use them, or that the same may be used, for any unlawful purpose, any magistrate, any police officer or any other public servant or any person employed or working upon a railway, aircraft, vessel, vehicle or any other means of conveyance, may arrest him without warrant and seize from him such arms or ammunition

Section 36 Every person employed or working upon any railway, aircraft, vessel, vehicle or other means of conveyance shall, in the absence of reasonable excuse the burden of proving which shall lie upon such person, give information to the officer in charge of the nearest police station regarding any box, package or bale in transit which he may have reason to suspect contains arms or ammunition in respect of which an offence under this Act has been or is being committed.

THE ANDHRA PRADESH AND MADRAS (ALTERATION OF BOUNDARIES) ACT, 1959

Section 24 Distribution of revenues. Section 3 of the Union Duties of Excise (Distribution) Act, 1957 (55 of 1957), sections 3 and 5 of the Estate Duty and Tax on Railway Passenger Fares (Distribution) Act, 1957 (57 of 1957), section 4 of and the Second Schedule to the Additional Duties of Excise (Goods of Special Importance) Act, 1957 (58 of 1957), and paragraphs 3 and 5 of the Constitution (Distribution of Revenues) No. 2 Order, 1957 , shall, as from the appointed day, have effect subject to such modifications as the President may, by order published in the Official Gazette, specify having regard to the transfer of territories effected by the provisions of Part II of this Act. PART APPORTIONMENT OF ASSETS AND LIABILITIES PART VI APPORTIONMENT OF ASSETS AND LIABILITIES

Atomic Energy Act, 1962

section 11 Where the Central Government acquires any plant referred to in clause (d) of sub-section (1), it shall also have the right to acquire any buildings, railway sidings, tramway lines, or aerial ropeways serving such plant.

THE CUSTOMS ACT, 1962

Section 2 (31) (c) "person-in-charge" means,— in relation to a railway train, the conductor, guard or other person having the chief direction of the train

Section 2 (42) vehicle" means conveyance of any kind used on land and includes a railway vehicle

THE MAJOR PORT TRUSTS ACT, 1963

Section 2 [f] "dock" includes all basins, locks, cuts, entrances, graving docks, graving blocks, inclined planes, slipways, gridirons, moorings, transit-sheds, warehouses, tramways, railways and other works and things appertaining to any dock, and also the portion of the sea enclosed or protected by the arms or groynes of a harbour

Section 3[1][a][i][6] Constitution of Board of Trustees. With effect from such date as may be specified by notification in the Official Gazette, the Central Government shall cause to be constituted in respect of any major port a Board of Trustees to be called the Board of Trustees of that port, which shall consist of the following Trustees, namely a Chairman to be appointed by the Central Government; 1[(b) one Deputy Chairman or more, as the Central Government may deem fit to appoint;] 1[(b) one Deputy Chairman or more, as the Central Government may deem fit to appoint;]" 2[(c) not more than nineteen persons in the case of each of the ports of Bombay, Calcutta and Madras and not more than seventeen persons in the case of any other port who shall consist of— 2[(c) not more than nineteen persons in the case of each of the ports of Bombay, Calcutta and Madras and not more than seventeen persons in the case of any other port who shall consist of such number of persons, as the Central Government may, from time to time, by notification in the Official Gazette, specify, to be appointed by that Government from amongst persons who are in its opinion capable of representing any one or more of such of the following interests as may be specified in the notification, namely the Indian Railways.

Section 6[d][v] Disqualification for office of Trustee.—A person shall be disqualified for being chosen as a Trustee, if he has, directly or indirectly, any share or interest in any work done by order of the Board, or in any contract or employment, with, by, or on behalf of the Board: Provided that no person shall be deemed to have a share or interest in such work, contract or employment by reason only of his having a share or interest in any licence by the Board, or right by agreement or otherwise, with the Board to the sole or preferential use of any railway siding or any berth for vessels in the docks belonging to the Board.

Section 35[2][a] Power of Board to execute works and provide appliances Such works and appliances may include wharves, quays, docks, stages, jetties, piers and other works within the port or port approaches or on the foreshore of the port or port approaches, with all such convenient arches, drains, landing places, stairs, fences, roads, railways, bridges, tunnels and approaches and buildings required for the residence of the employees of the Board as the Board may consider necessary.

or/and

Section 35[2][b] buses, railways, locomotives, rolling stock, sheds, hotels, warehouses and other accommodation for passengers and goods and other appliances for carrying passengers and for conveying, receiving and storing goods landed, or to be shipped or otherwise

Section 42[1][d]Performance of services by Board or other person A Board shall have power to undertake the following services receiving and delivering, transporting and booking and despatching goods originating in the vessels in the port and intended for carriage by the neighbouring railways, or vice versa, as a railway administration under the Indian Railways Act, 1890 (9 of 1890); 2[3[***]] 1[2[***]]" 2[(e) piloting, hauling, mooring, remooring, hooking, or measuring of vessels or any other service in respect of vessels; 4[and] 1[(e) piloting, hauling, mooring, remooring, hooking, or measuring of vessels or any other service in respect of vessels; 3[and]" 5[(f) developing and providing, subject to the previous approval of the Central Government, infrastructure facilities for ports.] 4[(f) developing and providing, subject to the previous approval of the Central Government, infrastructure facilities for ports.]"

Section 42[1][i]Responsibility of Board for loss, etc., of goods Subject to the provisions of this Act, the responsibility of any Board for the loss, destruction or deterioration of goods of which it has taken charge shall,— in the case of goods received for carriage by railway, be governed by the provisions of the Indian Railways Act, 1890 (9 of 1890)

Section 123[e] General Power of Board to make regulations.—Without prejudice to any power to make regulations contained elsewhere in this Act, a Board may make regulations consistent with this Act for all or any of the following purposes, namely:— for the guidance of persons employed by the Board under this Act; 1[(f) for the safe, efficient and convenient use, management and control of the docks, wharves, quays, jetties, railways, tramways, buildings and other works constructed or acquired by, or vested in, the Board, or of any land or foreshore acquired by, or vested in, the Board under this Act;] 1[(f) for the safe, efficient and convenient use, management and control of the docks, wharves, quays, jetties, railways, tramways, buildings and other works constructed or acquired by, or vested in, the Board, or of any land or foreshore acquired by, or vested in, the Board under this Act;]"

THE UNIT TRUST OF INDIA ACT, 1963

Section 19[4] Business of Trust accepting, collecting, discounting, rediscounting, purchasing, selling or negotiating or otherwise dealing with, any bills of exchange, hundies, promissory notes, coupons, drafts, bills of lading, railway receipts, warehouse receipts, documents of title to goods, warrants, certificates, scrips and other mercantile instrument.

www.ingramcontent.com/pod-product-compliance
Lightning Source LLC
Chambersburg PA
CBHW080655190526
45169CB00006B/2129